Welcome to Fear City

THE SUNY SERIES

HORIZONS OF CINEMA

MURRAY POMERANCE | EDITOR

Welcome to Fear City

Crime Film, Crisis, and the Urban Imagination

Nathan Holmes

Cover: Gene Hackman in *The French Connection* (1971). 20th Century-Fox / Photofest, © 20th Century-Fox.

Published by State University of New York Press, Albany

Printed in the United States of America

For information, contact State University of New York Press, Albany, NY
www.sunypress.edu

Library of Congress Cataloging-in-Publication Data

Names: Holmes, Nathan.
Title: Welcome to fear city : crime film, crisis, and the urban imagination / Nathan Holmes.
Description: Albany : State University of New York Press, [2018] | Series: SUNY series, Horizons of cinema | Includes bibliographical references and index.
Identifiers: LCCN 2017050738 | ISBN 9781438471211 (hardcover : alk. paper) | ISBN 9781438471228 (ebook)
Subjects: LCSH: Cities and towns in motion pictures. | City and town life in motion pictures. | Crime films—United States—History and criticism. | United States—Social life and customs—20th century. | United States—In motion pictures.
Classification: LCC PN1995.9.C513 H65 2018 | DDC 791.43/621732—dc23
LC record available at https://lccn.loc.gov/2017050738

10 9 8 7 6 5 4 3 2 1

Contents

Illustrations

Acknowledgments

When I think of how this book developed, changed shape, and then took its present form, a number of paths, and a large cast of people come to mind.

One trajectory begins with a group of friends watching American crime films in a ramshackle Milwaukee Avenue loft. Returning to Chicago from Paris on an abortive dissertation proposal research trip, I received a consoling text message from my roommate and friend Josh Goldsmith, which advised me to write about the movies we loved to discover together. He told me to entitle the project "This City Will Kill You." The name didn't stick but the general idea was all there in that text.

Another trajectory was my experience reading and learning from Tom Gunning, particularly his work connecting cinema, detective fiction, and urban visual culture. Tom incited me to think seriously about the crime genre as a form and his fierce dialectical thinking about cinema and modern vision, as well as his encouragement and support of this project are, I hope, evident on every page. I was also inspired by Ed Dimendberg's work on film noir and modern space and so was thrilled when he agreed to become a dissertation advisor. Many thanks to Ed for his careful readings and suggestions, and for introducing me to Eagle Rock's Cacao Mexicatessen. Jim Lastra, who combined his invaluable dissertation guidance and deep knowledge of cinema with personal experiences of the cities and films about which I was writing, was key in convincing me that I was moving in the right direction.

Many of these chapters took initial shape at the University of Chicago, where I was fortunate to join a community of students and scholars who, around the bad coffee and bagels of the Mass Culture Workshop, demonstrated an encouraging willingness to help me sort through my ideas. These include: Inga Pollman, Mara Fortes, Adam Hart, Ian Jones, Hannah Frank, Nova Smith, Katharina Loew, Noa Steimatsky, Mary Adekoya, Christina Petersen, Robert Bird, David Levin, Julie

Turnock, Kalisha Cornett, Richard Davis, Michelle Puetz, Artemis Willis, Lee Carruthers, Charles Tepperman, Clint Froelich, Caitlin McGrath, Sarah Keller, and many others. Miriam Hansen passed away shortly after the very beginnings of work on my dissertation, but her kindness was extremely important, and I hope that readers will detect her spirit here.

Murray Pomerance has been a kind and diligent editor, and I thank him for his deep understanding of the social life of cities, equanimity, abundant insights, and friendship.

Much appreciation too goes to James Peltz and Rafael Chaiken at SUNY Press for shepherding this book into publication.

I am grateful for the conversations I have been able to have over the years, often at Society for Cinema and Media Studies conferences, with scholars also inquiring into film, urbanism, and cultural spaces: Merrill Scheleir, Josh Gleich, Lawrence Webb, Erica Stein, Pamela Robertson-Wojcik, Mark Shiel, Malini Guha, Josh Glick, Sabine Haenni, Will Straw, Patrick Keating, and many others.

A portion of this book was supported by a Michigan-Mellon Post-Doctoral Fellowship on Egalitarianism and the Metropolis, and I was very happy to have the chance to discuss my work at the University of Michigan with Johannes Von Moltke, Caryl Flinn, Dan Herbert, Matthew Solomon, Benjamin Strassfield, and the wonderful Corina Kessler.

I am happy to have many colleagues who have become friends (and friends who have become colleagues), whom I can count on for new perspectives and discerning comment. Erika Balsom and Daniel Morgan were always up for reading a draft and offering their thoughts. Ongoing conversation about deception and revelation with Colin Williamson has been fundamental to my thinking in this book, and moving image media in general. For their always engaging observations and advice I want to thank Scott Preston, Jennifer Wild, Tim Kaposy, Andrew Pendakis, Kemi Adeyemi, Matt Croombs, and Owen Lyons. Cheers as well to Beth Woodward for coming through at the last moment with some important scans!

Perhaps the most significant friendship to the formation and evolution of this book has been Matt Hauske, the one person who has read, talked about, and re-read my work in all its iterations more than anyone else. It is impossible for me to think of this book ever happening without discussing film history and method with Matt over lunches at Salonica, or in the stuffy group workrooms of the Regenstein library.

Thanks go to my mother Janice and my father Mark, as well as Eben and Kahlin, who have always cheered me on. Finally, the true story behind this book is the support and dedication of Kristin Groff, and the love that continued to grow between us as I wrote and wrote.

Introduction

Crime Film and the Messy City

> Many a commercial film or television production is a genuine achievement besides being a commodity. Germs of new beginnings may develop within a thoroughly alienated environment.
>
> —Siegfried Kracauer, *Theory of Film*

❧

In 1974, Vincent Canby wrote a piece for the *New York Times*, titled "New York Woes Are Good For Box Office," that puzzled over the spate of films that had been made in the city over the last few years. What confused Canby was why so many recent films that portrayed New York so unfavorably—he cites *Serpico* (1973), *The Super Cops* (1974), *Law and Disorder* (1974), *Mean Streets* (1973), *Death Wish* (1974), *For Pete's Sake* (1974), and *The Taking of Pelham One Two Three* (1974)—were seemingly so popular:

> New York is a mess, say these films. It's run by fools. Its citizens are at the mercy of its criminals who, as often as not, are protected by an unholy alliance of civil libertarians and crooked cops. The air is foul. The traffic is impossible. Services are diminishing and the morale is such that ordering a cup of coffee in a diner can turn into a request for a fat lip. (1)

Pointing out that New York has been a mess for much of its history, Canby was less fretful about the negative portrayal of the city in these films than curious as to why, at this moment, the mess of the city had become a subject of interest. "Is being a mess box office?" he wondered. Pauline Kael also noticed the departure from the sentimentality that had marked depictions of the city through the 1960s, noting that the new crop of "urban gothic" films "provided a permanent record of a city in breakdown" (1971, 314).

Hollywood, as much as New York, was facing an economic crisis at the end of the 1960s, which it tried to remedy by re-inventing itself for a savvy youth market and cost-cutting wherever possible (Cook, 9–14). Location shooting in cities was attractive for feature filmmakers not only because it was thought to lend realism to a production—a quality that New Hollywood ardently pursued—but also because it was cheaper than shooting in a studio.[1] In New York, shooting a film on location was also easier than ever. In 1966, Mayor John Lindsay created the Office of Film, Theatre, and Broadcasting in order to streamline the process of granting permits to shoot on city streets, signaling the city's embrace of commercial film production.[2] Between 1966 and 1975 over 440 films were produced in the city. As significant as these developments were, however, they do not answer what is at the center of Canby's question: why is it that film audiences were interested in New York's mess?

Contemporary urbanity on film in the postwar era was one facet of mass culture's broader engagement with the decline of cities. Concerns over the visible changes to the city and the social transformations taking place there in the 1960s and 1970s were not only the purview of politicians, policymakers, and experts, they also echoed through newspapers and popular magazines, the nightly news, journals, nonfiction, and comic books. Like the Vietnam War, the urban crisis lent itself to a visual montage that combined images of the revolt of the inner city, the deleterious effects of urban renewal, and the incivility of a burgeoning counterculture and its attendant repression by police. Rising crime rates and de-industrialization came to be paired with an iconography of crumbling buildings, empty lots, junk strewn streets, and mysterious (frequently racialized) strangers.

At the same time, however, "downtown" was still associated with the cosmopolitan nature of urban life. Cities were still the ineluctable location of cuisine, fashion, art, music, the avant-garde, social and sexual experimentation, and, of course, cinema—all of which could be antidotes to anodyne suburban life. Commercial real estate developments drew on these associations while constructing edifices that began to hem downtown from the disorder of their surrounding environs. Opposition to the grand modernization projects undertaken by Robert Moses in New York helped to draw attention to the profuse architectural heritage harbored within the physical plant of cities, spurring the momentum of preservation movements. Preservationists and a new generation of urban planners and designers promulgated a new vision of the city, seeing it not as a space to be remade anew, but to be invested in for its existing complexity and semantic richness. In contrast to the expansive, top-down views of the city favored in images of modernist planning, new takes on American urbanism began at street level. Writers on urbanity such as Jane Jacobs (1961), Richard Sennett (1970), and Jonathan Raban (1974) argued that what others saw as mess was dense with significance and vitality. Against both the boosters of suburbia and the nouveau-agrarianism of the "back to the land" segments of the counterculture, Sennett's thesis was (and remains) that it was precisely the disorderliness of modern urban life, in fact, that supplied a path to freedom.

The messiness of urban life, both cherished and vilified, was largely itself an effect of suburbanization. At the end of World War II the mass production of housing on the periphery of cities, encouraged by a home buyer's market created through the generous financial assistance of the G.I. Bill, the Federal Housing Administration, and the construction of a connective network of expressways, augured the flight of the white middle classes from urban centers. At the same time, the waves of African Americans that had moved to northern and Midwestern industrial cities throughout the twentieth century faced increasing unemployment as manufacturing likewise moved to the suburban periphery and abroad. Persistent unemployment was exacerbated by the displacements of urban renewal projects—which James Baldwin famously dubbed "negro removal"—and the desiccation of social services brought on by the city's eroded middle-class tax base. Even those who could afford to move away from the city faced the prohibitions on racial mixing written into the Federal Housing Administration's manual,[3] redlining and real estate covenants (contracts preventing the sale of houses to non-white buyers), and the violent hostility of white suburbanites (see Sugrue, 2005). In 1961, the U.S. Commission on Civil Rights proclaimed that the suburbs were a "white noose choking the ghetto" and yet, despite the deep economic interdependence between them, the white suburbs not only declined responsibility for the plight of the inner city, they frequently worked to obstruct measures to improve life there, protesting busing programs that would bring inner-city school children to suburban schools, and staging revolts against the use of their taxes to fund social programs in the city. The suburbs instead became ground zero for the "silent majority" conservatism that rejected the liberal program of the Great Society and its policies for social reform. Despite the fact that it was federal initiatives that had made suburban life possible, and even though the suburbs and the city continued to be firmly economically interdependent, a deep social rift had opened. As the Kerner Commission, charged by Lyndon Johnson with investigating the root causes of urban uprisings, reported in 1968, the nation was "quickly moving toward two societies, one black, one white, separate and unequal." The incipient "culture of poverty" discourse promulgated by Daniel Patrick Moynihan and others, argued that the black inner-city family was caught within a "tangle of pathology" that inhibited outside assistance (1965, 47). As the nation shifted to the right, it also excused itself from the types of urban reform prioritized by postwar liberalism.

The social formation of suburbia was then, categorically anti-urban. Yet as familiar as this characterization may at first seem, a number of curious, and interrelated, wrinkles present themselves. First, of course, is the fact that both the suburbs and the central city are part of a larger contiguous fabric of urbanization. Though the suburbs may have occasionally trafficked in Jeffersonian visions of an agrarian life divorced from the corrupting influence of the city, in truth suburban life was still economically, physically, and experientially imbricated with the center (see Fishman, Castells). Second, because these two spheres remain so tied, the suburbs gained definition only negatively. That is, the suburbs were primarily distinguished by reference to, and circulation of, tropes of the central city such as crime, overcrowding, and pollution. Finally, the significant reason for this negative identity was that by the 1960s, the suburbs themselves had come to be broadly derided as the epicenter of American conformity, mass-produced banality, and cultural homogeneity. As the urban historian Becky Nicolaides (2006) observes, in the postwar era, a shift in cultural perception occurred wherein all of the damaging aspects attributed to urban life, in particular the impossibility of achieving authentic forms of community, shifted to the suburbs. Though dissatisfaction with suburban life was typical within baby boomer counterculture, it was also a recognized and risible target of middlebrow critique, from cartoons in the *New Yorker*, William H. Whyte's columns for *Fortune* that became *The Organization Man* (1956), and popular songs like Malvina Reynolds' "Little Boxes," (1963), The Monkee's "Pleasant Valley Sunday," (written by Carole King and Gerry Goffin), and even Dionne Warwick's "Papier Maché" ("Twenty houses in a row, eighty people watch a TV show. Paper people, cardboard dreams, how unreal the whole thing seems." [lyrics by Burt Bacharach and Hal David, 1970]).

Despite its material ties, the geographical distance of suburbia from the central city, the isolation of ghettos, and horizontal character of looping highways and shopping complexes enabled the notional separation of suburbia from downtown and the inner city.

In his study of postwar suburban culture, Eric Avila (2004) describes the gulf between the suburbs and the inner city (after a lyric from George Clinton) as "chocolate cities and vanilla suburbs." For Avila, popular culture helps to invent new types of whiteness by mediating the racial geography of separation and privatization, characterized through the sanitized worlds of Disneyland and the managed perspective of freeway systems that obfuscated views of the inner-city neighborhoods they passed through, preventing a comprehension of the multiplicity of urban lifeworlds harbored within the contemporary built environment. Yet as the incipience of anti-suburbanism demonstrates, the ersatz, vanilla culture of the suburbs was by no means monolithic. A quickly emerging disenchantment with the suburbs, in fact, produced renewed interest in the city as a place of contingency, heterosocial encounter, and autonomous reinvention; everything that the suburbs were not. This image of the city is captured in works ranging from WAR's "City Country City"—an extended track from their bestselling *World is a Ghetto* album (1972) that transitions between an unhurried pastoral passage to a more frantic rhythmic funk to signify a movement into the city—and Lou Reed's "Walk on the Wild Side," to Ralph Bakshi's *Heavy Traffic* (1973) and Paul Cadmus's painting "Subway Symphony" (discussed in chapter 4). Reed famously populates his song with characters who have converged on New York from Long Island and Miami in order to use the city to explore new identities and desires.

A sense of possibility extended to the city's material environment. In contradistinction to the monotonous landscape of tract housing, the central city, clutter and all, offered the experience of an architecturally variegated territory. More so than the automobile-centered suburbs, the city offered pedestrian experiences that necessitated negotiating labyrinthine spaces and contact with the people who moved through them. Whereas the suburbs promised order and peace but delivered homogeneity, the city, as Sennett framed it in *The Uses of Disorder: Personal Identity and City Life* (1970), issued a healthy chaos that calibrated to modern life's adventure of dislocation. As the residential and domestically-focused suburbs became the nation's *interieur*, the post-industrial city emblematized an indeterminate external world.

Given this context, an answer to Canby's question begins to come into focus. As "America's city," New York and its mess came to represent the status of the central city as a social and cultural project and as a space of social possibility. On the one hand, "mess" could designate the panorama of visual disarray and unrest comprising the non-suburban realm. On the other hand, mess also portended an emergent form of urban representation, one that confronted the prospects for urban life head on. To be sure, films like *The Out-of-Towners* (1970) and *Law and Disorder* featured plots trading on and amplifying anti-urban motifs. Yet shooting commercial features also encouraged filmmakers to open themselves to the multitude of representational possibilities afforded by the urban environment and to develop new ways of interpreting this territory.

Consider, for example, how the word "gritty" has become a byword for the films of this era; used most often in criticism and publicity to signal the use of seedy and unsavory milieus, such as the world of street hustling rendered by *Midnight Cowboy* (cinematographer Adam Holender, 1969). Yet within 1970s cinema, "grit" is more than just a thematic value, it is also a visual aesthetic. The term is most frequently used when describing the desaturated colors achieved by cinematographers who "pushed" film stock—underexposing by a stop during shooting and overexposing in the lab. A favored technique of cinematographers Gordon Willis (*Klute* [1971], *The Godfather* [1972]) and Owen Roizman (*The French Connection* [1971], *The Taking of Pelham One Two Three*), pushing is responsible for the way that daytime outdoor scenes become imbued in brackish tones of green and deep brown.[4] Part of the appeal of this technique was that it helped cinematographers better manage the shifting patterns of daylight at a location. In its kinship to the color and feeling of rust and mud, pushing makes the city textural, amplifying the chromatics of deindustrialization. In certain ways then, when we use the word grit, we are referencing a visual quality developed within 1970s practices tied to location production.

Grit, moreover, is a term that through the 1970s extends beyond film aesthetics to capture a broader sensibility toward the changing American landscape. As the utopian aspirations of architectural modernists like Le Corbusier, Mies van der Rohe and their adherents came under question, attention was turned toward America's vernacular landscape (for, example, in Robert Venturi and Denise Scott-Brown's pioneering *Learning from Las Vegas*). Part of this turn, inflected by the nostalgia that would mark postmodernism, aestheticized rusting industrial fixtures and factory interiors. Artists in New York who colonized the Cast Iron district that came to be known as Soho and Tribeca, for example, prized the rawness of the factory floors they converted to lofts, often leaving artifacts of industry exposed. An article for the American Institute of Architects' *AIA Journal* entitled "Rediscovering the Gritty Cities" also exemplifies this turn. Published less than ten years after Robert Smithson's ironic travelogue "Tour of the Monuments of Passaic, New Jersey" in *Artforum*, the article features photos and text that establish grounds for a reappreciation of the architectural forms to be found in industrial towns of that state, as well as those of Pennsylvania, Maryland, and others along the rust belt. The authors draw attention to the variety of street designs, housing types, and shopping districts to be found in these cities, even gesturing toward familiar forms of urbanism occurring there: "Hoboken may be the liveliest downtown of them all," they write, "stimulated by the newest ethnic group—the large Latin population—and young couples from Manhattan buying brownstones" (Procter and Matuszeski 27).

Looking over Canby's list of messy New York films, one genre predominates: the crime film. It is not difficult to see why: crime fiction and urbanity have been deeply connected, from the detective story, to the gangster drama, to film noir. During an era in which the intense antipathy directed toward the city mixes and mingles with a renewal of interest in the city as a cultural space, crime film would rush in to reflect the anxieties, delusions, and fantasies surrounding urban life. In representing the city as a zone of danger and criminal enterprise, the crime film necessarily asks us to look at its surfaces closely, to re-experience it. As the architectural critic Geoff Manaugh has argued, "crime is a way to *use* the city," a way, in other words, to explore and re-purpose buildings and streets, to destabilize dominant understandings of inside and out, private and public. The same could be said for the form and genre of crime cinema and the city. Detective films, police procedurals, and gangster films orient us to the unseen or unnoticed aspects of modernity—the details subsumed in the crowd, surreptitious patterns of circulation. In crime narratives traditional distinctions between background and foreground dissolve, bringing us closer—bringing us *into*—the city.

Crime film is a form disposed to accessing and examining urban society. Some scholars who have looked at the relationship between the crime genre and the city, particularly during the era of the 1970s (and 1980s) have suggested that crime films primarily reinforce an anti-urban, white supremacist ideology (see, for example Kellner & Ryan 1988). Representing black and Latino ghettos as drug-ridden territories ruled by violence, hemmed in only by a necessarily martial police force, films from *The French Connection* to *Fort Apache, The Bronx* (1981) legitimize the culture of poverty discourses (and policies) that animate both liberal piety and right-wing revanchism. It is imperative no doubt to regard urban formations as both the product and object of systems of power and domination. This is particularly important in relation to what we call crime. Crime is a term that has been made slippery through its historically shifting social construction. In the modern era, the power to name the acts that can be called crime has been held by the ruling classes and wielded to sustain their interests through the regulation and control of poor and marginalized populations. What spaces after all, immediately come to mind when the word crime is uttered? Is it the corridors of Wall Street or the domestic realm, the sites of so many of the crimes of our modern world, or is it streets, parking lots, underpasses, and parks? What I am calling the urban imagination involves returning to the very public grounds of crime's social construction, its pre-empirical formation beyond the statistics, the social science, and the color-coded city maps. In this book I locate this associational realm of the imagination in the margins of journalism, popular visual culture, urban sociology, and, most centrally, popular cinema, and argue that there is more to see and hear in the 1970s crime film if we do not rely solely on interpretive approaches that seek to either redeem or condemn.

The sense of the term "imagination" used here is not the modern, transcendent conception, which regards imaginative images and processes as wholly separate from the world, but rather the older, more immanent sense in which the imagination necessarily partakes of reality. As the anthropologist David Graeber puts it, this conception of imagination sees it as "a kind of circulatory system through which perceptions of the material world would pass, becoming emotionally charged in the process and mixing with all sorts of other phantasms, before the mind could grasp their significance" (21). Attending to crime cinema's urban imagination is a way to emphasize the virtual, expressive, fantastical, creative, and occasionally utopian dimensions of film that fuse with actual locations, events, social realities, and material conditions, to create cinematic experience. Exploring this realm involves looking beyond strictly narrative meanings, toward the recurrent images, tropes, motifs, gestures, and backgrounds that comprise the crime film. In doing so, this book reveals that the crime films produced at the beginning of the 1970s were hardly as clear-cut as common descriptions like "anti-urban" or "dystopian" suggest—or, at the very least, that we should use these terms as points of entry rather than as a way of shutting down discussion.

At the end of the 1960s, the question on the minds of many, from the counterculture, to right-wing editorials, was: is the city, in all its messiness, actually livable? Is the city a sociogeographic formation that will continue into the future? Implicit in this question was an interest in what kinds of life were made possible by the city. When people returned to city centers, they sought out ways of life within formerly industrial spaces; they formed alternative, subcultural communities that thrived with minimal conveniences. So, too, did dominant culture once again come to value architectural heritage, refurbishing urban infrastructures for purposes of consumption and entertainment. The "downtown renaissance" that occurred in varying degrees across American downtowns was underpinned by a revaluation of urban life. How, in what is almost unanimously regarded as a resolutely anti-urban nation (see White & White, Conn), did it come to pass that Americans returned to the city? One answer, this book suggests, can be found in the urban imagination that courses through the crime films of the 1970s.

The connections between crime, film, and urbanity explored in this book is partially inspired by a persistent thread found within the work of Siegfried Kracauer. Throughout his major works, from his 1920 writings as a cultural critic collected in the anthology *The Mass Ornament* (1995), to his post-World War II books *From Caligari to Hitler: A Psychological History of The German Film* (1947) and *Theory of Film: The Redemption of Physical Reality* (1960, 1997), Kracauer explores a connection between the surfaces of urbanity and mass cultural representation, film in particular. In *Caligari*, Kracauer analyzes a cycle of "street films" in the Wiemar period—Victor Grune's *The Street* (1923), Bruno Rahn's *The Tragedy of the Street* (1927), Joe May's *Asphalt* (1929)—in which characters express their discontent with bourgeois domesticity by seeking sensation and vice on city streets. Even if many of these films concluded with characters returning home, submitting themselves to the realm they abandoned, for Kracauer their images of pavement, crowds, and traffic demonstrated that "in the Germany of the time the street exerted an irresistible attraction," and that "Life . . . is not worthwhile within the boundaries of the 'system'; it comes into its own only outside the rotten bourgeois world" (1947, 158, 159). In his later work, Kracauer expands *Caligari*'s mode of analysis to theorize film as a medium predisposed toward material life. The significance of urban imagery he discerns in *Caligari* becomes in *Theory of Film* evidence of the way that the camera is able to gather in and put on display a physical world that a culture of rationality has unduly abstracted. Moving between D. W. Griffith, Italian neo-realism, and documentary, he presents a case for cinema as a medium whose functions of recording and revealing allow spectators to re-experience material phenomena (*Theory*, 41–74).

The detective story, and crime films more generally, are of sustained interest for Kracauer. In the 1920s, he wrote a book on detective novels, *Der Detectiv-Roman: Ein philosophischer trakat*, a portion of which was translated and published in *The Mass Ornament* ("The Hotel Lobby") and, after emigrating to the United States in 1941 he wrote one of the earliest essays on what came to be known as film noir ("Hollywood's Terror Films: Do they Reflect an American State of Mind?" [1946, 2012]). In *Theory of Film*, Kracauer (much like his close critical acquaintances, Erwin Panofsky and Robert Warshow) isolated the crime genre for the ways its subject matter was explicitly "cinematic" in nature. That is, crime plots emphasized movement, detail, "things normally unseen," and "the flow of life"—the latter a nebulous concept meant to emphasize the "stream of material situations and happenings . . . a material, rather than a mental continuum" (71). Sleuthing and thrillers for Kracauer were narrative forms that successfully match and open themselves toward particularly cinematic subjects like contingency, the surfaces and objects of physical life, and movement. The detective searches for "material clues normally unperceived," necessitating the use of close-ups; the scientific nature of detection "justifies the attention . . . to physical detail." Finally, Kracauer writes, "it is inevitable that detection should take on the form of a chase," a form of emplotted motion that, like dance on film, reveled in spontaneous human movement through the everyday world.

In thinking through the popular dimensions of Hollywood cinema, this book also adopts Kracauer's concept of the "homogenous cosmopolitan audience," first introduced in the essay "The Cult of Distraction," in order to think through how the aesthetics of mass culture carry the power to connect audiences of disparate backgrounds (1995, 325). For Kracauer, mass cultural forms like cinema were defined by their power to dissolve traditional cultural distinctions. The homogeneous cosmopolitan audience, exemplified by the four million people of Berlin, was one in which "everyone has the *same* responses, from the bank director to the sales clerk, from the diva to the stenographer" (325). Written in 1926, Kracauer's concept of audience usefully frames the continued growth of Hollywood over the ensuing decade and corresponds with Theodor Adorno and Max Horkheimer's commentary on the unanimity and cohesiveness of the American culture industry (94).

Post-war developments in socio-spatial arrangements and the increasing differentiation of media forms and markets have made it difficult to conceive of culture on a mass basis. In the late 1960s and 1970s, changing patterns of exhibition and market segmentation augured new forms of segregation within popular cinema. As multiplex theaters emerged in the suburbs, the centralized run-zone-clearance system of theatrical booking, wherein films would open in downtown theaters before radiating to neighborhood and rural theaters, was gradually abandoned (Cook, 399). Theater chains that were prohibited from simply divesting themselves of underperforming downtown cinemas created the conditions for a cycle of popular film aimed at a black audience. In *From Sweetback to Super Fly: Race and Film Audiences in Chicago's Loop*, Gerard Butters brilliantly traces how black-oriented cinema—commonly known as Blaxploitation, a label that unfortunately erases the many non-exploitative films produced for black film-goers during this era—in Chicago played a significant role in galvanizing black audiences and reinvigorating downtowns as black cultural spaces.

Although the emergent power of youth audiences had realigned Hollywood's priorities in the late 1960s, the industry held onto an understanding of itself as a mass cultural form, and many of its products in the 1970s reflect a will to rebuild the mass audience that had made it so successful in the past. Many films produced in the 1970s, crime and action films in particular sought out (and found) audiences in both the cities and the suburbs, from *Klute* and *The French Connection*, to *Shaft* (1971) and *Detroit 9000* (1973). In fact, as this book will show, this traversal between the city and the suburbs becomes, in films like *Klute* and *Death Wish*, a central theme. Further, it was the crime film, more often than other genres, that was capable of making this traversal because its narratives invariably represented the urban spaces in which people of different identities and backgrounds mixed together. While acknowledging and building on the important scholarship connecting specific experiences of gender and race to film and urban life, this book hews more closely to the massified experiential stratum of film spectatorship elaborated by Kracauer, elucidating recurring urban images and motifs in films that traversed the apparently incommensurate social realms of the chocolate cities and vanilla suburbs in order to emphasize the shared, rather than divergent aspects of the urban imagination. Such an emphasis is not meant to erase the fact that the city is experienced in very different ways by different social groups, but rather to draw attention to the coagulation of mass culture, film and urbanity that forms the common basis of this variegated experience, the way that different people used the same films to see *into* their sense of the city. It is from this common ground that we can begin to understand how the meaning and shape of the American city transformed.

The remainder of this introduction develops Kracauer's line of thinking about the crime film, connecting it to the historically specific dimensions of American urbanity and urban discourse in the 1970s to set the stage for the chapters that follow. Here I show that the crime film's openness toward a material continuum as a generic form enabled a reflexive space for American audiences to grapple with the materiality of urban transformation, and that, at the same time, changes within understandings of urbanism itself provided a unique opportunity—a special sort of messiness—within which crime films could flourish.

The Basic Armature of the Crime Film

Of the crime films on Canby's list, each could be said to fit within a well-established subgenre like the police procedural (*Serpico*, *The Super Cops*) or the underworld drama (*Mean Streets*), or to develop new variations on the urban thriller (the vigilante film with *Death Wish*, the suspenseful hostage/heist plot with *The Taking of Pelham One Two Three*), or offer comedic takes on familiar crime film tropes (*Law and Disorder*, *For Pete's Sake*). In fact, this short list covers only a small portion of the films made in New York in the late 1960s and early 1970s that thematize criminality in some way. We might also include, *The Incident* (1967), *Madigan* (1968), *The Detective* (1968), *Coogan's Bluff* (1968), *No Way to Treat a Lady*, (1968), *A Lovely Way to Die* (1968), *Cotton Comes to Harlem* (1970), *Born to Win* (1971), *Little Murders* (1971), *The Anderson Tapes* (1971), *Panic in Needle Park* (1971), *Come Back, Charleston Blue* (1972), *Super Fly* (1972) *The Hot Rock* (1972), *Across 110th Street* (1972), *Shaft's Big Score* (1972), *The Seven-Ups* (1973), *Badge 373* (1973), *Cops and Robbers* (1973), *Black Caesar* (1973), *Gordon's War* (1973), *Three Days of the Condor* (1975), *Report to the Commissioner* (1975), and *Dog Day Afternoon* (1975). The list grows even larger if we move beyond New York to include all of the location-shot crime films made during this period in cities such as San Francisco (*Point Blank*, [1967], *Bullit* [1968], *They Call Me MISTER Tibbs!* [1970], *Dirty Harry* [1971], *The Organization* [1971], *The Laughing Policeman* [1973], *Magnum Force* [1973], *The Mack* [Oakland, 1973], *The Conversation* [1974], *Freebie and the Bean* [1974], *Mr. Ricco* [1975]), Los Angeles (*The Split*, [1968], *Sweet Sweetback's Baadasssss Song* [1971], *The Bus is Coming* [1971], *The New Centurions* [1972], *Cisco Pike* [1972], *Hickey & Boggs* [1972], *The Outside Man* [1972], *Trouble Man* [1972], *The Stone Killer* [1973], *The Outfit* [1973], *The Long Goodbye* [1973], *Busting* [1974], and *Newman's Law* [1974]). Crime films that featured other major American cities include: Chicago in *The Spook that Sat By the Door* (1973), *Three the Hard Way* (1974), and *Uptown Saturday Night* (1974); Detroit in *Detroit 9000*;Cleveland in *Up Tight!* (1968); Philadelphia in *Trick Baby* (1972); Washington, DC, in *Top of the Heap* (1972); Boston in *The Boston Strangler* (1968), *Fuzz* (1972) and *The Friends of Eddie Coyle* (1973); Seattle in *The Parallax View* (1974) and "*McQ*" (1974); and even Galveston, Texas, in *Together Brothers* (1974), among others.[5] The prevalence of crime subjects within urban-set films is perhaps unsurprising, the world of crime has been a durable source of popular fascination and a key to understanding the mysteries of the modern city. Crime genres of all sorts have always formed a significant portion of cinematic production, not least because both criminals and the investigators that invariably follow them are avatars of the visual—from the deceptions of camouflage and disguise to the eye for microscopic detail, signified by the magnifying glass, that penetrates inscrutable appearances. Relatedly, crime endows the popular dimension of film with topicality and social import. Though crime narratives may take place in any period or setting, crime films tend to be contemporary-set stories, frequently sensationalizing current events circulating within other popular texts, from novels to newspapers.

On the one hand there is a striking continuity in the forms of urbanity extended by crime cinema. It is not difficult to discern connective threads between the naturalism of *The Musketeers of Pig Alley* (1912), *The Asphalt Jungle* (1950), and *Mean Streets*; the urban exploitation of *Traffic in Souls* (1913) and *Death Wish*; the reformism of *Regeneration* (1915), *Dead End* (1937), and *Serpico*; or the kinetic action adventure of the *Nick Carter* (1908, 1909, 1910, 1911) series and *Shaft* and its sequels. On the other hand, there is an historical specificity encoded in these texts, one that relates to the currents within popular culture they drew on, the urban context in which they were made, and the sociological discourses on crime they make reference to. Raoul Walsh's *Regeneration*, the story of a lower-class criminal from the Bowery reformed through the efforts of a social worker makes sense against the political backdrop of Progressive-era America. While sustaining this reformist mode, *Serpico* places itself in relation to the transformation and professionalization efforts of the New York City police force in the late 1960s and early 1970s, as well as with the Knapp Commission hearings into police corruption.[6] Charting the urban imaginary of the crime film involves acknowledging its proclivity for directly referencing topical social issues, its intertextual relations with other popular arts, as well as its dialogic relationship to the crime as a generic form.

As a cultural object that has historically opened itself to topical issues and contemporary environments, the crime film invites us to look at it as both a distinct form and as a form open to being shaped by social, historical, and urban forces. Although all popular films define themselves both through relatively fixed textual features and the historical contexts in which they're produced, the crime film has, more than most other genres, foregrounded the latter, even while sustaining the former. Thus, to provide an accurate account of the flourishing cycle of crime films in the early 1970s involves a method that weaves between close analysis and a historicism that places visual codes within an evolving network of cultural meanings.

The urban and sociological disposition of the crime film is widely recognized but it has more often been presumed than specified. Gangster films and noir have tended to dominate genealogies of the crime film, subsuming the resilience and formal particularities of subgenres like the police procedural and the heist film, as well as the specificity of particular periods beyond the postwar noir cycle. Granting balanced force to both form and context has animated a small body of work on crime films, including essays by Tom Gunning (1995, 1997, 2009), Vivian Sobchack (1998), Murray Pomerance (2013), and the collection *Mob Culture: Hidden*

Histories of the American Gangster Film (Grieveson, Sonnet, Stanfield, 2005). Edward Dimendberg's *Film Noir and the Spaces of Modernity* (2002) is perhaps the most sustained study of the interaction between crime narratives and urbanity. Dimendberg's interdisciplinary intervention is to detour the questions of formal and stylistic essentialism that had dominated one branch of noir scholarship while also deepening an understanding of noir's historical relationship to the built environment that had been glossed by others. By pointing to the significance of noir's material grounds—backgrounds, settings, milieu, location, visual perspectives on urban spaces—Dimendberg's work also follows in the critical tradition of Kracauer. The method of *Film Noir and the Spaces of Modernity* also pairs nicely with Sobchack's essay "Lounge Time: Postwar Crises and the Chronotope of Film Noir, which uses Mikhail Bakhtin's concept of the chronotope (the literary figuration of time-space) to illustrate "lounge time"; the way that the prevalence of waiting around in bars, nightclubs, and diners in noir film hyperbolizes the empty temporality and homelessness endemic to postwar culture. In the work of both scholars, character motivation and psychology is de-centered in order to give greater prominence to the enveloping urban contexts that the noir cycle registers.

Influenced by this work, but moving beyond noir, the present study is also situated within a growing body of scholarship that eschews the putative anthropocentrism of narrative film in order to attend to a material environment that has frequently been cast as a neutral, non-determinative background. For American cinema this emergent scholarship has given a fuller presence to the proto-suburban landscapes of 1920s Los Angeles slapstick (Wolfe, 2011), electric lighting in noir (Keating, 2015), the streets of Times Square in 1960s sexploitation films (Gorfinkel, 2011), skyscraper films (Schleier, 2009), and apartment plots (Wojcik, 2010). Such approaches ramify a new take on film genre that departs from the syntactic/semantic framework productively established by Rick Altman (1999) in order to invite us to look at the worlds and environmental contexts that Hollywood films have furnished for our exploration. This work also sustains the sensibility of Kracauer, who, first watching American films from afar, found within their fiction a material world dense in sociological detail. In "Why France Loved Our Films," he wrote "May I mention too, those scenes from the completely average film *Mannequin* (1937), in which Joan Crawford, walking down a cheap staircase, switches off, from habit, the bulb, and afterwards, in the elevated train, talks and talks to her young lover. Behind such fragments of New York life the immense city itself seems to appear" (36).

In attempting to specify crime film's relation to the urban environment, one immediately confronts the problem that what is usually called a crime film in fact encompasses a number of subgenres, each with distinct and sometimes overlapping sets of conventions, formulas, plot situations, and iconography. Gangster films, social problem pictures, prison films, heist/caper films, psychological thrillers, police procedurals, detective films, serial killer films, and a number of others crowd within the classification, bobbing in and out of prominence depending on the historical period. Noir, a period strictly defined by crime films produced between the early 1940s and the mid-1950s exerts an inordinate gravitational force on the idea of the crime film—expanding, depending on the variable employed, across years, decades, continents, and generic categories. The present work is less interested in creating a classificatory framework for crime's subgenres and their hybrid forms in order to describe what crime films *are* and hence how the films of the 1970s fit or do not, than in describing what crime films *do* (and have done) with the urban environment at a particular moment. Thus, it is not an essential character for the crime film that is sought, nor a prescription for how crime films should deal with the city, but rather a tracing out of the particular *affinities*, within crime films, for urban settings.

The most pronounced affinity between the fictional form of crime and the modern city is expressed through the detective story. Though the detective story has antecedents in gothic and sensation literature, as well as other narratives of discovery and revelation (from *Oedipus Rex* to *Hamlet*), the stories of Edgar Allan Poe are commonly cited as the definitive point of emergence. Prior to creating the character of C. Auguste Dupin, Poe wrote "The Man of the Crowd," in which a narrator who has been sitting in a coffee house, classifying passersby, becomes so struck by a strange man he cannot help but follow him. For Walter Benjamin, "The Man of the Crowd" represented an "X-ray" of the detective story because it contained a basic armature—"the pursuer, the crowd, and an unknown man who manages to walk through London in such a way that he always remains in the middle of the crowd" (27)—that would be sustained in the more formalized investigative adventure literature to follow. Benjamin refers to Poe in the course of his essay on the Paris of Charles Baudelaire, who was also drawn to Poe's story, and who would go on to suggest the wanderer as an emblematic figure of modern life. Detection, however, gave form and narrative direction to the more aimless classifying gaze of the flâneur, allowing for a literature both distinctively urban and visual to continue.[7]

The critic and mystery writer G. K. Chesterton also recognized the detective story's itinerant nature, stating that the movement and visual scrutiny of the detective comprised a poetic approach to the surfaces of urban environment:

> Men lived among mighty mountains and eternal forests for ages before they realized that they were poetical; it may reasonably be inferred that some of our descendants may see the chimney-pots as rich a purple as the mountain-peaks, and find the lamp-posts as old and natural as the trees. Of this realization of a great city itself as something wild and obvious the detective story is certainly the Iliad. No one can have failed to notice that in these stories the hero or the investigator crosses London with something of the loneliness and liberty of a prince in a tale of elfland, that in the course of that incalculable journey the casual omnibus assumes the primal colors of a fairy ship. The lights of the city begin to glow like innumerable goblin eyes, since they are the guardians of some secret, however crude, which the writer knows and the reader does not. (1901, 119–120)

For many critics and commentators on detective stories—and even narrative art more generally—it is the solution (or resolution) of the mystery that forms the principle area of interest. In turn, the detective has frequently been cast as a heroic paragon of logic, the detective story teleologically advertising the normative virtue of sober reason.

Yet, understanding the detective story as a parable of rationality confuses its content with what is its final effect: the solution that recasts, and indeed re-tells, everything we have seen before it in a process of making logical that which seemed inconceivable (for example, homicide by orangutan in the middle of nineteenth-century Paris). It neglects everything that precedes the solution, what Benjamin suggests is the story's "basic armature": a crowd, a strange encounter, a parade of visual detail, a pursuit. Kracuaer agrees: "The eventual discovery of the criminal," he observes, is functionally necessary but "more or less in the nature of a letdown" (*Theory* 275). Chesterton too corrects this forgetfulness, reminding us that for much of the detective story, just as we are involved in a journey across the city, so too, before everything has settled again, we are in a heightened, often anxious, state of awareness that animates spaces, people, and objects.

That this type of narrative and its basic armature would in turn flourish within cinema is unsurprising: both the detective story and film were formed within the crucible of urban modernity and both were premised on examining and interpreting the hieroglyphic fabric of the urban environment. Theoreticians as diverse as Jean Epstein, Rudolf Arnheim, André Bazin, Erwin Panofsky, and others commented on cinema's capacity to vivify, defamiliarize, and renew a cognition of the world in much the same way that Chesterton, writing shortly after cinema's emergence, wrote about the detective story. Crime stories and film technology intensified each other's spatial representations. In mystery films, Panofsky writes, space is "doubly charged with time as the beholder asks himself not only 'What is going to happen?' but also 'What has happened before?'" (1992, 239).

A doubling could also develop by folding narrative intrigue into film's documentary images. Consider, for example, American Mutoscope & Biograph Company's *The Black Hand* (1906), the story of the abduction and ransom of the young daughter of a butcher by a notorious gang (coded as Italian immigrants). The kidnapping sequence begins with the intertitle "The Threat Carried Out" then provides a wintry image of a Lower East Side street in which a continuous traffic of bodies streams into view from both the depths and the edges of the frame. This deep shot establishes itself as a documentary view as a number of onlookers stop to gaze directly at the camera; the realistic street scene a contrast to the stagey, studio-shot scenes that have preceded it. Eventually, the butcher's daughter emerges from the background and begins to interact with a man searching for something on the sidewalk. In a moment, a carriage pulls to the side of the road, and the searching man helps snatch the girl. Here, the dense visual detail and actuality of the mise-en-scène amplifies spectatorial suspense. The knowledge that a threat is about to be enacted charges the frame, demanding anticipatory investment. Unlike documentary street scenes that invite us to comfortably watch the crowd's variety, or, as one early film catalogue puts it, "study its many interesting phases," (quoted in Gunning, 1997, 35), here we are tensed in our inspection. The kidnapping itself enacts a paranoia that Gunning argues is at the center of the modern cinematic thriller: the ability to see or to read a scene of terror but the inability to control it (57). But the scene also gains power through a reality effect. The weight of the descriptive detail supplied by the mise-en-scène mirrors the crowded perceptual field of the modern urban environment. The anticipation of a threat to be carried out introduces a game of visual cognition that the scene itself always seems to win at—the kidnapping is underway before we can discern its outlines. Still, the shot of the busy street has a synchronic effect different from our everyday experience. As spectators (relatively) safely ensconced in our seats, we can really look at these streets and their people, even if danger is omnipresent. This game of description and anticipation is sustained, as I will show, in urban crime thrillers of the 1970s like *The French Connection*, a film which deftly intertwines documentary and fictional elements to similar effect.

The descriptive aspects of detective and mystery genres are further elaborated by the literary theorist Tzvetan Todrov. In his essay "Typology of Detective Fiction," (1977) Todorov identifies the prominence of description and milieu in the American hardboiled tradition defined by the work of Dashiell Hammett, Raymond Chandler, and others. Developing a suggestion by the experimental writer Michel Butor, Todorov argues that earlier formulations of the detective story like the whodunit could be separated into two stories that roughly correspond with the formalist distinction between *fabula* and *sujet*, story and plot (45). The first story, the murder, has already happened, and is nestled inside the second story, the story of the investigation. The detective's investigation that is, involves a plotting out of what exactly happened before. This requires, Todorov states, a certain transparency of narration. "[T]o keep the second story from becoming opaque, from casting a useless shadow on the first, the style is to be kept neutral and plain, to the point where it is rendered imperceptible" (47).

Both this narrative organization and adherence to neutral description, however, are transformed in the hardboiled thriller. For the thriller fuses the two stories, or "suppresses the first, and vitalizes the second" (47). The concern of Hammett's and Chandler's detectives is usually not just a single murder, but a crime that is ongoing, a crime that the investigator is very much enveloped by, rather than apart from. One effect of this change is to privilege the narrative significance of the environments moved through by the investigator, downplaying, in comparison with the whodunit, the claims of the past on the present: "No thriller is presented in the form of memoirs: there is no point reached where the narrator comprehends all past events, we do not even know if he will reach the end of the story alive. Prospection takes the place of retrospection" (47). Unlike the whodunit, the detective thriller is oriented towards the present rather than the past; this present, moreover is less secure, more dynamic than the ground on which the detective of the whodunit enunciates the crime, for in the thriller crime and danger are ongoing and environmental.

Though he is describing differentiations among literary forms, Todorov's distinctions help to explain how it is that the thriller rather than the whodunit has been the dominant format within the broad assemblage of subgenres making up crime cinema. If film is understood as a medium disposed to showing over telling, it follows that it would gravitate toward a form given to description and milieu. Though, particularly within noir, flashback narration is prevalent, it is has less often been used as a tool for a detective's recounting of a crime.[8] More common, from the gangster film to the heist film to the police procedural, the narrative places protagonists in worlds and situations of encompassing danger, facing anxiously forward, rather than back. While the question of what has happened before lingers, the thriller places the viewer within a dangerous and uncannily mysterious present. Consider that in the preponderance of recent Sherlock Holmes films and TV series (Guy Ritchie's *Sherlock Holmes* [2009] and *Sherlock Holmes: Game of Shadows* [2011], as well as the BBC's "Sherlock" [2010–]) elements of danger, suspense, and sensational action are showcased as much as, and often more so, than Holmes' famous ability to reconstruct the story of a crime, as is a densely detailed London milieu.

As in the *Black Hand*, the crime thriller more generally has frequently depended on actual urban sites for its effects, the streets of Paris in Louis Feuillade's *Fântomas* (1913–1914), for example, or the sewers of Los Angeles in *He Walked by Night* (1948). This principle was further elevated within the semi-documentary procedural cycle of the late 1940s, which broke away from the standardized street designs on studio lots to seek out different varieties of setting. Films like *The House on 92nd Street* (1945), *Boomerang!* (1947), and *The Naked City* (1948) foregrounded the use of locations through voiceover and documentary montage in order to enhance their claims of authenticity. As one critic wrote of the postwar vogue for realism: "in a long-brewing reaction against phony studio sets and 'actors,' [Hollywood] found a new, newsreel, newspaper reality in the semi-documentary technique—actual locations, peopled by men and women whose 'glamour' came from within not without" (Phillip K. Scheuer "Movie Realism at Peak in 1948" [26 December 1948] D1). The attraction to urban location was not solely the verisimilitude offered by identifiable topography and landmarks, they also counted on accruing visual interest through the infinite variations of physical infrastructure gathered within the modern city, a heterogeneous and intersecting collision of pedestrian passages, edifices, and transportation corridors, bridges and tunnels, grand public buildings and tiny commercial alcoves, park spaces and abandoned lots, palatial residences looking over this built landscape, and dark underground recesses hidden from view. As James Sanders points out, cinematographers and location scouts began to fulfill more significant roles in a film's overall look than the production designer (whose job had been mostly aligned with studio-based practices), assuming responsibility for selecting sites that would be both consistent with, and add variety to, a film's design (342–43). In the threading of diegesis with locale, documentary views become infused with intrigue and, conversely, intrigue gains power from veritable settings. In turn, the city as a visual experience becomes defamiliarized and renewed. As much as the city may be inevitably become psychic space, it is foremost a material space, one that both enables and delimits visuality and grounds possibilities for action.

The full range of urban contexts—cultural, social, material—participated in by the crime film has been circumscribed in part due to the aforementioned tendency to focus on gangster films and noir. Popular surveys of American crime films have tended to follow up examples from early cinema like *Musketeers of Pig Alley* and *Traffic in Souls* with the gangster and social problem films produced by Warner Brothers in the 1930s, groupings of detective films (the *Thin Man* [1934, 1936, 1939, 1941, 1945, 1947] series, for example), and the film noir cycle of the 1940s and 1950s. Noir is then typically followed by neo-noir, which extends between the late 1960s into the present. Although such periodizations identify the major works and cycles of crime film they also tend to obscure the continuity of crime genres across film history. Between and within this periodization, detective films, prison films, heist films, and even gangster films, have been durable but evolving staples of genre production. Crime genres have also been carried along by the transnational currents of global film culture, leading to variations on the forms within different cultural contexts. From French *policiers*, Japanese *yakuza* films, and Italian *polizichetti*, to Mexican noir, Hong Kong cop films, and Scandinavian procedurals, almost every national film culture can lay claim to a distinct cycle or crime tradition that both reciprocates older forms and adds unique stylistic patterns. Yet here too, such genres invariably contextualize themselves within localized iterations of urban modernity. As much as *M* (1931) or *Stray Dog* (1949) offers a glimpse into the peculiar social spaces of Berlin and Tokyo, their narrative basis in crowds and the dynamics of urban circulation are globally comprehensible.

Does every film plot including a murder count as a crime film, or does criminality need to be the dominant concern? Definitions of the crime film tend to vary widely, even within critical and scholarly discourse. The film noir period of the 1940s and 1950s, however, has come to exert an incredible gravitational pull and the vast commentary and debate over the cycle has often obscured the contexts and traditions sustained within noir and after it.[9] One effect of the volume of this discourse is that the crime films produced in the 1960s and 1970s appear to be resuscitations of noir style, when in fact they are merely extensions of the urban crime thriller that preceded noir and was sustained through the original cycle.[10] Crime films appearing after the cycle are construed as "neo-noir," a bulky classification that tends to obscure both their inheritance and transformation of longer standing generic traditions. Certainly *Marlowe* (1969), *The Long Goodbye* (1973), *Chinatown* (1974), and *Farewell, My Lovely* (1975) draw on the 1930s hardboiled fiction that was the basis for 1940s noir but stylistically they mostly lack the expressionist geometry and chiaroscuro that most would associate with the original cycle.

A common definition offered for neo-noir by Alain Silver and Elizabeth Ward (1992) bypasses the films of the 1970s altogether, claiming that the neo-noir cycle can be traced to filmmakers in the 1980s that are "cognizant of a [noir] heritage and intent on placing their own interpretation on it" (398). This definition echoes commentary that has connected neo-noir with the aesthetics of postmodernism. Oftentimes neo-noir is seen as a genre that nostalgically recreates the sense of a different era; a style that, as Fredric Jameson notes of a paradigmatic neo-noir, *Body Heat* (1981), "permits them to do without most of the signals and references which we might associate with the contemporary world, with consumer society—the appliances and artefacts, the high rises, the object world of late capitalism" (1998, 9). For Jameson, neo-noir becomes a key example of the depthlessness of postmodern culture, its tendency toward surfaces and simulacra. Yet though this description may be apt for a handful of films produced at the beginning of the 1980s, it is only on shaky ground that it can be applied to crime films produced a decade earlier.[11]

Understanding the crime films of the 1970s, particularly the early 1970s, within the broader tradition and development of the crime film, opens up the possibilities for seeing layers of extension, expansion, and innovation that are related, but not dependent on noir. Indeed, although urban crime thrillers of the early 1970s extend some of noir's thematic tendencies, they do not often traffic in the self-conscious and nostalgic style that has been ascribed to neo-noir. In fact, the films of this time sustain a tradition of interest in exploring the "late capitalist" object world that Jameson sees as excluded from 1980s neo-noir: a built environment replete with high-rises, highways, urban renewal, shopping plazas, bars, and subways. These spaces, in turn, are doubly charged by what Todorov understands as the thriller's tendency toward prospection over retrospection. Not only is the specificity of the physical environment supplied through mise-en-scène, its presence becomes vivified via narratives disposed towards moving through the city, orienting and disorienting figures within it, with the legibility and illegibility of surfaces and people. The surfaces of the city invested in by the urban thriller are different (but perhaps adjacent to) the surface sensibility Jameson ascribes to postmodernism. The effect of depthlessness, for example, achieved by an Andy Warhol lithograph, derives from its strategic effacement of a referent, an untethering of the sign from a signifier. But the urban thriller's tendency to description and prospection, mitigates the free-floating aesthetic experience derived from pop art or other forms of self-identified postmodernist art. This book claims, in other words, that although the detective films of this period—from *Mickey One* (1965) through *Chinatown* and *The Long Goodbye*—begin to traffic in what is recognized today as the pastiche and nostalgia characteristic of postmodernism, many location-shot thrillers still made (implicit and explicit) claims to access and expressively interpret the actual, material conditions of the contemporary city.

The shift of the detective from a figure of the urban, material, modern to the (dematerialized) postmodern also depends on what element of the detective story is emphasized. In a certain way, the detective story may be understood primarily as an epistemological quest in which reason is brought to bear on a messy reality in order to produce the truth. This understanding of the detective story branches off toward the formalism of Agatha Christie's locked-room mysteries, and the rigid rules of the genre set down by S. S. Van Dine in the 1920s.[12] It is a postmodernist skepticism of the detective story understood as a parable of reason's power—its incredulity toward the suggestion of objective or absolute truths—that lies behind the development of the frustrated detective of neo-noir; the detectives of *Chinatown* and *Night Moves* (1975), for example, for which the solution to a crime becomes meaningless in the face of a mounting pile of even messier truths.

Yet the view of the detective story as based around the triumph of reason tends to abstract the experiential dimension of confronting, scrutinizing, and rooting through a messy reality, the questing *process* of interpretation that often dominates the story itself. Alain Robbe-Grillet challenges this transcendent-reason notion of the detective story, pointing instead to the ways these stories move us closer to the externalized object-world:

> The evidence gathered by the inspectors—an object left at the scene of the crime, a movement captured in a photograph, a sentence overheard by a witness—seem chiefly, at first, to require an explanation, to exist only in relation to their role in a context which overpowers them. And already the theories begin to take shape: the presiding magistrate attempts to establish a logical and necessary link between things; it appears that everything will be resolved in a banal bundle of causes and consequences, intentions and coincidences . . . But the story begins to proliferate in a disturbing way: the witnesses contradict one another, the defendant offers several alibis, new evidence appears that had not been taken into account . . . And we keep going back to the recorded evidence: the exact position of a piece of furniture, the shape and frequency of a fingerprint, the word scribbled in message. We have a mounting sense that nothing else is *true*. Though they may conceal a mystery, or betray it, these elements which make a mockery of systems have only one serious, obvious quality, which is to *be there*. (1965, 22–23)

For Robbe-Grillet, things and objects in the detective story would initially seem to be overwhelmed by the context of an overarching narrative. But gradually the story "begins to proliferate" such that the uncanny there-ness of things is thrust forth. It's not just that the detective story flips background to foreground, it destabilizes the opposition between them by suffusing the diegesis with their potent force. Even within the postmodern era of the frustrated detective, a messy, disordered object-world plays a key role.

According to Robbe-Grillet, the detective story is paradigmatic of a new form of writing that could do away with signification, psychology, and depth. His other model for this new type of writing, notably, is cinema. The implicit triangulation Robbe-Grillet makes between the detective story, the material world, and cinema echoes Kracauer's sense that sleuthing was a narrative frame with a tendency to gather in specifically cinematic motifs, in particular the "endless" material world Kracauer labels "the street," a site which designates "not only the street, particularly the city street, but also its various extensions, such as railway stations, dance and assembly halls, bars, hotel lobbies, airports, etc." (62).

Narratives of investigation not only create images of a material world, they offer the opportunity to reflect on the experience of living in this material world. In bringing up the chase, Kracauer is cognizant of the basic armature of detection and also the fact that as narrative, the detective film incorporates the elements of forward-facing prospective action and intrigue outlined by Todorov. "This complex of interrelated movements," Kracauer writes of the chase, "is motion at its extreme, one might also say, motion as such—and of course it is immensely serviceable for establishing a continuity of suspenseful physical action" (42).[13] In addition to recording the world, the chase also works to create the impression of open-endedness in the way it creates a contiguous geography, demonstrating the "solidarity of the universe" (64). Kracauer acknowledges the ideological function of such an action, its persistent role (from D. W. Griffith onward) in displacing the social contradictions arising through drama onto a physical plane. Though this may be true, the aim of Kracauer's film theory, as Miriam Hansen (1997) has shown, is to illuminate cinema's capacity to help us re-experience the physical world—a world so often given short shrift by a cultural predisposition toward psychology and the metaphysical. Within the detective thriller, scenes of chase occur frequently, and not just as penultimate narrative events. More than that just ideological displacement then, the chase may be read as one of the many tropes that remind us of the material realm within which the detective operates and reveals. The preeminence of chase is also what allows detective films—despite their intellectual markings—to be aligned with the more visceral genres of action and sensation.

The basic armature of the detective story—encounter, observation, and pursuit—comprises the key mode of urban representation across the chapters that follow. It is joined by the crime film's claim to sociological topicality. In their analyses of film cycles, Richard Maltby (2012) and Peter Stanfield (2013) have delineated topicality as a key feature of Hollywood film production, distribution, and exhibition, defining it as the transient, ephemeral, and indeed obsolescent appeal of popular films to the contours of their particular historical moment (Stanfield 216). Inasmuch as a crime film is a form always open to aspects of urbanity, as a cultural commodity, it also gears itself to historically specific, and easily forgotten, features of urban experience. Although the connection between crime films and society is commonly made in scholarly discourse, it has often occurred within the framework of sweeping thematic analyses or reflectionist arguments, which see film as mirroring or reinforcing broad sociopolitical patterns.[14] Such arguments can be illuminating but they frequently subordinate form and visual technique to preexisting historical narratives.[15] As Vivian Sobchack has pointed out, this tendency in noir scholarship has favored allegorical and metaphorical readings, rather than literal approaches that "ground both the internal logic of the films and the external logic of the culture and allow each to be intelligible in terms of the other" (130). To take the route suggested by Chesterton, Todorov, Robbe-Grillet, and Kracauer would be to understand the crime film not like a mirror or even necessarily a dark mirror, but like an X-ray, a magnifying glass, and a lever—tools, in other words for prying open and exposing the city for view.

By instead looking to historically situated aspects of 1970s urbanity—its banal modernity and new cultural spaces, the fad for undercover "hippie" police, the phenomenon of mugging—this book reveals aspects of city life that have been previously neglected, showing 1970s crime cinema to be a synchronic snapshot and an archive of forgotten urbanism. This book places these films in relation to the urban context that was their location, setting, and subject. What types of contact did these films make with the forms of experience available in the urban crisis? From where did these films gather their images and rhetoric, and how did they interpret it? Additionally, what types of expressive forms did this context take within crime film? To offer a focused historical image of the crime film involves not only identifying the generic forms it traffics in, but also triangulating it between the circulations of imagery and discourse that formed an urban imaginary and material context, the cities in which these films were shot, that formed its vision. To see this clearly, however, requires a closer look at the changes in American cities in the postwar era, and the changes in the way that cities were understood.

Back to the Streets

As highways looped through suburbia, canaled through the inner city, and dead-ended in the parking structures of urban cores, metropolitan expansion continued unabated in the 1960s, offering even vaster tracts of housing, commercial corridors lined with car dealerships, supermarkets and fast-food, and fields of parking lots abutting each other to create a patchwork of asphalt, concrete, and small ribbons of grass. Peter Blake derisively called this landscape, "God's own junkyard," the title of his book on the problem of urban planning gone awry. Yet despite a growing unease with metropolitan sprawl evinced by Blake and others, the external world of contemporary life in the 1970s could still be epitomized by the downtown landscape of the central city, a space of blind corners, soaring ranges of vertical construction, and whirling crowds of strangers. This distinction held, partly, because a new cultural politics demanded a conceptual division between city and suburbs (figure I.1).

Beginning in the 1960s, Barry Goldwater, Ronald Reagan and, later, President Richard M. Nixon helped to voice the new conservative discourse of "law and order," taking Democrats to task on a national level on the failure of Great Society programs to stem the problems of the inner city. Law and order became a catch-all term that, in addition to designating growing levels of street crime, also covered the panorama of 1960s social disorder, from inner-city uprisings and anti-war protests to juvenile delinquency and any type of countercultural expression (loitering, for example) perceived to be non-normative. According to historian Michael W. Flamm, the power of this discourse was "precisely its amorphous quality, its ability to represent different concerns to different people at different moments" (4). Conveniently fungible, "law and order" was a phrase that also resounded with the moral clarity of western myth at a time of intense confusion, a precursor to the more sophisticated arsenals of campaign imagery adopted by Reagan in 1980, and George H. W. Bush in 1988. Crime, rather than Vietnam, was the deciding factor in the 1968 presidential election, notes Flamm. Whereas Nixon and Humphrey's views on the war were fairly similar, they diverged in their approach to the growing issue of crime. "Crime and disorder were the fulcrum points," Flamm writes, "at which the local and the national intersected. Anxious whites now saw how national policies affected their neighborhoods; eager conservatives discovered how to exploit local fears" (9) The conjunction of "crime" and "streets" was a powerful national figuration of the modern urban landscape, another way for suburbia to claim itself as a social space different from the city and to deflect, however superficially, the broader social problem of de facto

Figure I.1. *Newsweek*, November 1971.

racial segregation onto fears over personal security. Yet it is possible to see in later subcultural developments—punk's adoption of the signifiers of criminality for example—that the indeterminate anxiety ascribed to the urban environment did in some ways hold a seductive power. What makes "crime in the streets" such a potent phrase is the way it ties, not unlike the "broken windows" theory of urban policing, an indefinite, fearful, and borderline experience to a generic but actual place, animating that place with an uncanny, imaginative power.

The external public realm was not only the intractable site of rising social disorder and criminal activity in the national imaginary, it also became a new object of inquiry within various forms of environmental thought, both specialized and popular. Throughout the 1960s, the geographer Melvin Webber developed the concept of "community without propinquity," the idea that the necessity of place and physical proximity to the process of community forming had been overemphasized. In "The Urban Place and the Non-Place Urban Realm," (1964) Webber argued that undue focus on the "physical city, conceived as an artifact; upon the spatial arrangement of activity location conceived as land-use pattern; and upon the urban settlement, conceived as a unitary place," had neglected the dynamic processes and relationships that now connected people across cities, regions, and nations (93). As communications and transportation technologies enabled spatial distance to be more easily overcome, physical places receded from importance as the defining basis of community. Within this transformation, new questions arise: what experiences or understandings could be attached to physical environments whose social functions had become dislocated, or, in the term aptly used by sociologist Anthony Giddens (1990) to describe an analogous set of social processes, "disembedded"?

Similar questions arose as the practices and vision of modernist urban planning came under intense scrutiny. At the nexus of modernism and capitalist modernity metropolitan regions expanded haphazardly—urban renewal, commercial sprawl, and the unchecked development of automobile-centered infrastructure produced dizzying spatial disarray. Dismay at the visual disorder and inhumanity of late modernist planning was conveyed in books like *The Exploding Metropolis* (1958), edited by William H. Whyte, Kevin Lynch's *The Image of the City* (1961), *The Last Landscape* (Whyte, 1968), *Streets for People* (Rudofsky, 1969), *God's Own Junkyard* (Blake), *Life Between Buildings* (Gehl, 1971), *After the Planners* (1971), and *Close-Up: How to Read the American City* (Clay, 1974), and was ubiquitous in the pages of architecture and planning journals and the popular press. The 1960s and 1970s also saw a veritable explosion of urban fields in sociology, social psychology, and political science that reinvigorated what were felt to be the hidebound orthodoxies of urban planning. Top-down planning processes became repeatedly challenged by emerging grassroots conservation movements, most famously by the opposition to the demolition of Penn Station in 1963, and subsequent protests, led by Jane Jacobs and other Greenwich Village residents, against the large-scale engineering projects that typified the reign of Robert Moses.[16] Jacobs' popular book *The Death and Life of Great American Cities* (1961) mounted significant resistance to the social engineering dimension of modernist super blocks, arguing for the vitality of densely populated, mixed-use, and pedestrian-centered neighborhoods. The success of preservation and neighborhood-oriented movements is attested to by the layout of the New York City Planning Commission's 1969 *Plan for New York City*, which now mixed the graphs and tables typical of planning documents with lively photographs of street scenes in the various boroughs. Architecture critic Ada Louise Huxtable explained the contextual impetus for the *Plan*'s approach in the *New York Times*: "the textbook scientistic-Utopian planning of long-range policies based on statistical extrapolations and translated into massive rebuilding schemes has proved such a conspicuous failure in the last 25 years that doctrinaire planning, and its adherents, are in considerable disrepute and disarray." The *Plan*'s new approach instead "deals with processes; with the forces of growth and decay and the inconstant and troubling human factors that underlies the city's serious disorders—things that cannot be pinned down on charts or graphs" ("Plan Is Regarded as Break with Tradition" [16 November 1969] 84). William H. Whyte played a significant role in authoring the New York City plan, and through the 1970s would go on to conduct a variety of street studies around Manhattan that would lead to *The Social Life of Small Urban Spaces* (1980) and, in turn, *City: Rediscovering the Center* (1988). In the twilight of the catastrophe of urban renewal, new approaches to urban design were to be sought closer to the ground.

The cardinal problem associated with modernist planning had to do with its logics of scale and perception, the way in which expansive open spaces engulfed individuals and made pedestrian traversal both arduous and overwhelming. Kevin Lynch's influential insight in *The Image of the City* was that principles of urban design—"design" itself being a scaled back idea of planning (Harvey 66)—should flow from the perceptual, on the ground experience of individuals navigating the built environment. After interviewing citizens in Boston, Jersey City, and Los Angeles, Lynch proposed that the composition of built spaces should take into account a typology of forms—paths, edges, districts, nodes, and landmarks—to better help people navigate and orient themselves. Designers also began to consort with popular currents in modern psychology. As urban historian Mariana Mogilevich explains, designers "saw attention to individual development and experience as a way to effect social change and a way out of their service to universal and hegemonic categories of standardized users" (23).

As criticism of urban planning practices mounted in the 1950s and 1960s attention shifted to the relationship between individual subjectivity and the environment in emergent academic fields like urban studies, urban anthropology, proxemics, ekistics, ecological psychology, environmental studies, and environmental psychology. For urban designers, the idea of a distinction and a relationship between an individual's consciousness and the built environment "provided the possibility of design's contribution to the greater liberation of the people, in the vein of 'sixties freedom' of personal fulfillment," but also "potentially made way for a more individualistic and privatized conception of urban space" (Mogilevich 23). This movement, in fact, is allegorized by the character of Paul Kersey (Charles Bronson) in *Death Wish*. Kersey, notably, is played by an architect in the film and is depicted in several scenes presiding over scale models of urban developments like an archetypal modernist planner. In his turn to vigilantism, however, Kersey's experience of the city takes a sharp turn toward the individualistic and subjective, the film now focusing, as I explore in chapter 4, on his perceptual experience of dimly lit streets and parks.

As *Death Wish* indicates, there was a darker side to the incipient culture of psychologization. What Christopher Lasch (1978) famously named the "culture of narcissism," also contained a paranoid underside that complicated experiences of public space and the experiences of people within that space. The issue of propinquity identified by Webber related closely to the cultural ascendance of what Richard Sennett calls the "tyranny of intimacy"; the ever growing suspicion of all relations between people that did not in some way involve bonds of warmth or personal disclosure. Sennett's *Fall of Public Man* (1977) demonstrated that this state of affairs was arrived at through the gradual foreclosure of a vital public sphere that was participated in through collectively understood codes of performance and visual display (i.e., gesture, comportment, or costume). The urban public realm of the eighteenth- and nineteenth-century coffee house or tavern involved a sophisticated production of signs that created conditions for enlivening interactions between strangers. The escalating rhetoric of the self and its authenticity in the twentieth century, however, impaired activities common to the external terrain of city life that involved impersonal interactions between strangers.

This unease is rooted as much in the ideology of intimacy as in Webber's notion of community without propinquity. Webber's ideas initially seem more suited to the digital contours of twenty-first-century social relations than the relations of the 1960s, but what he captures is the sense of dematerialization portended by the emergence of the post-industrial age. If bodily proximity had ceased to become the natural setting and stage of social relations, what did it become? What codes dictated interpersonal social relations within physical space? What could we now make of the external public realm? Moreover, if unmediated interpersonal relations now assumed increased value, what did it mean to be close to someone whom one did not know, or even to be within a space, like the city, where strangers were known to gather? It is within this context of a growing gap between inside and outside that an urban imaginary centered on crime finds a place.

A number of thinkers picked up on the novelty, strangeness, and uncertainty surrounding the public realm. The emergent disquiet inspired a variety of interpretive approaches dedicated to looking closely at the dynamics of everyday social life. This work includes, for example, Edward T. Hall's conception of "proxemics" (social distance) in *The Hidden Dimension*; Lyn H. Lofland's close study of codes of behavior in *The World of Strangers: Order and Action in Public Space*; as well the thickly descriptive analyses of various urban scenes—from the Chicago art world and police riots to con games and pornography shops—in the fledgling journal *Urban Life and Culture* (1972–present).

Perhaps the most influential scholar in the emergent study of everyday urban life was Erving Goffman, who across numerous books and essays beginning in the 1950s developed a dramaturgical perspective on social relations that denaturalized encounter and public behavior in order to reveal the hidden structures of social conduct. Whereas Sennett described what practices had fallen away from the public sphere, Goffman examined what had rushed in to take their place on the obverse of intimacy.[17] After a period of silence in the late 1960s, in 1972 Goffman returned with *Relations in Public: Microstudies of the Public Order*, a series of essays concerning the dynamics of interaction in modern public realm. For Marshall Berman, this new work solidified Goffman as the "Kafka of our time," and unlike the academic detachment of his earlier work, signaled that Goffman had indeed "experienced the Sixties" and was now more explicitly positioning his analysis within history rather than conceptual abstractions (Berman "Weird But Brillant Light on the Way We Live Now" [27 February 1972] *New York Times*, BR1, BR10).

In *Relations in Public* Goffman forthrightly identified the historical specificity of his micro-logical approach, writing that public life as an object of study and concern had come the fore as a result of

> a complex unsettling expressed variously in the current unsafety and incivility of our city streets, the new political device of intentionally breaking the ground rules for self-expression during meetings and contacts, the change in rules of censorship,

> and the social molestation encouraged in the various forms of "encounter group" and experimental theater. Indeed, concern about public life has heated up beyond our capacity. (ix–x)

Like the law and order conservatives (but without the eye toward political machination), Goffman recognized the dense significance of criminal activity, filling *Relations in Public* with anecdotes of smugglers, bank robbers, con artists, and muggers drawn from newspaper articles, popular nonfiction, and spy novels. For those politicians intent on fashioning a "silent majority," the overhanging motif of crime in the streets was useful for its fogginess. But this obscurity was precisely where Goffman began his analysis—not to diffuse the generalized moral panic over social breakdown, but to de-sublimate its hidden conventions. In the book's longest essay, "Normal Appearances," Goffman explored how it was that individuals both interpreted and produced the appearance of normalcy in public places, such a judgment significant in determining the presence of potential threats or the relative safety of their immediate surroundings, or, more simply put, how we might come to suspect that something is up, the lengths that people will go to from preventing us from thinking something is up, and why we do not think something is up more often. His questions moved beyond the normative values of social science by seeking to explain not how to maintain social order, but how social order was maintained at all. In that Western society was increasingly, and justifiably, testing the apparatus of civility, what generalizable codes governed our perception and navigation of the byways and passages of public life?

Crime, for Goffman, gave special access to these codes. The success of a gang of thieves dressed as construction workers who pull off a jewel heist on a busy street illustrates our tendency to disattend to "stocked characters . . . non-persons, mere background figures who function within a different frame of reference from co-users of the streets" (307–08). The low simmer of this paranoid imagination develops into a boil as Goffman shortly moves on to uniformed personnel, such as police men, who are "allowed the run of otherwise private places." "Here too, of course," Goffman dryly observes, "we find a role that often is used as cover by thieves, police agents, and rapists" (308–09).

Through the somewhat unorthodox (for sociology) method of culling data from reports of elevator attacks, blackmail, and smugglers, Goffman portrays successful crimes as precisely designed and carefully staged. In order to work, criminals must produce normal appearances so to better conceal themselves from their object until the last possible moment. Essentially, Goffman was interested in what, in an effort to remain invisible and undecipherable, crime makes visible about the surfaces of social life. The dissimulation, gain of trust, and tests of perception involved in criminal games—from con artistry to mugging to murder—threw into relief the outlines of social codes in a culture that was seeking to abandon them.

The implicit argument developed in "Normal Appearances" has nothing to do with deviance or pathologization, nor with seeing in criminal acts a dark mirror of our own psyche. As Goffman explains in a footnote:

> The argument is that the important thing about criminals—and other social desperadoes such as children, comics, saboteurs, and the certified insane—is not what they do or why they do it . . . the importance of these strays is not in the cue they provide as to what, in our heart of hearts, we do also, but rather in the contrastive light their situation throws on what, in doing what we do we are doing. What is accomplished during such acts? What do these doings actively presuppose? (260n19)

Crime, that is, hyperbolizes social dynamics, throwing into relief the habits and assumptions of our behavior. It is an act, for Goffman, that has the effect of bringing to the surface and rendering visible submerged presuppositions.

Crime Film in the Streets

The mounting zeal of law and order, the changing scale of focus on urban life and design, and the uncanny dynamics of the public social realm, forms the force field within which a new urban mise-en-scène comes into view. Crime in the streets was not just a byword for law and order conservatives based on a surge in urban crime rates, it was an image, one which allowed a consolidation of political support that would culminate with the success of 1980s conservatism, a reactionary formation that continues into the twenty-first century. For Goffman, however, the multiplicity of crime unfolding in public space was a way to understand the micro-logical dynamics of an emerging social order in which impersonal relations were infused with suspicion. Crime films were also being made in these streets. There is little doubt that these films may have helped to advance the conservative agenda (see Macek). More subtly, they also perhaps play a role in forging the imagery of urban fear that paved the way for the fortified designs of the downtown renaissance. But to see these films only by the retrospective light of the bad urban future that is our present is to neglect the uncanny propinquities, strange strangers, and weird physical spaces that were transmitted from downtown locations to national screens. It also neglects the ongoing lure of the city that through the 1970s, 1980s, 1990s and beyond brought all sorts of people willfully marginalized by the right to the city to forge identity and community.

This book will make clear that the crime film's openness to urbanity, tendency to spatial description and place-based sensation, as well as its sociological, mass cultural appeal make it uniquely suited to capture and transmit, frequently at the microscopic level preferred by Goffman and Kracauer, the social dynamics lodged within the urban crisis. If we understand crisis to mean turning point, it is clear that this juncture in American urban history also represented an opportunity for the city—opportunities that would be later taken advantage of by architect-developers like James Rouse and John Portman as much as they would by urban artists and subcultures.[18] This book presumes that a sense of ambivalence and uncertain opportunity form the foundation of an urban imagination that can be found within the crime films of this period. To open this dimension up, to really uncover how these films extend and connect themselves with these broader cultural energies and material realities, means looking closely at the images of the city they present, but also how these images reflect or respond to a diverse range of motifs constitutive of the urban imaginary at this moment.

This book covers a handful of films produced within the cycle of urban crime films made after the first flashes of the urban crisis, between 1970 and 1976.[19] Location production of crime films did not end after 1976, nor did urban crisis—in fact, for cities like Detroit, Buffalo, Chicago, St. Louis, and Newark the crisis deepened and continues into the present in even more complex forms. However, the production of crime films shot on location in cities swells during this time, both those made for the Blaxploitation market and those searching for a more diffuse audience. In larger cities, the insurrectionary fires were temporarily quelled—often through militaristically enforced forms of segregation—while their causes continued. This six-year stretch also represents the historical center of a transitional period in which modernism is said to have come to an end and what was called (for better or worse) postmodernism begins. Although there is good reason to be ambivalent about the historical break with modernism and modernity claimed by the gamut of postmodern periodizations, it is undeniable that as discourse about culture, postmodernism gains significant presence in the 1970s and 1980s.[20] This discourse, notably, focused on developments in architecture, the built environment, and media culture. The destruction of the Pruitt-Igoe housing projects in St. Louis in 1971 signaled the death of modernism to architecture critic Charles Jencks while, at about the same time, Robert Venturi and Denise Scott Brown were conducting the trips to Las Vegas for Yale Architecture students that would result in *Learning from Las Vegas*, their celebration of vernacular commercial architecture. The confusing layout of John Portman's Bonaventure Hotel in Los Angeles was for Fredric Jameson emblematic of postmodernism, "the cultural logic of late capitalism," and the difficulty of "cognitively mapping" (a concept of scale and perception borrowed from Lynch's *The Image of the City*) contemporary geopolitics.

Meanwhile, the success of *Jaws* (1975) and *Star Wars* (1977) ushered in the era of the blockbuster, ostensibly saving Hollywood financially with the help of post-Fordist production models, whilst also displacing the creative bloom of New Hollywood. As studios scaled back the number of feature films released every year, they began to invest more and more in event-based, high-concept spectacles and cross-promotional marketing strategies. From a vantage point at the end of the 1970s, Nöel Carroll observed that the films of the seventies and eighties—from *Star Wars* to *Raiders of the Lost Ark* (1981) to *Body Heat*—became increasingly reliant on nostalgia, allusion, and a recycling of styles from Hollywood's past (1982). And, in contrast to what Thomas Elsassaer (1975) identified as the "pathos of failure" marking New Hollywood, traditional heroes rematerialized. *Rocky* (1976), shot on the streets of Philadelphia, offered a new, white, working-class hero for national audiences that aligned nicely with the emergent cultural politics of the Reagan era. Viewers followed Rocky (Sylvester Stallone) on his jog through the gritty environs of this hometown, spaces that were simultaneously made authentic and romantic by the smooth glide of Steadicam tracking shots (Webb 61–67).[21] The triumph of *Rocky*—its narrative, box office, and legacy of sequels—signaled an end to the failure so prevalent in New Hollywood, as well as to the cinematic estrangement of the urban environment that marks the era I examine here.

The investigator-avatars of the cluster of location-shot crime films made in the early 1970s tread on a different ground, one that precedes the advent of postmodernism's predominance. They hold in common an ambiguity about the fate of the city that reverberated with phrases like "benign neglect" and "planned shrinkage" and evince a moment prior to the complete split of the city into downtowns for white shoppers, tourists, and executives and destitute ghettos for poor people of color; the borders of each assiduously patrolled. The group of films this book looks at closely—*Klute* (1971), *The French Connection*, *Serpico*, *Detroit 9000*, *The Taking of Pelham One Two Three*, and *Death Wish*, as well as several others—are distinguished by an anti-nostalgic tendency that marks them off from the postmodern style that would close the 1970s. The root of nostalgia is homesickness, and what I believe these films can be seen to acknowledge is the strangeness of an environment that through a destruction of context (either through suburbanization or urban renewal) and a decline in traditional forms of propinquity has been made to seem less and less like home, but also curious, worthy of investigation.

1

Parking Garage, Apartment, Disco, Skyscraper

Alan J. Pakula's Banal Modernity

In an interview with Richard T. Jameson, Alan J. Pakula stated that he "loved to use architecture to dramatize society" (16). Hearing this, one might be might be inclined to think that Pakula is referring to a famous scene in his *All the President's Men* (1976), wherein a camera pulls up from hundreds of little slips of paper to reveal a bird's-eye view of the floor of the Library of Congress. As significant as Washington DC's landmarks may be to that film, however, it was another, much more ordinary seeming space, that became impressed on the national imagination:

> A GIGANTIC UNDERGROUND TYPE GARAGE
>
> Cut to:
>
> WOODWARD ENTERING THE GARAGE. It's an eerie place, and his heels make noise and if you wonder is he edgy, yes he's edgy. He comes to the ramp leading down to lower levels, hesitates
>
> Cut to:
>
> THE RAMP. It seems to descend forever.

Cut to:

> WOODWARD starting down. HOLD on him as he walks. Down he goes, the shadows deepening, then disappearing, then covering him again. He continues on. (Goldman 254–55)

By the 1960s and 1970s parking garages had already been familiar urban forms for many years. The mass production of automobiles, beginning in the 1920s, rendered street parking unviable and necessitated buildings dedicated to stacking vehicles. The ubiquity of parking structures by the mid-century testified not just to the ascendancy of the automobile, but also to the ways in which the central city changed to accommodate the suburban periphery. A 1965 study reported that 73.2 percent of downtown parking in the United States was being used by office buildings, indicating the influence of automobile commuters on the downtown landscape (McDonald 61). But, whereas in the 1920s and 1930s buildings for parking had been imbued with the modernity associated with the culture of motorization, by the 1950s their design had assumed a moribund uniformity. When cold-resistant engines obviated the necessity of protective enclosure, open-deck designs became predominant, eliminating the architectural façades that had once tied them into the townscape (46). By the late 1960s architects began to use screens to ornamentally sheath the naked utility of the open-air structures, disguising the extent to which downtowns had become warehousing districts for automobiles.

Placed undercover or underground, the parking garage has been a consistently suppressed feature of the urban landscape since the mid-twentieth century. Although many cities feature aesthetically appealing garages designed by top-flight architects (in Bertrand Goldberg's Marina City complex in Chicago, for example) the generically designed parking garage is typically a type of vernacular Brutalism. Concrete and seemingly anti-human—or at least antisocial—in the most literal sense, the alienating effect of the interior space of parking structures is amplified by the fact that they are environments that feature few concessions to the pedestrian traffic they functionally produce. Their crude functionality only adds to the converse effect of the attempt to erase the visibility of the parking garage from the cityscape: once inside, one feels emplaced nowhere—in a space under or parallel to the city with no real footing, only an exit to move toward, if it can even be located within the numerous identical levels and recursively looping ramps. Profoundly anti-contemplative for many, despite being a bastion of relief between traffic congestion and the modalities of white-collar labor, parking garages are designed to be moved through (preferably in a car), not thought about.

Built for movement not inhabitation, the banished, liminal interior of the parking garage is a concrete metaphor for the spatial negativity of what Henri Lefebvre calls "abstract space" (50).

Protesting the pejorative fate of the parking garage interior, Shannon Sanders McDonald's recent history of parking structures as evolving architectural forms begins its final chapter by asking why the parking garage "has come to represent people's deepest fears, instead of their dreams?" (249). Noting it as a transitional space, "a private environment where time and space merge," she opines: "The garage is experienced as a void between events, where the mind can reach towards new visions—if we allow it to" (297n45). Though perhaps not in the way McDonald intends it, this call to fill in the empty space of the parking garage with "new visions" has been repeatedly met by cinema. Since the beginning of their ubiquity in the urban landscape, generic parking garages have figured centrally in genre film and television; first perhaps to connote contemporaneity, but later, curiously, as a setting for shadowy exchanges of goods or information, violent physical confrontations and assaults (see for example, *I Am a Fugitive from a Chain Gang* [1932], *Double Indemnity* [1944], *The Lady From Shanghai* [1947], *Chicago Deadline* [1949], Joseph Losey's version of *M* [1951], *The Driver* [1978], *Robocop* [1987], *Fargo* [1996], *The Bourne Ultimatum* [2007], and *P2* [2007]), and even sadistically tinged sexual encounters (*Body of Evidence* [1993]).[1] As an architectural space into which we see only with difficulty, and where the efficient storage of vehicles seems to trump the needs of the human body/cogito, the parking garage becomes the preeminent site upon which to figure clandestine and nefarious activities that are building blocks of crime thrillers. Mobilizing an architectural potential for undetectable violence and a suggestion of the forbidden and unseen, cinema both hyperbolizes the parking garage's everyday refusal of human life and redeems it as a space of urban experience, however dreadful. Yet, as much as the parking garage on film becomes an imaginative space, this imaginativeness is grounded by the crude facticity of the structures themselves. The historical formation of the parking garage, its status as a liminal, abstract, and occluded space of urban modernity, grounds the way it can be visualized within film narratives, and perhaps even what kinds of things can be visualized there.

❧

All the President's Men, in its famous portrayal of Bob Woodward's anonymous meetings with the figure who came to be known as "Deep Throat," features one of the most striking, if not definitive, cinematic uses of the parking garage. Woodward (Robert Redford) initiates the first rendezvous by placing a red flag in a flowerpot on his outdoor patio (a detail, Woodward and Bernstein's book notes, that followed Deep Throat's written instructions). Later on, he ventures into the DC night, changing cabs in the midst of the theater crowd at the Kennedy Center to avoid potential pursuers. In a very long shot, Woodward is shown exiting his taxi at what seems to be his final destination: a dark, nondescript structure that fills the screen, squeezing him and his cab into the top left corner of the frame. After descending the structure's exterior stairwell, the miniscule Woodward enters, a move not conveyed through the standard conventions of the establishing shot. The point where Woodward exits from the taxi rearranges axiomatic body-space representations wherein a vehicle is typically exited at the front of a building at its base, and where a low angle might for a moment compare the vertical scales of individual to building (as seen repeatedly with Gary Cooper, for example, in King Vidor's *The Fountainhead* [1949]). Instead, Woodward is first beside the structure at what would seem to be its upper level before he descends to enter it. The strange effect of this visual composition—a dwarfed body scrambling through strange pathways around a dark and inscrutable structure—is the result of a reversal of the anthropocentric bias of conventional shot composition, the building here seeming to be the figure rather than the ground of the shot. This protracted one-shot sequence indicates that the strange dominating power of modern functional architecture is intertwined with the way it configures the human body as, at best, incidental to its mammoth utility.

Cutting to a shot of this building's interior we now see that it is of course a parking garage, a dark recessive space lit sporadically with bright fluorescent tubes to render it variously gray, dark-gray, and pitch-black. Woodward emerges out of the darkness and walks into the foreground, the sounds of the soles of his shoes echoing loudly against the concrete walls and floors as he comes into view and scans his surroundings (figure 1.1). A cut to a reverse angle shows even more of the garage, capturing the pattern of concrete columns, smattering of monochrome cars, and fluorescent lights that recede, blacken, and disappear in the distance. Here, Woodward enters from behind the camera to survey the layout. Cut now to pair a close-up of a pair of watching white eyes, part of a face whose features are almost entirely obscured by darkness. Woodward is wandering confusedly but the distinct sound of a cigarette lighter is suddenly heard and, spinning around, he spies the shadowy figure standing beside a column. The sound that immediately precedes this visual is therefore keyed as both an auditory message ("I want to be heard") and a beacon ("This is where I am"): this is "Deep Throat" (Hal Holbrook), the man he came to see.[2]

Figure 1.1. *All the President's Men.* Woodward's view of the parking garage.

Although the 1974 book based on Woodward and Bernstein's reports for *The Washington Post* refers to the content of Woodward and Deep Throat's meetings, the garage functions merely as a backdrop in the book's story rather than a palpable location. Occasionally in the novel, the two men kick the wall, sit on the garage floor, or place their hands on a car, but aside from these minute spatial references the place is primarily conceived as an empty domain in which informational exchange can secretly happen—significant in signaling that these meetings are clandestine but insignificant for its particular properties. In the book, in fact, Woodward and Deep Throat meet once, and quite successfully, in the more sociable environs of a tavern outside of the city. But in the film they meet only in the parking garage. The inspiration to amplify the visual presence of the garage in the film arguably came from Julian Allen's paintings for the *New York* magazine series "The Secret Illustrated History of Watergate," (figure 1.2) published in the spring and summer of 1974, portions of which are included as clippings in a "Visual Research Materials" folder amongst the film's production files.[3]

As happens, too, in the film version of *All the President's Men*, Allen's painted illustrations portray Woodward in a recessive concrete darkness, a shadowy figure walking toward him. Allen and a number of other artists were hired by *New York* design director Milton Glaser and editor Clay Felker to provide painted imagery that would capture Watergate's key moments (Heller 2002, 145). At the time when it was published, Allen's paintings for the series constituted a significant contribution to

Figure 1.2. Julien Allen Painting of Woodward's meeting with Deep Throat for *New York* magazine's "Illustrated Secret History of Watergate," June 1974.

the visual inventory of the scandal. As graphic design historian Steven Heller recalls:

> During Watergate the world struggled to conjure images of the besieged Richard Nixon and his henchmen in their banal illegal acts. Julian brought them all to life. The inspired choice of Julian to make concrete Watergate's most private and secret moment [sic] gave all us readers of *New York* magazine a chance to see what was only suggested . . . I can't think of Watergate without seeing Julian's images. (Heller 5)

The visualization of Watergate that Pakula creates with cinematographer Gordon Willis extends Julian Allen's aesthetic, with the filmmaker and editor Robert L. Wolfe building and augmenting suspense in the parking garage scene first through a series of hidden notes and signals then in discreet passage to a precise location as yet unknown to viewers. Yet, whereas Woodward's movement to his destination is captured in an elliptical montage of discrete scenes and locations that fragment the length of his journey, (leaving the house, the opera crowd, exiting the taxi), once inside the parking garage time begins to be expressed in more durational consecutive moments, each successive moment felt one after the other in longer takes.

The camera's perception and point of view is for the most part joined with Woodward and the visibility of the garage is delimited by the disproportionate zones of luminescence in the space, even when the film cuts to a close-up of Deep Throat's eyes before Woodward has spotted him. Prior to this disclosure of Deep Throat's presence we may be given to anxiously wonder if Woodward is alone here. The power of the sequence derives from the uncanny banality of the space and the way it seems in these moments to have been built doubly for the storage of automobiles and for games of hide-and-seek such as this. Further, it is an ideal site to demonstrate cinema's ability to modulate darkness and light in order to produce uncertainty, to provoke anxiety and build suspense by suggesting elements on a narrative level but withholding them in the immediate field of vision. It is in the filmmaker's attention to the ambience of the meeting site that it becomes possible to see how what Hayden White calls "historiophoty"—"the representation of history and our thought about it in images and filmic discourse"—both forms and sustains the historical imagination (1193). In *All the President's Men*, the parking structure becomes inextricably linked to Deep Throat's knowledge and communication, not just a meaningless building, not just a node of informational exchange but precisely the imagined site of Watergate's disclosure, of history itself.

It would have been difficult to predict that a parking garage in the nondescript business district of Rosslyn, Virginia, would one day bear a historical plaque describing the meetings between Bob Woodward and Mark Felt/Deep Throat. Perhaps more surprising is the fact that the significance of the parking garage to the Watergate story might have gone unnoticed if it were not for the creative effort of Julian Allen and, in turn, Pakula and Willis, who shot the parking garage scenes for *All the President's Men* thousands of miles away from their original location at a parking structure in the ABC Entertainment Complex at Century City, Los Angeles.[4] In emphasizing the rather banal sites of Watergate's unfolding—a hotel, the open-plan office of the *The Washington Post*, a banal parking garage—*All the President's Men* brings generic space into the realm of historical meaning.

❧

The garage in *All the President's Men* is but one of the spaces of banal modernity that recur within Pakula's 1970s thrillers, and its representation exemplifies the director's interest in depicting the ways that contemporary built environments impinge, crowd, and otherwise squeeze the individual body, as well as the way that the particular experience these material spaces provide subtly shapes an isolated and estranged spatial consciousness. As Woodward's foray into the parking garage demonstrates, Pakula marshals the conventional prospective poetics of the thriller—its forward leaning anticipation of threat—into ways of bringing everyday spaces into visibility.

As *Klute* and *The Parallax View*, the other two films in what have been called his "paranoia trilogy," demonstrate, Pakula was drawn not only to iconic, nationally significant sites, but also a more anonymous contemporary urban topography. Pakula's professed interest in architecture as a dramatic social space is especially evident in *Klute*, the first in the paranoia series (which could also be extended to include his later films, *Rollover* [1981] and *The Pelican Brief* [1993]). The film tells the story of a private detective, John Klute (Donald Sutherland) investigating the disappearance of a suburban businessman, Tom Gruneman (Robert Milli) in New York City. Klute's investigation leads him to a call girl, Bree Daniels (Jane Fonda) who may have information about Gruneman and the two soon develop a relationship.

As a detective story, *Klute* conveys viewers through a selection of New York locales, in the process tracing the outlines of a social geography that imagined new boundaries between city and suburb, and which harbored new fears about the relation between interior and exterior space. Although existing studies of the film by Christine Gledhill and Fredric Jameson have picked up on this unique spatial aesthetic, their analysis suggests a movement away from the historically specific environments the film represents (through either ideological structure or allegory), toward a more mythical or abstract understanding of the settings.[5] With the benefit of greater historical distance (Gledhill and Jameson's analyses were developed in the mid-1970s and early 1980s, respectively), however, there is an opportunity to understand *Klute* in relation to actual urban environments and the types of experience they offered. *Klute*'s integration of familiar living spaces, spaces of nightlife, and sites of corporate modernism demonstrate a prescient attunement to the ways that cinema absorbs and translates cultural space. I examine these sites in particular detail here not to make a claim for *Klute*'s realism but rather to reveal the way its expressive modes made it aesthetically appealing for audiences enmeshed in the anxious hum of ordinary modernity.

Designs for Living

Unlike other urban thrillers, *Klute* centers primarily on living spaces, not the public realm of the street. With only a few scenes depicting movement through city streets, the film instead emphasizes the characters' preference for being situated and enclosed in privacies. Yet these spaces—the Gruneman household, Bree's apartment, and a few others—are never truly enclosed, but constantly subject to obscure incursions from the outside.

The Gruneman's

Although the greater part of the film is set in New York, the fact of the suburbs looms everywhere in the story, playing with and often undercutting the notion of an absolute separation between the two spheres. This has to do with the film's intent to trace out a libidinal economy connecting licit suburban corporate life with city-based sex and culture industries. The suburban environs of Tuscarora, Pennslyvania, where the Gruneman family live and where John Klute works as a police officer, are too far away from New York to constitute a proper commuter town but near enough to fall under its powerful magnetism. It is "commuters" that are understood to make up Bree Daniels's core business. Thus, where the suburbs are understood to be a place of domesticity and pious procreation, this film suggests that the city is where repressed energies may safely be loosed. In exploring this distinction, *Klute* does not reify it as an aspect of an insoluble city/country divide. Rather, by portraying the routine practices of male business travelers—a publicity tagline for the film suggestively implied "Lots of guys swing with a call girl like Bree"—it indicates they are part of a shared ecological system. Both the missing man sought by Klute in New York, and the depraved executive revealed to be the film's villain, Peter Cable (Charles Cioffi), work for the grandiosely nondescript Toll-American Corporation. With locations in Tuscarora and New York, Toll-American signifies the blandly corrupt edifices of capital that bind the suburbs to the city through both finance and sex.

The constant allusions to the suburbs in *Klute* are given a particular reference point in three short elliptical scenes set within the Gruneman household at the beginning of the film. The first begins with a shot of a Thanksgiving meal at the Gruneman table. Klute and Cable are present, and Holly Gruneman (Betty Murray) lovingly toasts her husband Tom across the table. Tom smiles back and now cutting back to Holly we see her sipping her white wine. But a subsequent reverse shot returning to Tom's place shows his chair empty. We have jumped ahead to a nighttime scene around the dining room table in the near future. Holly is being questioned about Tom's disappearance and his authorship of an obscene letter. Klute is again present, as is Cable, who faces away from the table looking out a window. A few scenes later, we are again at the Grunemans', this time on their lush backyard patio. It is six months later and Betty seems to be in a catatonic state as an FBI agent informs her, "There are thousands of honest, decent men who simply disappear every year." The settings of these scenes are crucial because as well as propelling the narrative toward the city they introduce a riddle central to the film. Why do thousands of men disappear, perhaps of their own volition, from such bucolic and paradisiacal environs?

Although it does present an idealized tableau of middle-class domesticity, the suburban mise-en-scène constructed for the Gruneman household also functions to bring into sight an architectural topos that will be carried over into the film's urban settings later on. The Thanksgiving dinner is staged in front of floor-to-ceiling plate-glass windows that open out onto an unfocused, yet sylvan exterior. Within the dining room, large potted and hanging plants of all varieties frame the scene, sustaining the chromatic motif of greenery even when the scene jumps to nighttime and the backyard darkens. Standing in front of their window, The Gruneman's friend Cable is placed in a position he will subsequently assume in the film many times, but in an office high above the city rather than in a suburban home.

Plate-glass, of course, was a ubiquitous mid-century building material, most often used to promote the modernist ideal of uniting outdoor and indoor space. As the architectural historian Sandy Isenstadt has shown, the integration of plate-glass into suburban architecture faced the difficulty of negotiating the inward-facing orientation to the hearth that dominated the design and discourse of the American home. Promotional strategies allayed anxieties of exposure by heralding the provision of a view—not a view toward the uncertainties of the outside world but a controlled view of the private landscape of the backyard. Thus, Isenstadt points out, picture windows could "bring the outdoors indoors without making the private public" (226). Additionally, although plate-glass itself was an emblem of modernism, by providing the private resident a visual relation to the outdoors "it was promoted as a means to compensate for having to live in a technological society" (226). It is, however, just this outside society that all of a sudden comes rushing back in to the Gruneman household, indicated by a bucolic view that suddenly darkens through sudden a cut from a late afternoon Thanksgiving meal to the nighttime interrogation. The synthesis of family, community, and the natural world promised by modern suburban design is economically conveyed by the Thanksgiving dinner but quickly foreshortened by the cut to the same dining room at night. A series of obscure outside forces is introduced: a disappearance (why? to where?), an obscene letter to a call girl in the city (lurking and spatially extensive perversion). The formerly verdant backdrop afforded by transparent glass is dark—with the familiar shift from exterior sunlight to electric indoor light it is the inside that is now exposed to the outside. A strange path has opened to the larger outside world. The Gruneman house is suddenly not a home.

Bree's

The primary home setting of *Klute* is Bree's New York apartment, a space that, unlike the Grunemans', has never seemed to have sanctity to begin with. It is introduced through an establishing shot that shows Bree climbing a set of steps on a street lined with row houses. As the camera tilts upward, the neon sign for a funeral home becomes an ominous portent within the frame. Cutting to a dark interior foyer, Bree enters and peers upward with a look of trepidation. Ascending tones on the score present themselves, cueing us to her disquiet. After she finally lets herself in and settles in for the night, the phone rings. On the other end is a "breather." The camera pulls back from the distraught Bree, surrounding her in the darkened space of her apartment, ascending tones and voiceless singing returning to the score.

As Pamela Robertson-Wojcik notes in her book on apartment-based films, *The Apartment Plot*, Bree's home is continuously marked as a space threatened by exterior forces: "Rather than a container or shell . . . Bree's apartment [is] particularly porous" (173). Indeed, Bree is assailed from all sides. Not only subject to threatening breathers, her phone conversations are also tapped by Klute, who takes up residence three floors below to begin his investigation. Cable watches her through the window from across the street, and also stalks her roof. In addition to its vulnerability, the apartment is also a physically mutable, unsettled space. First introduced during the night in almost complete darkness, it takes on a drab character the next morning as Bree moves through her daily routine. Later vandalized by Cable, the apartment's contents are disaggregated, the apartment turned inside out. In the context of Bree and Klute's developing relationship, its folksy furnishings become prominent. At the film's end, Bree is moving out, and the space is emptied of her belongings.

Bree's apartment set was designed by George Jenkins and built at the New York studios of Filmways in East Harlem. Not unlike a scaled-down version of the parking garage in *All the President's Men*—on which Jenkins also served as production designer—the apartment is built to be dark and recessive.[6] Essentially rectangular, the one-room layout features a bed at one end, a kitchen and fireplace along one wall, a vanity and small bathroom on the other, and a rocking chair at the opposite end. The set dressing arranges brownish-toned antiquarian elements like a Beaux Arts light fixture, a metal bed frame with looping ornamentation, a rocking chair by the fireplace, and a quilted bedspread. These objects connect Bree to rooted, traditional forms of life, and serve as motifs that stand in opposition to the sleek, transitory functional spaces through which she circulates, like a mod hotel room with a transformable sofa bed. The folksy feel of the apartment is also utterly contemporary for 1971. Its integration of neo-traditional elements is consistent with décor trends popularized through the ad hoc artist's-loft aesthetic. A 1970 *House Beautiful* profile of the loft of pop artist Robert Indiana, for example, shows rooms lined with old signs and commercial ephemera juxtaposed with early American furniture and a Victorian bed (Sverbeyeff), a cheeky rejoinder, perhaps, to minimalist trends of the time. Bree's apartment is urbane in this way, but also monochromatically drab. Thus, Jenkins's design suggests Bree's apartment, in its sophistication in the face of downward mobility, as a site in which contradictory forces play out.

Biographical aspects of Jane Fonda's life at the beginning of the 1970s impress further layers of meaning onto her character's apartment. *Klute* was filmed during the period of Fonda's heavily publicized political radicalization. The following year she would be famously dubbed "Hanoi Jane" for her activism in the anti-war movement. Onscreen, Fonda had transitioned from wholesome modesty to an increasingly sexualized openness, particularly via the films she made with her then-husband Roger Vadim: *The Game is Over* (1966) and *Barbarella* (1968). The press tended toward bemusement and casual misogyny in its scrutiny of Fonda and her political transformation during this time. Months before *Klute* was released, she appeared on the cover of *LIFE* (April 23, 1971) with the story inside leading snarkily with "Nag, nag, nag!: Jane Fonda has become a non-stop activist." The films that Fonda appeared in during these transitional years were often as not apartment plots, including *Sunday in New York* (1963) with Rod Taylor, *Any Wednesday* (1966) with Jason Robards, and *Barefoot in the Park* (1967) with Robert Redford. *Klute*'s apartment setting presents viewers with Fonda in a familiar terrain, but it is a terrain that has tonally shifted, not unlike Fonda herself, in response to social change.

In its intertextual relations to what Wojcik labels the "single-girl apartment plot," *Klute* is at the vanguard of the evolution of a certain imagination of a single woman's life in the city. Its downbeat vision would soon be followed by films like *T. R. Baskin* (1971) with Candice Bergen, *Looking for Mr. Goodbar* (1977) with Diane Keaton, *An Unmarried Woman* (1978) with Jill Clayburgh, and *Girlfriends* (1978) with Melanie Mayron and Anita Skinner. The single-girl film, however, also becomes part of a larger subset of 1970s apartment films, mostly set in New York, which register the increasing stress born by citizens as the result of street crime. In dark satires like *Little Murders* and *Law and Disorder* everyday harassment and routine violence combine to make going outside unbearable. As criminals start to infiltrate apartment corridors and elevators (in *Law & Disorder* a burglar even swings in through the window to steal a television while a resident makes a sandwich in the kitchen), the perilousness of apartment life induces agoraphobia and claustrophobia simultaneously.

The shadowy visualization of apartment life in *Klute* places the film in stark contrast to the pop aesthetic of the apartment comedies of the 1950s and 1960s. Although this is understandable given the generic differences between thrillers and comedies, it also indexes a shifting understanding of the apartment as a space in which inhabitants attempt to close themselves off from the outside world. The high-rise apartment of the pimp Frank Legourin (Roy Scheider), for example, is filled with modern furniture, op-art wall hangings, mirrored columns and track spotlighting—a typical bachelor pad. But the scene that takes place there is shrouded in darkness: Legourin's face is covered in shadow in front of walls illuminated by electric blue light. Thin lines of daylight from drawn blinds behind him underscore Legourin's insistent nocturnality and possible drug addiction. Given that Legourin is Bree's ex "old man," it is possible that this is the Park Avenue apartment that Bree alludes to having previously lived in when she was "in the life" on a more full-time basis.

Dark spaces gain a weight in *Klute* that fall heavily around its characters, emphasizing the potentially alienating effects of enclosure. *Klute* has often been described as a neo-noir, and indeed Pakula admitted that it was "modeled after the characteristics of a forties crime thriller" (Ciment 36—translated by author). Accordingly, he conceived of Bree's studio apartment as a "world without sunlight" (Brown 97). Jenkins's set design appropriately offers only two small windows and a grubby translucent skylight. Willis, who became known as the "Prince of Darkness" for his subsequent work on *The Godfather* (1972), is largely responsible for the dark images that dominate the film, most of which occur in indoor sequences. In these shots, Willis works in the manner of an Expressionist woodcut artist, using what appears to be a single light source to sculpt out only the partial shapes of a face or body. Indeed, the mise-en-scène of *Klute* is marked by solitary sources of light: lamps, candles, flashlights that shine brightly but are not technically powerful enough to motivate bright illumination. The darkness Willis achieves is less graphic, or geometrical, than the high-contrast cinematography commonly associated with 1940s and 1950s noir. As in *The Godfather*, his forced development allows the registration of darkened, but not completely black, visual details, thus producing a sense of a depth and physical variegation. Willis's dark spaces are volumetric rather than two-dimensional.[7]

This aesthetic announces itself most forcefully in a scene where Bree sits down at her own dining-room table, lights candles, and then switches off an overhead light, reducing the diegetic lighting to only candles. Even with the overhead source light on, the room already appeared dark. Fonda was lit with a strong overhead light that made it possible to see a refrigerator and stove along the right of the frame and make out the shapes of lampshades and a bedframe in the background. After she switches the source light off, Willis's dimmer overhead emulates the source light of the candles, but dim shapes and lines of the furnishings continue to be discernable—the appliances, for example, can still be made out on the right. Thus, increasing grades of darkness are implied rather than absolute light or dark—Willis's darkness is not a black void, but a defined chromatic space within which physical textures can be discerned. The overall effect of this shot, and others like it in the film, is to weigh the environment with material elements. This is not to say that the mise-en-scène eschews graphic elements. According to Pakula, his instruction to Willis, specifically for the initial meeting between Klute and Bree, was "to take the Panavision screen and wipe out all the horizontals and over the shoulders so that [Bree] is a tiny figure . . . always being squeezed and isolated." This effect is also achieved throughout the film through Willis's atypical production of densely dark space. Bree is crowded and pressed on her by her surroundings. This aesthetic of darkness combines with the recessive architectural design to produce a fearful expansiveness—there is darkness but there is also always possibly something within the darkness.

The uncanny feeling of the outside's accessibility to the interior is most extensively developed in a sequence of pursuit that has Klute chasing down a figure heard walking on Bree's roof. Climbing to the roof and dropping down into a building next door, and equipped with a flashlight, Klute searches a series of dark abandoned rooms in vain. The speed of the cutting combined with fragmentary dark images disorients spatial relations, making it difficult to discern whether we are looking at pursuer or pursued. Once Klute enters the adjacent building, the visual field is linked to his flashlight, thus, to a degree our vision is yoked to his. Sensing he is close to his quarry, Klute calls out Gruneman's name, fixing his gun and the flashlight on a closed door. There is an abrupt cut to a long-shot of a man in a suit caught by the flashlight beam, slowly kneeling to evade being seen, and indeed not seen by Klute although he is seen by us. Klute's gaze remains on the doorway, not toward the part of the room into which his flashlight has strayed. Retracing his steps he moves to another floor of the building, kicking down a door to find a small group of youths in an empty room decorated with graffiti (the script labels this scene a "teenage pot party").

The visual logic of this pursuit sequence, the presence of Peter Cable kneeling in the shadows in particular, is utterly incomprehensible in an initial viewing, and thus achieves a nightmarishly unhinged dimension. The doubling nature of pursuit, in which the pursued maps out a route that a pursuer must follow, underscores the doubling and tripling of the male characters. Klute is calling out Tom's name, but it is actually Cable he is unknowingly chasing. Because spatial relations are so tangled, the image of a man in a suit makes the impression a jarring reflection. It seems at first that the kneeling figure may be Klute himself, seen suddenly in a long shot. The confusion of the scene literalizes the tripartite character overlap between Klute, Cable, and Gruneman, each a darkly suited shade of the other, each in some way appearing or disappearing from presence in this story. Moreover, it is unclear in this disorienting inverted space if this building is different from Bree's place or if the space we are in is on the opposite side of her walls. These abandoned rooms with their detritus and exposed plaster and chaff signify an outside that is also a distorted reflection of her apartment in ruin (an image that turns out to be somewhat prophetic given that she is later vandalized).

The privileging of interiors as spaces of personal expression pervades American culture. Shielded from the uncertain torrents of the outside world, interiors are understood as spaces allowing the reflection of selfhood. As Wojcik shows, however, in her analysis of the "temporary modernity" of the single-girl's apartment, it is just as likely that interiors can be the rehearsal spaces where identity may be tried on. As a consumer category, identity is assembled from the images of mass culture, a fact frequently illustrated by the magazine clippings that surround women's vanity mirrors. Fonda was a practitioner of Method acting and during the production of *Klute* she requested to be able to sleep at the studio on the set of Bree's apartment. As Jenkins recalls, Fonda used this immersive experience to help decide how Bree's living space would be decorated:

> Jane, being the extraordinary person that she is, wanted to spend nights in this apartment before we started shooting, so she could really feel at home in it, and decide if the props that I had provided were the things that Bree would own. We had a guard in the studio all night while she was sleeping in this set. We had built a ceiling over it and she could lock all the doors and windows. Every morning I would meet Jane quite early at the studio. The guard would let me in, and Jane would have put outside the door of the set four of five props that she thought Bree would not have. I would come in and sit down, and she would tell me about the additional things she had decided in the night that Bree would keep in her apartment. (Jenkins 44)

Fonda would contribute to the set the prominent picture of John F. Kennedy, as well as the book *Sun Signs* that Bree reads in bed (Wojcik, 284n9). Inhabiting the set "as" Bree, supposedly allowed Fonda to better design the surroundings. However, one of *Klute*'s dominant threads concerns Bree's struggle with her identity, her sexuality, and with the various roles she plays as call girl, as actor, and as a model. When she is asked by a casting director "Do you know yourself? . . . Really really know yourself?" Bree admits that she forgets herself when she acts (arguably the first step in method acting). Fonda, knowing the crisis of identity Bree confronted in the story, was thus faced with decorating the set with items that reflected an identity on shifting sands, a woman interested in forgetting herself. Within such a context, objects like the image of JFK, imbued with tragedy, testify to a kind of blank non-identity, an object estranged from, rather than intimately extensive of, identity. Like the single-girl apartments of 1960s cinema, Bree's is a shabby stop-gap, but instead of being on the precipice of romance and normative monogamous habitation it is vulnerable to threatening forces both outside and inside, presaging something much darker and more uncertain.

Disco Inferno

Bree's apartment and the film's various living spaces establish Klute's pervasive sense of unhomeliness, a sense that is also underscored by the film's sparse construction of exterior city space. Unlike conventional urban thrillers, outdoor scenes in the film are rarely strung together through movement to suggest a contiguous space (excepting Bree's introductory walk to her apartment). Instead, the urban realm is presented through fragments—Bree striding through a lobby, Bree and Klute standing next to Central Park or at an outdoor market—that establish the city as isolated and fragmentary rather than sequential and harmonically organized. This style tends to metonymically imply urban culture rather than explore or describe it. Often such culture is also alluded to through stereotype. When Bree teases Klute: "Did we get you? Huh? Just a little bit? Us cityfolk, the glitter, the wickedness?" We seem to be in the realm of the mythic divide between the moral turpitude of the city and the purity of the country (Gledhill even suggests that Klute is a virgin). Yet these lines are clearly hyperbolic, playing on, rather than reinforcing, the representations of urban life so often mobilized through various types of anti-urban discourse. Bree is in fact shown to be acutely aware of the sexual network that connects the city and the suburbs, and which forms the bulk of her business: males from a failed nirvana looking for a hotter life. "What are you?" she asks Klute, occasioning a typology of her suburban clients, "A talker? A button freak? You like to have your chest walked around with high heel shoes? Then you have us watch you tinkle? Or do you get it off wearing woman's clothes? Goddamn hypocrite squares!" But although *Klute* does frequently work through allusive dialogue rather than description, and is restrained in its use of the establishing shots and aerial views so often used to build out an urban milieu, it does not completely lack for anthropologically specific details of public urban culture. Indeed, a particular aspect of contemporary culture shows up in notable clarity in this film, one involving entertainment, consumerism, and a recreation area for sexual identity: the disco.

The iniquity and hedonism stereotypically ascribed to the city through various puritanical and conservative representations did contain germs of fact. Indeed, this aura would be embraced and appropriated by the postsexual-revolution city, begetting new material bases for sexual possibility. As George Chauncey has shown, during the late nineteenth and early twentieth century New York's public sphere was very much a place "where an extensive gay world took shape in the streets, cafeterias, saloons, and apartments . . . and gay men played an integral role in the social life of certain neighborhoods" (355). A period of increased regulation and unfavorable cultural shifts beginning in the 1930s led to decreased gay presence in the city's cultural life, a time that has come to be associated with the notion of "the closet." However, gay visibility was renewed in the 1970s, in part because of the mass political mobilization following the Stonewall riots in 1969, and in part due to the mass popularization of the culture of gay nightlife through the disco.

Though commonly understood as a musical genre, disco emerges first as a culture of dancing within nightclubs and semi-private lofts. These nighttime cultural practices joined with a flourishing culture of sexual freedom that made new spaces for both homosexual and heterosexual culture. For example, in 1965, as the commercial availability of birth control was normalizing sexual promisicuity, Alan Stillman opened the first location of T.G.I. Friday's in New York. Stillman's original intent was to capture the commingling spirit of an apartment cocktail party in a public bar. He encouraged unaccompanied women by brightening the typically dark space of the barroom with Tiffany lamps—inaugurating a décor scheme that, with the addition of hanging plants, would be reiterated in the incipient vogue for "fern bars." T.G.I. Friday's soon saw lines out the door and would become the vanguard of a burgeoning singles culture that would continue to spread through the 1970s and 1980s (Twilley & Ninivaggi).

Single women would also make up a significant portion of the clientele at the first gay-oriented discotheques in New York. As the dance music historian Tim Lawrence points out, there were a number of reasons for the presence of women in the cultural spaces of gay men, one being that New York state law prohibited all-male dancing and stipulated one woman for every three men. There was also, Lawrence writes, "the motivating considerations of fashion, companionship, and sex, with women functioning as style gurus, best friends, and even bed partners for many gay men" (2003: 31). In addition to their sexual variety, the network of discotheques emerging around the city harbored an ethnic diversity that was early on encouraged by the diversity of musical styles favored by DJs—especially their proclivity to soul and Latin music.

Of course, nightclubs and spaces for dancing have been recurrent motifs in popular cinema, so it is unsurprising that contemporary iterations of these new spaces would become incorporated into films such as *Midnight Cowboy*, *Diary of a Mad House Wife* (1970), *Serpico*, *Report to the Commissioner*, *Looking for Mr. Goodbar*, *Cruising* (1980) and others. In film noir such spaces function as part of a larger chronotope that Vivian Sobchack has called "lounge time." Bars, nightclubs, cocktail lounges, motels, diners, and boarding houses appear again and again in noir, Sobchack argues, because they amplify a broader sense of postwar displacement and dispossession unable to countenance dominant idealizations of "home." By the 1960s, however, nightclubs and dancing spaces morph into more jubilant sites transmitting youthful and countercultural energy. Though always set in spaces of unproductive leisure, music and dancing on film, particularly when combined with a montage of psychedelic visuals and disorienting camera work, seem to summon the possibility of transcendent realms and temporalities outside the self. Instead of lounges, these spaces become heterotopic "happenings" or "freak outs," which stage ecstatic opposition to dominant straight culture. *Play Time* (1967), *Riot on*

Sunset Strip (1967), and *The Party* (1968), are a few archetypal examples of the unraveling power of the "happening" in various sites, and pre-date what would form the ultimate depiction of a psychedelic happening (albeit one not set in a nightclub): *Woodstock* (1970).[8]

The discotheque as a particular social space takes shape at both the culmination of 1960s psychedelic culture and the post-Woodstock beginnings of an increasingly gay and heterosocial urban nightlife. Although they are brief, *Klute*'s nightclub scenes fill out the film's socioeconomic topography, bolstering its coherence with contemporary transformations. Klute and Bree first appear at the nightclub on the trail of Arlyn Page (Dorothy Tristan), a call girl once close to Bree who reputedly worked with Gruneman. Positioned along a longer investigative thread, the club appears as part of a descent into the city's sexual economy. Previously, they visited a high-class madam (Antonia Rey) doing business on a sunny rooftop patio, and Legourin's mod bachelor pad. Subsequently, they move further down the ladder of moral caricature, visiting "Momma Reese" (Shirley Stoler) who projects bawdy films in a confined apartment bordello while patrons cavort wildly around her. As much as the discotheque fits within this broader ecology, it is also, by dint of its connection with nightlife culture, tangibly connected to a social realm understood to straddle the licit and the illicit. The wide shot of the club that establishes the setting conveys a busy dance floor filled with young, smartly dressed dancers—a clientele that seems an extension of the modeling and acting world within which Bree is trying to legitimate herself. Yet this is also an operational base for an extensive prostitution ring, as Legourin's presence at the club later on implies.

The disco was the perfect setting for Pakula to describe the modern social sphere that Bree was intimate with. The club scenes for *Klute* were shot on location at Club Sanctuary (also known simply as The Sanctuary) a former Baptist church in Hell's Kitchen that had been converted into a discotheque. The interior design of The Sanctuary featured religious iconography emphasizing carnality—a large mural depicting angels and devils engaging in intercourse—and traditional church furnishings appropriated to suit the needs of dancing: pews rotated to face a central dance floor and an altar converted into a DJ booth. For its décor and its musical curation, The Sanctuary is acknowledged within histories of disco as a key point of origin (see Lawrence, Shapiro, Aletti). The idea of dancing to recorded rather than live music was still a relatively new phenomenon in 1970. Though the atmosphere of disco developed in part out of 1960s rock concert aesthetics, its use of heavily amplified recorded music in the place of performers unfastened participants from the orientation to a centralized spectacle. The DJ credited with pioneering techniques of blending records between two turntables in order to ensure an uninterrupted flow of music at ever escalating tempos was Francis Grasso, who honed these skills during his tenure at The Sanctuary as The Sanctuary's resident DJ. Grasso's percussive mix of soul, psychedelic rock, African drum music, and Latin created an unremitting and ever-increasing pulse that became preferred within gay disco culture. The owners of the club's nightlife impresarios Seymour and Shelley, hired a mostly gay staff and the club soon became known as a gay friendly establishment. As one Sanctuary patron recalled:

> I thought it was the most glamorous place I had ever seen, and it was always packed to the rafters. The whole setup was very decadent and the experience of seeing Francis on what had once been the altar with his long hair, muscular body, and skin-tight t-shirts was just amazing. He looked like a Minotaur to me—a creature of sorts. Of course, the fact that we were on acid enhanced the visual aspect of it all. (Lawrence 30)

Pakula's selection of The Sanctuary, though to a degree fortuitous, was also on trend; it fit within emergent cinematic representations of urban nightlife. As a reporter interviewing Fonda from the "raunchy discothèque" described it: "The Sanctuary is deep in the seedy part of town now known to millions of moviegoers as Midnight Cowboy country" (Knelman 27). For straight suburban audiences, therefore, it would connote both authenticity and turpitude; or, perhaps, authentic turpitude. The actual site, notably, was also diegetically apposite: the nightclub was located only a few doors down from the row of houses outside the funeral home where Bree is shown to enter her apartment. Though this proximity is likely the result of practical considerations (enabling the shooting of two set-ups from a single base location) and would elude many spectators, it coheres with a general social geography. Hell's Kitchen, as Robert A. M. Stern et al. point out, is a neighborhood at this time associated with a "theatrical clientele and later a lower class population," who lived in row houses that "had been broken up for single room occupancy" (316)—an apt description of both Bree's apartment, the downward trajectory of her career, and the patrons of the nightclub.

As much as the décor of the Sanctuary served a mythic vision of the city's "glitter and wickedness," it also suggests concrete social transformation. In several shots it is clear that the dancers are a disaggregated, uncoupled mass. The norm of couples dancing (pervasive in classical Hollywood representation) had been gradually rolled back through the

1960s, and dance floors had moved toward providing experiences that oscillated between the individual and the crowd, rather than mechanisms for reinforcing heterosexual pairing (Lawrence 2009: 199–200). The single pair discernable in an establishing shot, notably, are male, a fleeting allusion to The Sanctuary's gay orientation. While the gayness of The Sanctuary is hardly explicit in the film, the crowd and dancing scenes, including a lateral tracking shot that moves down patrons sitting on the pews, do provide a sense of the club's sexual and ethnic diversity, as well as highlight it as a space designed to encourage new forms of social mixing. These are the city folk of whom Bree considers herself a part.

Bree's association of city folk with "glitter" and superficiality among other sins, points up the significance of surfaces and externality that disco and 1970s nightlife culture would push and develop. As it gained in popularity and moved from out-of-the-way clubs and underground, semi-private lofts into more moneyed echelons, disco culture shifted from its countercultural origins. The mass publicity surrounding clubs like Studio 54 connected disco with celebrity and artifice, rather than collectivity. This association grew partially from the aesthetics of its music. Disco music proper would layer lush strings and sweet vocals over a mechanized and relentless beat. Andrew Holleran's disco-era novel *Dancer from the Dance* (1978) captured the self-alienation at the center of disco's receding horizon of pleasure:

> They passed one another without a word in the elevator, like silent shades in hell, hell-bent on their next look from a handsome stranger. Their next rush from a popper. The next song that turned their bones to jelly and left them all on the dance floor with heads back, eyes nearly closed, in the ecstasy of saints receiving the stigmata. Some wiped everything they could off their faces and reduced themselves to blanks. Yet even these, when you entered the hallway where they stood waiting to go in, would turn toward you all at once in that one unpremeditated moment (as when we see ourselves in a mirror we didn't know was there), the same look on their faces: Take me away from this. (qtd in Shapiro 137)

Though produced in the very early days of disco, *Klute*'s representation of this social scene anticipates the compulsion and disappointment that would define 1970s nightlife.

The second of *Klute*'s two nightclub scenes has Bree returning in a drug-induced stupor. Having learned that Arlyn has fallen into drug addiction, Bree and Klute track her to a run-down tenement. The shock of finding her former friend manic for a fix throws Bree into a spiral of fear and self-loathing. She bolts from Klute's car and jumps on the subway. Reappearing at the club, she has clearly also found a fix for herself. Perspiring, Bree teeters through the throng (figure 1.4), gaining the attention of men, but steadily moving across the dance floor toward Legourin and Trina (Rita Gam) who are seated on what look to be gilded thrones. Legourin puts his hand on her head in what seems at first a gesture of affection, but then roughly pulls her head up by her hair, forcing her to look him in the eyes before replacing her head on his shoulder. Bree's slippage away from Klute and back toward the world she has been moving away from, is paired with an ersatz monarchy and perversely exploitative figuration of family: a madam mother/sister (Trina), and a pimp patriarch.

Klute, it must be remembered, is in many ways an exploration of the various roles of performance in Bree's life and of the various ways she uses performativity to control the space she finds herself in. The film bears out her confession, made in one of the film's therapy scenes, that being a call girl allows her to be the best actor in the world. In a hotel-room meeting with a Chicago commuter, she moves smoothly past the doorway, ensuring the necessary monetary transaction without missing a beat in an unfolding seductive progression and artfully blocking out the dramatic space. Lest we begin to believe she is not at work, she is. A well-remembered shot shows her looking at her watch whilst moaning in pleasure. Her flair for using mundane space dramatically is further illustrated in a scene where she visits her long-standing client Mr. Goldfarb (Morris Strasberg), an elderly garment manufacturer to whom she gives vicarious erotic thrills by recounting what Pakula labels as a "Schniztlerian" story of her encounter with an elderly gentleman at Cannes as she languidly removes her sequined dress, proficiently enacting a particularly Europeanized feminine ideal (Pakula is alluding to the Viennese novelist Arthur Schnitzler [Brown, 97]). The film encourages us to view both these scenes as performance by alternating between stage and backstage views. In the scene with Goldfarb, Bree is introduced, per Pakula's direction to Willis, via a "glamour shot" modeled on the style of Josef von Sternberg's close-ups on Marlene Dietrich (Pakula qtd in Brown 107). The shot, however, sticks out from the more distanced shot scales of the unfolding sequence, reminding us again that this is a performance for a diegetic audience.

At the disco, however, Bree's performative acumen begins to break down. Bree's journey across the nightclub floor occasions one of Fonda's more fascinating physical performances, one that resonates with the descriptions of the nightlife culture within which Bree is framed. In a single reverse-tracking shot that pulls through the nightclub crowd this carefully constructed self-presentation visibly fractures, oscillating wildly between staged and unstaged. The camera holds still on Bree as she first moves rhythmically, "letting it all hang out" and smiling at an admirer before abruptly breaking the moment by frowning and looking away in frustration. With her hands on her hips, she briefly attempts to save face by flashing the stranger a smile and then moves on. The music filling the space is composer Michael Small's acid-tinged version of proto-disco, with lyrics that repeat "Take me high, take me higher. . . ." Continuing through the club, Bree stumbles, falling almost directly into the lap of another stranger, whom she briefly makes out with as his male friends look on appreciatively. They move together toward the dance floor, but she loses him in the crowd after pushing toward a girlfriend she recognizes (a cameo by Warhol's trans-ingénue, Candy Darling). Amplified through Fonda's ingenious performance is the fragmentation of Bree's self-management, her carefully segmented identity—what Erving Goffman called the "bureaucratization of the self" (56)—collapsing within a single space. But this space, rather than being dramatically heightened in its own right, is rendered banal by Pakula's obsessive attention to Bree as she moves through it.

It is not incidental that this space should be a discotheque. As Sobchack points out, the affinity of cinema for nightclubs lays partly in the conduciveness of their layouts to dramatic intrigue (155). A nightclub contains a spectrum of social zones, a dance floor for the intensification of specular/erotic display, tables that encourage comingling, and an array of "backstage" areas out of the public eye. Like the lounge-time of noir, this is a cultural space divided away from the pressures of the social world but one that, within film, prismatically refracts and hyperbolizes a multitude of social forces within itself. The disco, a hip night-world of young professionals, seemingly carried away by their sexual desires, is an interior space structured for letting it all hang out, whatever "it" all is. Straight identity can be dispensed with in a carnivalesque atmosphere of free love and a continuous flow of music. Yet Fonda reveals, in moments of Bree truly losing herself—i.e., in not knowing what self to present, in existing in the interstices of selfhood—that The Sanctuary is likewise a space where social performance is unceasing, where dancing and flirting can be a calculated, possibly unconscious, maneuver for creating and eliciting desire in a way that is homologous to the operations of the call girl. Indeed, this is precisely why this nightclub is shown to be a base of operations for Trina and Legourin: it is at the nexus of an emergent sexual marketplace in which both gays and singles have become paying consumers. Despite the film's unfortunate insistence on Bree's prostitution as an individual compulsion (primarily via the therapy sequences) rather than socially and materially determined, this scene brings into the night spaces and night times of the 1970s Walter Benjamin's suggestion that it is the prostitute who reveals the dynamics of social relations under capitalism (1996: 171, 188).[9] In turn, we are offered a premonition of disco, nightlife, and singles culture to come: a heterosocial zone of pleasure and ecstasy in throbbing, unceasing, and unraveling repetition, a space of lifestyle that drains life.

Peter Cable: The Disappearing Man

In truth, there seem to be no havens *Klute*, not at home, not in the privacy of one's apartment, not in the sanctuary of modern nightlife. This being said, the film's villainous man in black, Peter Cable, maintains refuge, solitude, and control in a skyscraper. Where Ben Bradlee (Jason Robards) in *All the President's Men*, (ultimately a man in a suit) bursts heroically into the narrative and a supervisory role over Woodward and Bernstein's investigation, the villainous Peter Cable, similarly garbed and in a similar executive and supervisory position (he is Gruneman's boss and is reported to by Klute) constantly skirts the margins, ever recessive. He is also a character consistently identified with power and surveillance, and appropriately, this figuration accumulates architecturally. One of *Klute*'s most punctual and emphatic images is of Cable, repeatedly shown tens of stories above the city streets in a boardroom that gives him an eagle's view of the city below (figure 1.3). Though later in the film Cable is shown from a point of view outside the skyscraper, in these initial views he is presented as a reclining silhouette, a dark shape outlined by the gray New York sky. It is an image both ominous and ambiguous, symbolic to a degree in the eye-level view afforded Cable of cranes building the World Trade Center but also impressionistic in its *plein-air* effects: the mistiness surrounding the outdoor elements suggests both mountainous altitude and the foggy veil that shrouds Cable's character. Interior shots of figures in rooms backlit against outside spaces are recurring images and once again evince Willis's interest in, and adeptness at, shooting at light levels lower than the Hollywood norm.[10] To achieve the silhouette effect, Willis dispensed with the lighting conventionally used to fill in character's faces when they stood in front of windows, giving greater presence to the glare.

The motif of backlit images swells the presence of the outside on the inside, once again plumbing a spatial anxiety that is both claustra- and agoraphobic. In Pakula's other conspiracy films, all lensed by Willis, similarly patterned images appear in rather obscure places. In *All the President's Men* when Bernstein visits political "ratfucker" Donald Segretti

Figure 1.3. *Klute*. Peter Cable in boardroom with World Trade Center Tower in background.

(Robert Walden) at his apartment, Segretti and Bernstein converse leaning against the railing of an apartment deck that looks over a marina, shadowed by the bright California day behind them. Willis's cinematographic philosophy is rooted in a perceptual position toward filming on location, his credo being "See what you're looking at" (qtd in Steele 568). In practice, this means identifying the salient visual impressions that are given by a space and reconstructing them through lighting and cinematographic technique. For Willis, the essence of location shooting was not inherent in the location itself, but in the ways that location could be used in tandem with visual techniques to reconstruct reality:

> Some filmmakers I worked with in early stages thought that if you play a scene in an airplane, the plane should be in the air because the essence of the scene will be different. That's nonsense . . . it's a copout based on the feeling that its (sic) going to be better if I go with the reality. And the truth of the matter is, you never get reality that way, the bottom line is you get reality the other way, which is to reconstruct it. (Schaefer & Salvato, 301)

As Willis understands, film performs a translation of profilmic physical reality, which is broken down and rebuilt based on the properties determined through initial visual impressions.

Willis's cinematographic figurations for Pakula of people enclosed by glaring outside light are remarkable visual signatures, not least for the way they seem to draw on and circulate within broader image-contexts outside these films.[11] One such context is embedded in a pivotal sequence in *The Parallax View* (1974). At the midpoint of the story, Frady (Warren Beatty), an investigative journalist attempting to uncover a political assassination conspiracy, is invited to the offices of the Parallax Corporation—a re-coding of the Toll-American Corporation—to undergo a series of psychological tests. The main test, and the film's stunning visual centerpiece, is a brainwashing "film"—a montage of still photos set to music that Frady must watch alone in a darkened theater. This film-within-a-film, not unlike the brainwashing film in *The Clockwork Orange* (which was released contemporaneously in 1971), was expertly edited by Pakula to supposedly access, or produce, sociopathic tendencies in the viewer by pairing images together with text to create connotative chains of imagery (Home, Mother, Father, Nation, Sex, etc.). Buried in the middle of this montage is a photo of a silhouetted figure facing away from the camera towards a bright window. The inserted photo is of John F. Kennedy in the Oval Office, entitled "The Loneliest Job in the World," and taken by *New York Times* reporter George Tames in 1961.

A photo of Kennedy in a film that is *about* political assassinations makes sense, and there are, in fact, images of other political and historical figures in the film as well. It is notable, however, that the backlit presidential photo, in fact, became fashionably conventional in the 1960s and 1970s. Jacques Lowe took similar photos of John F. Kennedy and Robert F. Kennedy together, and there is also a famous image of Richard M. Nixon taken at Camp David in 1972, shortly after his reelection and as Woodward and Bernstein's investigation into Watergate was finally starting to attract serious public attention (figure 1.4). A UPI photo included in special issue of *Newsweek* (19 August 1974, 49) with coverage of Ford's inauguration and the Watergate affair, accompanies a piece on Nixon's future plans with a similar view of the ex-president, his back to the camera once again, strolling along the beach in San Clemente. The Camp David photograph taken by presidential photographer Ollie Atkins of a darkened figure looking out onto the snow-covered yard would shortly become a stock image for capturing the mood surrounding the fallen leader.[12]

These images of American presidents are strikingly similar to the way Willis patterns outdoor source lighting in his shots, shooting directly into day-lit windows in order to achieve silhouetted bodies dominated by outside glare. In *Klute*, this motif appears a number of times, once, for example, when Klute and Bree are in an apartment hallway on the trail of Arlyn and Bree is framed, in a long-shot and then a close-up, in the dark hallway that is powerfully lit by a door opened into daylight. The most recurrent framing of a figure against outdoor light in *Klute*, however, is of Cable. In three separate scenes Cable is shown in the boardroom,

Figure 1.4. Photograph of Richard M. Nixon taken by presidential photographer Ollie Atkins at Camp David shortly after his reelection in 1972.

each time listening to the tape recording of Bree that opens the film, each time positioned against large windows. In certain ways the motif of plate-glass settings that opens the film is sustained here, and thus is furthered the subtle continuity between the modern surfaces of urban and suburban life. Yet these images of Cable also supply a different relation to the outside. In some of the shots the silhouette effect is loosened, and Cable's face is partially lit. But in all of them the presence of the outside seems to overwhelm the image. Pakula's notes contain the germs of this representation: "Always shoot Cable against emptiness and abstraction. Never against anything human. I.e. Go from warm family photographs of Gruneman to Cable sitting against the world. Or in space."[13] These views characterize Cable's power through his distance from the world, much as in a great deal of Pakula's work, power is detailed through figures of dispassionate detachment. Indeed, from his seat at the boardroom table, Cable is able to control a series of retractable panels decorated with a depiction of the moon landing, emphasizing both his distance and his relationship with high-level techno-industrial interests. But as with the modernism of the Gruneman home, the un-homeliness of the apartment, and the sociability of the discotheque, there are qualities in these scenes that do indeed ground Cable within a material space.

Cable's boardroom scenes were shot at 140 Broadway (also known as the Marine Midland Building) about two blocks away from the site of the World Trade Center towers. Completed in 1967, just three years before *Klute* was shot, the building was designed by Gordon Bunshaft of the firm Skidmore, Owings & Merrill. According to his notes, Pakula had originally imagined Cable's skyscraper scenes being shot at Mies van der Rohe's Seagram Building, which had initiated the mid-century vogue for black minimalist skyscrapers that now dot the skylines of all major cities. The Marine Midland building is in many ways similar to the Seagram building. Both buildings embodied an aesthetic that Stern et al. label "corporate modernism," a style "epitomized by a single construction feature: the almost neutral, gridded glass-and-metal curtain wall" (53). *New York Times* critic Ada Louise Huxtable hailed 140 Broadway as the acme of sensible and beautifully clean modernist construction: "New York's ultimate skin building." "The skyscraper wall reduced to gossamer minimums of shining, thin, material," wrote Huxtable, "hung on a frame of extraordinary strength through superb contemporary technology" (*New York Times*, March 31, 1968, D33).[14] Like the Lever House, which Bunshaft also designed for SOM, the curtain wall of 140 Broadway recalls the rectilinear architectural motifs that feature prominently in Alfred Hitchcock's *North by Northwest* (1959); including the opening shots of the C.I.T. Tower that blend into the geometric credit designs of Saul Bass, and scenes making use of the United Nations building. In *North by Northwest* the graphic elements of International Style architecture underline the abstract vectors that will comprise the ranging movement of Cary Grant's Roger Thornhill. In *Klute*, however, Pakula's use of Corporate Modernism is much more static.

Like the plate-glass of the Gruneman home, the glass that sheathed mid-century skyscrapers was a feature connected to modernist ideals of transparency. In *Space, Time and Architecture: The Growth of a New Tradition* (1941), the critic and historian Siegfried Giedion outlined an agenda that would follow physics and painting to undertake modes of building that illuminated simultaneity in space and time. Architectural projects that followed these priniciples, such as Le Corbusier's Villa Savoie, produced buildings that featured a continuous passage to obscure distinctions between inside and out. As Richard Sennett has convincingly demonstrated, however, the utopian desire of architects seeking to unite interior and exterior via plate-glass privileged vision above the other senses. Though one could see outside through this glass, its double-paned thermal layers sealed office dwellers into a controlled environment that was cut off from the noise, smell, and haptic sense of truly being outside. In so doing, plate-glass designs, in conjunction with the vertiginous scale of steel-frame skyscraper construction, produced a new, truly modern form of detachment from the outside, one in which the eye, but none of the other senses, gained access across glassed boundaries. As Sennett puts it: "Fully apprehending the outside from within, yet feeling neither cold nor wind nor moisture, is a modern sensation, a sensation of protected openness in very big buildings . . . It is the physical sensation on which is founded the modern sense of isolation in a building" (1990, 108). Thus, in the designs of the International Style which come to dominate the American urban landscape, particularly the work of Mies van der Rohe, and the architects he influenced, new types of dislocation arise.

For Huxtable, one of the primary appeals of 140 Broadway was as "foil for the ornate masonry around it" (ibid.), yet in *Klute* the only other buildings visible from Cable's perch are the World Trade Center towers, soon to become the most dominant icons in the Lower Manhattan skyline. Instead of being a foil, the towers reinforce Cable's association with detached corporate and industrial interests. To achieve the anti-human effects he desired, Pakula isolated the building from its relations to the older buildings around it, focusing instead on sites connoting industry: either the Trade Center towers or, in another scene, the busy port traffic along the Hudson River. For all the ways it signifies its relation with the currents of the global economy, Cable's office space is ironically the most private interior in the film, the site apparently least susceptible to intrusion or penetration. This is evidenced both by his control of the retractable panels, which allow further seclusion, and in the way he blithely replays his tape recording of Bree aloud, certain that no one could be listening. Only toward the end of the film does an exterior perspective on the building reveal its black shell, the camera dramatically tilting downward from Cable to reveal his height from the city floor, hinting at the melodramatic defenestration that will soon spell his end at the film's climax.

Sennett notes that one notable feature of plate glass is the way its strength frustrates attempts at suicide "and lesser acts of spontaneity," that the height of skyscrapers otherwise make so attractive. This, he says, is ironic, in that the skyscraper designs of Mies and others typify "a soulless modern environment in which men and women are as cut off from each another as from the outside, an architecture if not of suicide, at least of despair." Such a notion accounts in some way for the desperate quality of Cable's villainy. Sennett's remark also recalls a playful image the architect Bernard Tschumi reproduces for his series "Advertisements for Architecture": a falling man who has been pushed out of an open window. Text accompanying the image reads: "To really understand architecture you might even have to commit a crime." A suggestion made by this ersatz advertisement is that architecture remains a dormant aspect of our experience, brought into vision only by—as a caption reads further—"the actions it witnesses." Although the window he eventually plunges through at the film's conclusion is located in Goldfarb's garment factory, not his boardroom, it is impossible not to envision him falling from a skyscraper, in an imaginary reverse shot. As much as Cable's isolated perch hyperbolically implies his power, it also portends his fate. And, as the country would soon to learn, even the highest offices of American power are not beyond impeachment.

But while in the era of Kennedy and Nixon particularly, the ends of American presidents are consistently framed as tragedy, Cable's end is pure movie melodrama. Through *Klute*, corporate modernism is placed squarely within contemporary melodrama's catalogue of motifs and the panoptic chamber of the villainous executive would continuously feature as an architectural trope in conspiracy and action thrillers through the 1970s and beyond.[15] As the critic and filmmaker Thom Andersen demonstrates in his film essay *Los Angeles Plays Itself* (2003), modernist homes across Los Angeles have frequently featured as the headquarters for film villains. Likewise for office and skyscraper spaces, which, as Merrill Schleier shows, were associated with corruption during the Depression before being enlisted as icons of technological modernism around the mid-century. By the 1970s, owing perhaps to a renewed skepticism toward modernization and finance, skyscrapers once again become bad objects, available to genre cinema as a shorthand caricature for the epicenter of malignant power. The most recent iteration of corporate America's disappearing man is Don Draper (Jon Hamm) in *Mad Men*, the introductory credit sequence of which animates a silhouetted male figure plunging from a modernist office tower.

In many ways, Cable is simply the dark expression of corporate modernism. Pakula indicated in his notes that he understood Cable as *Klute*'s MacGuffin, the Hitchcockian term for an object with no inherent value, whose sole narrative significance is to animate the investment and action of other characters in order to create plot. In this sense Cable is an immanent surface, a character animated by a death drive that, in comparison with Bree's more involute inner-life, is rather uncomplicated. Cable's villainy, however, also gains definition within an existing ecology of images that depict masculine political power in a particular relation between inside and out. In the expressive journalistic uses to which it has been put the cameo-style image of a figure confronting the bright outside world has often been more nebulous than its genre film counterpart. These silhouette pictures or alienation cameos, such as the aforementioned images of John F. Kennedy in the Oval Office or President Nixon at Camp David, were shortly becoming tragic expressions of failed power. But what in these images does a glaring outside signify, and to what does it appeal or respond to? A judgment by God? The concatenation of social forces responsible for the downfall of these men?

Paired with the shadowed figure, this illumination from without seems to indicate the terrifying and overwhelming outside world that the individual turns inwardly against. It may be the glare of mass media attention that always "sees" us, or else the torrent of claims made of or against a character. Cable, Kennedy, Nixon are all, in their own ways, disappearing men, but this force, whatever it is, is what they sought to disappear from and does not itself disappear. In years to come this overdetermined light image appears again and again, and within vastly different contexts. Within the science-fiction and fantasy films of Steven Spielberg, for example, a character poised in front of an overwhelming light source—the spaceships in *Close Encounters of the Third Kind* (1977) or *E.T.: The Extra-Terrestrial* (1982)—becomes a stylistic signature for portraying a sublime confrontation with life forms from beyond earth.

It is possible, however, to bring this figuration of light closer to the ground and to the everyday, to signal a fearful relation to or alienation from, the outside world. Another iteration appeared on the cover of *LIFE* magazine in November of 1971, as *Klute* was still in wide release (figure 1.5). It is an image of a woman peering out through curtains onto an urban landscape. Her face is shown in silhouette, and outside the window, slightly overexposed, are the roofs of urban apartments. A title reads: "The Cities Lock-Up: Fear of Crime Creates a Life-Style Behind Steel." The story within is entitled "Fortress on 78th St," and details how a growing fear of crime amongst New York City residents has led to an intensification of physical security measures in apartment buildings. Black-and-white photographs show various of these security measures taken inside apartment buildings (including locks and bars on windows and doors), residents tightly assembled in a living room to discuss crime, as well as the foreboding exterior landscape, from rooftops dotted with barbed wire and metal grates to the fish-eye view of a hallway as seen through the peephole on a door. Black and white is employed strategically to convey the mode of photojournalistic seriousness—it contrasts both with the vividly colored advertisements in the surrounding pages (one, for example, for Seagram's which shows a happy social gathering in an apartment much nicer than the ones in this article) and the color cover images of sports stars, Disneyworld, and even Jane Fonda used in previous months.

Figure 1.5. *Life*, November 19, 1971.

In *Klute*, Pakula creates an urban world likewise defined by a growing anxiety about the relationship between inside and outside. His urban thrillers reveal an urban topography in which spaces like the parking garage, Brie's apartment, the new space-time of nightlife, and Cable's glass-walled office, stymie the complacently imagined comfort of a clear boundary between inside and out. The architecture of modernism that once promised the possibility of a better world now structures everyday social fears and paranoia. What becomes increasingly clear through Pakula's repeated architectural motifs and the narratives that they surround is a situation wherein individual bodies have become overcome by their environs and less and less able to recognize a place for themselves in a changing outside world. Then again, in *Klute*, the villain was at the dinner table from the beginning. Perhaps no such place ever existed.

2

Everyone Here Is a Cop

Urban Spectatorship and the Popular Culture of Policing in the Super-Cop Cycle

> In times of terror, when everyone is something of a conspirator, everybody will be in the position of having to play detective.
>
> —Walter Benjamin, "The Paris of the Second Empire in Baudelaire" (*SW* 4: 21)

❧

FEARS OF STREET CRIME AND THE increasing dread associated with the public realm of American cities did not bode well for the already struggling movie business of the early 1970s. A June 1972 *Variety* headline blaring "STREET CRIME CLIPS SHOW BIZ" captured widespread industry worries that trepidation associated with city streets would prevent people from finding entertainment outside the home. "The urban downtown decay in city after city and the accompanying rise in muggings, knifings, gun battles are keeping people at home, behind locked doors," the article stated, "And that's bad, bad, bad, for show business" (Green, 5 June 1972, 1). The film industry, of course, was also in deep financial trouble. The youth factor understood to be behind the successful returns on offerings like *The Graduate* (1967), *Bonnie and Clyde* (1967), and *Easy*

Rider (1969), had all but fizzled, leading to speculations that new opportunities could be found in older audiences and amongst more affluent, educated classes (*Variety* "Teen Power Fades at b.o., 24 Februrary 1971, 1; see also Nystrom 24–26). Still smarting from expensive, overproduced, and culturally out-of-step flops like *Doctor Doolittle* (1967), and *Camelot* (1967), New Hollywood sought a fix both topical and affordable. One solution, ironically, was found in the very streets that audiences had been seeking to avoid.

In the late-1960s and mid-1970s there was a small resurgence in police-centered commercial features, most of which were both shot and narratively set in major cities. This cycle of cop films joined with Blaxploitation to make urban images omnipresent in commercial cinema. A splash of publicity stills entitled "Cheezit—Here Come the Cops!" published in the *New York Times* in November 1973, gushingly brought the reader up to speed on the trend, showing images from *The New Centurions* (1972), *Serpico* (1973), *The Laughing Policeman* (1973), *The Seven-Ups* (1973), *The Super Cops* (1974), and, for good measure, a classic photo of Keystone cops piled onto a police van. "In recent months the moviemaker's flirtation with fellows on the force has blossomed into a passionate love affair," the article proclaimed, "and it's become all but impossible to find a flick that doesn't probe the public exploits and private psyches of police" (Flatley, 25 November 1972, 169). In addition to the films mentioned above, this cop-centered cycle also includes *Bullit* (1968), *Madigan* (1968), *The Detective* (1968), *Coogan's Bluff* (1968), *Cotton Comes to Harlem* (1970), *They Call Me MISTER Tibbs* (1970), *The French Connection* (1971), *Dirty Harry* (1971), *The Organization* (1971), *Across 110th Street* (1972), *Fuzz* (1972), *Badge 373* (1973), *Detroit 9000* (1973), *The Stone Killer* (1973), *Cops and Robbers* (1973), *Magnum Force* (1973), *Electra Glide in Blue* (1973), *Law and Disorder* (1974), *Busting* (1974), *Freebie and the Bean* (1974), *"McQ"* (1974), *The Taking of Pelham One Two Three* (1974), *Newman's Law* (1974), *The French Connection II* (1975), *Report to the Commissioner* (1975), *'Brannigan'* (1975), and *Assault on Precinct 13* (1976). Filmed in New York, San Francisco, Los Angeles, and occasionally further afield in Detroit and Boston, the 1970s police cycle became a generic vehicle for bringing images of the contemporary city to national screens. Not only were New York and other cities encouraging production on their streets, shooting on location had become less technically difficult and thus more economically attractive to Hollywood. Variegated, non-studio settings also lent authenticity, and, as the success of *Midnight Cowboy* (1969) had demonstrated, though the movie-going public might be clinging close to home, they had developed a taste for virtual views of downtrodden city streets.

The *New York Times* article's inclusion of the Keystone cops image reminds readers that the police films of the 1970s represented a new look for a venerable style. The police procedural enjoyed waves of popularity between the 1930s and 1950s but its cache tapered in the 1960s during the ascendance of the spy thriller.[1] The 1970s police vogue was primarily inspired by the tremendous box-office success of *Bullit* and *The French Connection*, both produced by Philip D'Antoni. The New Hollywood cop cycle revived the procedural and rogue cop conventions of the late noir era, updating the genre via displays of violence and vice enabled by relaxed censorship, and by amplifying the obsessive, aggressive, and occasionally pathological nature of their protagonists. The now iconic poster image of Clint Eastwood's "Dirty" Harry character pointing his .357 Magnum almost directly toward the spectator is a recurrent publicity trope in the cop cycle of the period, appearing in promotion for *The French Connection*, *The Seven-Ups*, *Cops and Robbers*, *The New Centurions*, *Busting*, and *Magnum Force*. The confrontational motif, which recalls the close-up of a train bandit (Justus D. Barnes) firing directly at the viewer in Edwin S. Porter's *Great Train Robbery* (1903), highlights the cycle's reliance on codes from the western, a fact underscored by the casting in cop roles of rugged male stars like Clint Eastwood (*Coogan's Bluff*, the Dirty Harry series) and John Wayne ("*McQ*," *Brannigan)* who formerly played cowboys. Of course, crime films and westerns have always shared audiences (understood to be primarily male) and personnel (Samuel Fuller, Howard Hawks, Don Siegel, Anthony Mann, John Alton, Jimmy Stewart, Sterling Hayden, and Barbara Stanwyck to name just a few). In the 1970s cop cycle, however, the frontier of the western would be transposed onto the disorienting territory of urban crisis. Here, urban decay and the wreckage of urban renewal stood in for the indeterminate physical space of the frontier and a de-individualized inner-city underclass often as not figured as an unruly native population.

Although sharing its setting with Blaxploitation, the 1980s cop cycle was clearly coded for a white audience. The films' protagonists were invariably white and when they confronted the endemic problems of the contemporary city, issues of race and the structural causes for poverty and crime typically remained unanalyzed. When it was treated, criminality within black communities could be portrayed as the quasi-revolutionary expression of black separatism. This mode of representation indexed the forms of black nationalism that were defining new contours and spaces for black culture. However, it also perniciously aligned with a nascent "culture of poverty" which understood the problems of the ghetto as intrinsic to the black culture and thus provided the rationale for an ongoing withdrawal of social services from impoverished black neighborhoods.

Cop films validated the latter perspective by likewise treating the problems of the inner city as intractable. For instance, in a pointed moment of sociological insight, a rookie cop in *The New Centurions* (Stacy Keach) responds to his veteran partner's (George C. Scott) running account of the racial profile of their East Los Angeles beat by commenting: "Well, considering the intensity of living conditions . . . poverty . . . I'm surprised there's not more criminals." Unwilling to countenance this analysis, or simply unable to enter into its complexity, his partner responds: "Ah, it's just a city." The comment aptly captures the cycle's broader approach to issues of race: no one is to blame (least of all suburban whites); this is just how things are.

Within the context of the social upheavals of the 1960s, related episodes of violent repression, the mainstreaming of anti-establishment critique, and the incipient rise of law and order conservatism, the police officer became a highly visible and highly ambivalent figure in American culture—at best regarded with suspicion, at worst, a "pig." On the news and on the covers of national magazines, it was uniformed cops, most often white, who marched, rode horses, and viciously wielded batons against political insurgents. Just as, according to Derek Nystrom, the construction worker was appropriated, following the hard-hat riots of May 1970, as "the new figure of conservative reaction," (71), so too could cops be used strategically to signify an emergent right-wing working class. Relatedly, within popular culture police were often used as figures that allowed for the playing out of the political enmities animating the period. One of the most popular television series of the 1970s, "All in the Family" (1971–1979), for example, based its satirical social commentary around the confrontations between the youthful liberal ideals of Gloria and Michael "Meathead" Stivic (Sally Struthers and Rob Reiner) and the unreconstructed bigotry of Archie Bunker (Carroll O'Connor), a cop. In a similar way, the characters of police in the 1970s cop cycle often function less as figures of heroic investment than as ambiguous agents, haplessly tasked with navigating crime-ridden territories and a social terrain marked by incivility.

As the political historian Michael Flamm shows, the success of the law and order discourse espoused by figures like Barry Goldwater and George Wallace—the latter of whom was responsible for the dissemination of the popular "Support Your Local Police" bumper sticker—stemmed from its rhetorical conflation of the civil unrest of the 1960s with rising urban crime rates. The twinning of these phenomena was reinforced through the expression so commonly used in the postwar era: "crime in the streets." The phrase became useful in the context of law-and-order discourse because it could trigger a host of resonant anxieties regarding social disorder. Crime in the streets might mean black revolt on the evening news, the mugger roaming the neighborhood, or loitering teenagers. It was doubly powerful, however, because it provided a dramatic locale: it furnished the material urban stage—the streets—on which a host of anxieties could be set.

Although many Americans might harbor reservations about law enforcement, cops were inarguably the figures understood to be on the frontlines in the battle against crime in the streets imagined by middle-class spectators. When narratives about the contemporary public realm were told, therefore, police were the most apposite avatars—especially for cultural forms geared to white audiences. But police were not only appropriate in the sense of social realism; they were also appropriate generically. Tied to the detective story and narratives of urban sensation, police were ideal figures through which to convey audiences into the urban milieus that not only stoked anxiety but its persistent companion, fascination. Narratively qualified as investigators, cops function as figures of urban observation and circulation, figures for imagining what it is to see and move through the contemporary city.

The first part of this chapter surveys what I call the super-cop cycle, paying close attention to the ways in which the dialectic of police visuality and visibility relates to contextual aspects of 1970s urban policing and is developed within fact-based procedurals. Though coded for white audiences, I argue that these films are more politically ambiguous than one might expect, more about conveying viewers into uncertain urban milieus than establishing respect for law enforcement activities taking place there. The second part of this chapter looks closely at what I regard to be the ur-text of the super-cop cycle, *The French Connection*. The incredible popularity and resonance of this film, I argue, has to do with the ways it incorporates the reciprocity of seeing and being seen into its many sequences of foot pursuit. More so than any other film in the cycle, *The French Connection*'s appeal lies in the way that it is marked by the interrelated problems of visualizing oneself, orienting oneself, and perceiving others in the city. Although undoubtedly a police film rooted in the procedural mode, *The French Connection*'s visual aesthetic resonates with prevalent fears and suspicions of, but also fascination with, the public realm of the street as a field of looking behavior.

Rise of the Super Cops

The popular idealization of law and order helped to usher in policing figures that could displace the porcine image of bigoted cops that proliferated during the 1960s. In the newspapers and magazines, on television, and in the movies, this new figure was christened the "super cop." In the popular press of the early 1970s, super cop is a title given to both screen cops and their real life counterparts. Just as Eastwood's Dirty Harry Callahan and Steve McQueen's Frank Bullit are dubbed super cops, so too were many of the actual police officers, such as Frank Serpico and Eddie Egan who received press coverage for their real-life exploits and then gained cinematic stardom. So too is Frank Rizzo, the right-wing police chief of Philadelphia who proudly identified as a super cop in his successful 1972 run for mayor. The term wasn't always applied affirmatively or without tongue-in-cheek. A mayoral race between former Detroit police commissioner John Nichols and black candidate Coleman Young in 1973 was characterized as "Super Cop vs. Super Liberal" in the local left-wing press (*Fifth Estate*, 29 September 1973, 1). An exposé on Detroit's notoriously vicious police department in the New Left organ *Ramparts* was ominously titled "Detroit's Super Cops: Terror in the Streets" (Kohn, December 1973). "Super cop" was thus a rather ambiguous identifier—it might connote heroism, but in a period of a growing incredulity toward the stock figures of American heroism (soldiers, cowboys) it might also be used to interrogate heroism's masculine rule of violence. A cop who was super, in other words, could be a cop dedicated to recuperating traditional American values against those who would tear them down, or, alternately, an agent of the state who used extraordinarily vicious means of policing. In a certain sense, it was just this polysemy that made super cops an ideal basis for popular film.

Institutional corruption provides an even more direct historical intertext for the cop cycle, particularly the New York-centered films. Between 1971 and 1972 the Commission to Investigate Alleged Police Corruption, better known as the Knapp Commission, disclosed the routine forms of police misconduct that pervaded the New York Police Department. Like the Kefauver hearings on organized crime in the 1950s—responsible for a cycle of urban crime films in their own time—the Knapp Commission hearings were televised and received national press coverage. In particular, the testimony of Frank Serpico and David Durk of the NYPD relayed stories of police corruption, payoffs, protection rackets, and petty graft, renewing calls for police reform. Yet, as the films directly based on the hearings—*Serpico*, *The Super Cops*, and Sidney Lumet's later entry *Prince of the City* (1981)—also reveal, the Knapp Commission refused to explore the structurally embedded forms of corruption that extended higher and deeper into departmental ranks.

While revelations of widespread police corruption would seem infertile soil for the representation of heroic police, in fact, as in the case of *Serpico* and *The Super Cops*, they became the basis for conceiving of individual cops as lone figures of moral certitude rising above an institutionalized climate of everyday graft epitomized by police "grazing" ("grass eaters" was the Knapp commission's figurative term for the police officers who routinely accepted small payoffs). Police, in other words, could now be represented as anti-authoritarian. In the fallout from the Knapp Commission hearings, the super-cop trope was employed to invoke a new type of law enforcement figure. An article for *U.S. News & World Report* entitled "Police for the '70s—Cities' Search for 'Supercops'" details the problems faced by police forces in developing "a new generation of 'supercops' to handle complex, sometimes explosive, situations with a strong hand, yet fairly and with understanding" (3 December 1973, 38). Here, the super cop becomes an idealized figure representing ongoing police reform and professionalization. Police departments of the 1970s, this article explains, demand police who are educated, integrated (by both race and gender), and skilled in community relations. Of course, as the *Ramparts* article on Detroit's super cops shows, the fully weaponized, paramilitary styling of the modern police force could also induce new fears about police power. Such fears are realized in *Magnum Force*, in which Harry Callahan tracks a formation of vigilante motorcycle cops who roam the streets of San Francisco in militia-style formations.

Police attempted to affiliate themselves with the zeitgeist in other ways as well. To mitigate what were increasingly legitimate apprehensions about out-of-control cops, law enforcement aimed to align itself with identity-based politics, promulgating a discourse of "minorityism." Popularized by police commissioners like Los Angeles's William Parker and New York's Michael J. Murphy in the 1960s, minorityism appropriated language from new social movements to present cops as "the most downtrodden, oppressed, dislocated minority in America" (Parker, qtd in Fogelson, 239). "The police officer too belongs to a minority group—a highly visible minority group," Murphy stated, "and is also subject to stereotyping and mass attack" (qtd in Lipset, 80). Minorityism itself was more in line with a neoconservative backlash that would gain steam throughout the 1970s, but it contributed to a confused structure of feeling within popular culture, one which enabled police figures to adopt the garb of counterculture and assume its posture of rebellion.

In his study of the 1970s police exposé as a literary genre, Christopher Wilson argues that figures like Frank Serpico and Robert Leuci—the latter being the cop on whom the book (Robert Daley, 1978) and film *The Prince of the City* are based—embody the discourse of law enforcement minorityism. In Wilson's analysis, these chronicles cast their protagonists as "nostalgic representatives of an already lost city," exploiting their Italian white-ethnic identity and tight community ties to lend authenticity to stories that, somewhat incongruously, affirmed extensions of managerial power taking place behind the scenes (351). On the surface, Serpico as performed by Al Pacino, appears to epitomize urbane, anti-establishment values. Yet the self-enterprising policing that came so naturally to Serpico, suggests Wilson, in fact embodied the officer of whom police departments dreamt: highly educated, competent, and autonomous only to the extent that his activities were always in line with broader departmental objectives.

What exactly the objectives of big-city police were, however, remained a question. The urban milieu of the super cop in the early 1970s is defined by the declining returns of mid-century law enforcement innovations like the FBI's Uniform Crime Reports (UCR) and centralized coordination, and by de-industrialized cities that pitted a top-heavy public service sector (including law enforcement) against the complex problems of a city in fiscal crisis with a poverty-stricken inner-city populace (Wilson 356). As police historian Robert Fogelson notes, although crime prevention was widely understood to be the primary function of postwar policing, there were in fact few opportunities or tried-and-true methods for dealing with urban crime. Standardized crime reports offered little help, he observes, not only because "they were extremely inaccurate, but also because, in the absence of a coherent theory of criminal behavior, they were virtually unfathomable" (233). Thus, "big-city police, no matter how well organized and ably staffed, probably cannot do very much about the incidence of crime in urban America" (Fogelson 234). Added to this lack of direction was the fact that the police force patrolling inner-city areas remained overwhelmingly white. In the aftermath of ghetto riots in the 1960s, a number of cities stepped up efforts to recruit black police, but only a few cities showed demonstrable changes in the racial composition of their police departments (*New York Times* 25 January 1971, 1). The disappointing truth beneath law enforcement's appropriation of the super cop's modernizing veneer was the fact that, not only were the superintendents of the ghetto overwhelmingly white, they also didn't really know what they were doing there.

In a certain sense, the heroic modifiers applied to police within the public sphere could be seen as a way to assuage anxiety over the social disorder that seemed to be taking over the city. Contemporaneous claims that cop films were as reactionary as law and order rhetoric, and even fascistic were common and often not unfounded. Eastwood's Harry Callahan expressed views that clearly echoed contemporary conservative critiques of the justice system's leniencies in the wake of the criminal rights movement. Pauline Kael, who tended to like action films, labeled *Dirty Harry* a "right wing fantasy" (113). The executive producer of *The*

French Connection was G. David Schine, a prolific anti-communist and advisor to Joseph McCarthy. Schine's presence was remarked upon in Michael Shedlin's ranging critique of the film in *Film Comment*, which argued that it epitomized the propagandistic nature of the American culture industries. These perspectives in many ways embody the cultural parochialism necessary at a time when conservatism seemed to be foreclosing the political gains of the 1960s. Historical distance, however, reveals the nuance and polysemy within the super-cop cycle, as well as the broad acknowledgment that police could be as disordered as the precincts they patrolled.

Films like *Cops and Robbers* and *Law and Disorder*, for example, form part of an anti-super-cop strain that satirized the absurdities of modern urban policing. *Cops and Robbers* iconoclastically depicts two disillusioned beat cops (Cliff Gorman and Joseph Bologna) who have become so fed up with low wages and futile battles with urban chaos that they have resorted to casually sticking up liquor stores while on duty.[2] Deciding to scale up their operations, they stage a bank heist that exploits the access and anonymity provided through their uniform. In *Law and Disorder*, Carroll O'Connor and Ernest Borgnine star as members of a group of residents of a crime-ridden, high-rise apartment who form their own auxiliary police force headquartered in the building's basement. Gaining access to a squad car, Borgnine's character gleefully peals around an empty baseball diamond and then invites his motley crew of ersatz officers to pile into it; they cruise the streets of New York not unlike Keystone cops for the 1970s. Other more downbeat entries, including *The Laughing Policeman* and *Report to the Commissioner*, deal rather squarely with the demands and toll of modern urban policing on officers, often as not representing the various inefficacies of modern law enforcement, including its entrenched corruption and inability to deal with a racially divided city.

Focusing on the social and political views expressed by individual characters also blinded commentators to how a film's visual discourse could be providing a contrastive, less cogent perspective on the social landscape. Director Don Siegel was renowned for his moral and political ambiguity, and *Dirty Harry* is of a piece with *Invasion of the Body Snatchers* (1956) in its resistance to strict ideological interpretation (in *Invasion*, the pod people might be understood as communist infiltrators or McCarthyites, depending on one's inclination). Understanding Harry Callahan as a heroic super cop means disregarding his obsessive and excessive violence and disavowing the ways that his savagery doubles those of the vicious serial killer he seeks (McGarry 92). Although *Dirty Harry* introduces its title character high atop a building that gives him a commanding panoramic daytime view of San Francisco, his ensuing investigation, as Josh Gleich has argued, consistently pulls him down into cinematographically darkened territories pervaded by visual uncertainty. Harry is a police detective, in other words, who is shown to be unable to negotiate the strange ungovernable forces that define modern urban society (Gleich 333–50). At the end of the film (the only one of the Harry series that Siegel directed), Harry is far from the city center that provided him the synoptic view at the film's opening. Having chased the Scorpio killer (Andrew Robinson) across the grounds of an empty factory, he now stands at the edge of a muddy slough into which he tosses his badge. The camera pulls out into a soaring helicopter view that places him as a solitary figure embedded within knotted highways and industrial sprawl. As Gleich demonstrates, *Dirty Harry* resists and denigrates San Francisco's more iconic, touristic spaces in order to turn toward interstitial spaces such as this. The vertical power imputed at the downtown opening is revealed to have been narcissistic fantasy. Although he seemed to surf above the fray, we now realize how enmeshed within this urban mess this cop really is.

The 1970s cop film faced stiff competition from television, the medium that had come to provide the procedural with its most stable home. Boosting the sordor of the genre via urban vice was one way for cinema to compete with the ongoing popularity of cop shows like "Adam-12" (1968–1975), "Dragnet 1967 (1967–1970), "The Streets of San Francisco" (1972–1977), "Police Story" (1973–1977), "Kojak" (1973–1978), and an increasing number of made-for-television movies that brought the procedural template of "Dragnet" (1951–1959) and "The Naked City" (1958–1963) into contact with new social themes and urban contexts. Cop films could take advantage of the MPAA ratings system that had replaced the production code to show what network television could not.[3] A poster tagline for *Busting* read: "What this movie exposes about undercover vice cops can't be seen on your television set," making abundantly clear the strategy to outdo TV cops. The poster depicts an image of co-stars Elliot Gould and Robert Blake literally bursting through the torso of an exotic dancer, flanked by a bikinied masseuse on the left and a man holding a fan of bills on the right. The tagline continues: "BUSTING . . . only at a movie theater!" Although promising a cop exposé, it is clearly the world of vice they work within, as much as the outsider cop personae, that is being sold here on the margins, demonstrating that cinematic police narratives were as much a mode of conveyance through underworld urban locales as they were character studies.

In certain ways, super-cop cinema can be seen as an extension of cop television. As with the films, cop television was, to various degrees, predicated on portraying crime fighting narratives occurring within urban locations. But 1970s cinema provided a number of different directions in which to take the cop formula, and too the possibility of moving it away from the rigidly defined conventionality of televisual codes. The tongue-in-cheek tone of the *Times*'s "Cheezit" article might initially seem an incongruous mode for characterizing a genre presided by moral seriousness and gritty masculinity, but it reflected the cycle's tonal spectrum, which occasionally shaded into comedic territory. Although depicting serious matters of modern urban policing, *Cops and Robbers*, *Busting*, *Freebie and the Bean*, and *The Super Cops* were spiced with the witty back-and-forth dialogue of weary cop partners, anticipating the trend for the comedy-laced, heavily sequeled buddy cop films—*Lethal Weapon* (1987, sequels released in 1989, 1992, 1998), *48hrs* (1982, sequel released in 1990), *Beverly Hills Cop* (1984, sequels released in 1987, 1994), and *Stakeout* (1987, sequel released in 1993)—that would become ubiquitous in the 1980s and 1990s. Assimilating the rogue cop tradition established in 1950s films like Otto Preminger's *Where the Sidewalk Ends* (1950), Fritz Lang's *The Big Heat* (1953), and André de Toth's *Crime Wave* (1954), the buddy cop films of the 1970s create a cop partner dynamic in which the bonds of friendship transcend the organizational corruption and absurdities of everyday police labor. Frequently shown caught between institutional breakdown and an unforgiving postindustrial beat, cops on film could be tagged with a survivalist, ironic, and anti-authoritarian identity highly compatible with police minorityism and the authenticity-seeking male culture of the era.

As the films spun out of the Knapp Commission hearings illustrate, a significant aspect of super-cop popular culture was indeed the range of reality effects that could be achieved by bringing true-to-life urban policing to the big screen. Strangely, but perhaps not unsurprisingly, the real-life police officers whose experiences were parlayed onto screen endeavored to stay within the realm of show business rather than return to policing. Eddie Egan and his partner Sonny Grosso, on whose exploits *The French Connection* and the subsequent *Badge 373* are based, shortly gave up on law enforcement in order to pursue careers in film and television. The detectives had served as consultants on *The French Connection*, helping director William Friedkin re-write Ernest Tidyman's screenplay so as to more authentically reflect police idioms. Grosso and Egan were also given roles in the film, as was Randy Jurgensen, an NYPD detective who would be a key consultant for Friedkin's *Cruising*, as well as an actor in many of the director's subsequent films. Egan, who filed for retirement from the NYPD in 1971, would go on to star in *Badge 373*, *Prime Cut* (1972), "Mannix" (1967–1975), *Night of Terror* (1972, TV), "McCloud" (1970–1977), *Let's Go For Broke* (1974, as himself),

Cop on the Beat (1975, TV), "Police Story" (1973–1979), *To Kill a Cop* (1978, TV), and a number of other productions, mostly for television. Grosso also found work developing stories (*The Seven-Ups, Strike Force* [TV, 1975) and acting (*The Godfather* [1972], *The Seven-Ups, Report to the Commissioner*) before transitioning into a successful career as a television producer. LAPD detective-turned-author Joseph Wambaugh also made successful forays into film and television writing. In the *Time* magazine review of Peter Maas's *Serpico* novel Wambaugh is credited as having initiated the "current cop craze" (Ferrer, 28 May 1973, 102). Wambaugh created "Police Story" and also wrote scripts based on his novels—*The New Centurions* (1971), *The Blue Knight* (1972, filmed for television 1973, TV series 1975–1976), and *The Choirboys* (1975, filmed 1977).

The boundaries between fiction and actuality become somewhat blurred as real-life super cops entered the contingent hyper-reality of media fame and the cop craze took on the appearance of manufacturing, rather than merely transmitting, cop exploits. The trajectory of *The Super Cops* in certain ways typifies—but also hyperbolizes—the slippages between fact and fiction characteristic of the phenomenon, and the iconoclastic, anti-institutional autonomy of the cops it tended to represent. The film is based on the larger-than-life story of NYPD officers Dave Greenberg and Robert Hantz, chronicled in L. H. Whittmore's 1973 book *The Super Cops: The True Story of the Cops Called Batman and Robin*. Reputedly gaining their super hero monikers from the Bedford-Stuyvesant residents in the neighborhood they patrolled, Greenberg and Hantz originally attracted public attention in 1972 after it was revealed that they had made over 600 collars together, mostly on drug-related charges, since 1968. Still rookies, they reportedly earned their cartoonish nicknames for the way they employed grappling hooks, rooftop sojourns, disguises, and a number of other off-the-cuff techniques to thwart criminals. In one of the many over-the-top stories that fill the book, the officers get word that Mafia assassins are waiting for them in a car outside their precinct. Hantz takes to the roof of the building and Greenberg sneaks out to commandeer a city bus and they ambush the men where they sit. Although boasting of carrying out arrests completely by the book, Hantz and Greenberg nonetheless earned the scorn of their superiors, who would frequently attempt to separate them or put them on traffic patrol in order to inhibit their prodigious arrest efforts.

While they attracted the attention of the D.A.'s office, Internal Affairs, the F.B.I., and even the Knapp Commission, corruption charges never stuck to the men. In Michael F. Armstrong's book chronicling his days as chief counsel to the Knapp Commission, serious suspicion is cast on the nature of Hantz and Greenberg's exploits. Armstrong recounts a meeting with an African-American police officer named Lenny Weir who told him that Hantz and Greenberg

> preyed in particular on the black community, bullying, arresting, and shaking down all kinds of people in all kinds of circumstances. For example, he said, the two would regularly stop as many as a dozen young blacks, line them up against a wall, smack them around pretty much at will, and confiscate any contraband. They also took any money they might find" (79). According to Weir, their nicknames were "derisive appellations" within the black community they bullied, with the pair "apparently missing the intended irony" (79)

Armstrong also outlines the suspicious involvement of the pair in the shooting of two low-level drug dealers. As described in Whittmore's book, the shooting was self-defense and the drug dealers were part of an "international drug ring" that Hantz and Greenberg were in the process of blowing wide open (qtd in Armstrong 80).

In a *New York* profile pre-dating the publication of Whittmore's book, however author Julie Baumgold described Hantz and Greenberg as "copyright cops," tangled in the arc of super-cop stardom. The article offered a glimpse into the bizarre apotheosis of cop vogue:

> They are quite caught up in the whole Eddie-Egan-Soon-to-Be-a-Major-Motion-Picture-Syndrome. In fact, just a few days ago Egan himself said to Hantz, "You guys are coming up fast. You're pushing me." The author of the book about them says, "They're not only cops, they're entrepreneurs." And so there are timeline conference calls to the palmy bowels of Hollywood on its cop kick; show-biz lawyers, literary agents, foreign and paperback rights, the Doubleday contract, trust funds, leaves of absence for promotional tours and to be technical consultants to M-G-M on the film, lengthy tape-recorded sessions full of their exploits. The media maw has opened for them with a big grinful of capped teeth as they—the last heroes—sit in decorated rooms talking about hitting flats, making collars and the junkies of Heartbreak Hotel. (Baumgold 30–31)

The article outlines, in some detail, the men's newfound penchant for designer clothing and material goods—Greenberg purchased a Cadillac "fraught with hair-trigger security devices and plastic 'POLICE' sign on the dashboard, and recently went off to Boston to buy $4000 worth of

California threads" (31)—as well as a variety of homosocial tics: although seemingly oversexed, they would go on double dates but rarely talk to their female partners. Photos accompanying the article show Hantz and Greenberg engaged in a drug bust and re-staging their infamous rooftop-to-rooftop leaps in Bedford Stuyvesant (figure 2.1). They are dressed, however, not in police blues but rather in stylish white leather loafers, white slacks, and leather jackets, cops literally cut from a different cloth.[4]

In posing its putatively hip subjects within the milieu of urban decay and playing up their knowledge of its obscure byways, the *New York* piece on Hantz and Greenberg disclosed, in a rather hyperbolic way, the reliance of the super-cop phenomenon on the built environment of the modern city. Although in *Dirty Harry* the modern city becomes a zone of opacity for Harry, in the publicity surrounding *The Super Cops*, similar spaces are represented much like playgrounds for cop action. As depicted in the film version directed by Gordon Parks (who in his career as a photojournalist covered similar territory), the urban environment patrolled by Greenberg (David Selby) and Hantz (Ron Leibman) literalizes the precariousness of urban policing in the manner of 1920s slapstick. In

Figure 2.1. "The Super Cops," Dave Greenberg and Robert Hantz, photographed for *New York* magazine.

the film's action sequences, Selby's gangly, almost awkwardly adolescent frame and Liebman's expressive, caffeinated bounciness come to the fore. In short-sleeved police blues one size too large and non-regulation white sneakers (for silently creeping up on targets), these talky, wise-cracking cops contrast the silent ruggedness of Eastwood, the elite corps of *The Seven-Ups*, and their ilk, marking themselves as hapless figures in this complex inner-city terrain. Just as often as Greenberg and Hantz rappel from rooftops or drop from elevated subway rails to the street below, so too do they tumble over each other in alleys, updating Keystone antics for the era of post-industrialism. The physicality of Greenberg and Hantz, like their negotiation of legal red tape in the precinct house, appears largely improvisational. When they employ ropes it is hardly in the iconic style that Parks depicts John Shaft (Richard Roundtree), swinging through windows with guns blazing, but rather in the skittish manner of freshman gym class.

Such urban pantomime reinforced the affiliation of *The Super Cops* with a campy, pop imagery redolent of the super hero television series from which they took their nicknames. Posters for the film depicted the protagonists in a series of vignettes framed by boldly colored comic-book lettering. Within this pop-inflicted publicity, foregrounding the film's urban iconography was as important as delineating the heroic feats of the protagonists. In one of these illustrated vignettes, Hantz and Greenberg even swoop down onto criminals from atop the wrecking ball of a crane. The scene in the film to which this image refers has Hantz and Greenberg chasing Mafia hoods into a tenement apartment building that is in the process of being razed. The cops exchange gunfire with the men in empty rooms as a wrecking ball breaks through the brick walls around them, parts of walls and ceilings tumbling down to cover them in dust. As the crooks try to flee the building, the staircase collapses and they disappear (and presumably die) in a cloud of dust. Motioning to the crane operator through a large hole in the side of the building, the super cops ride the wrecking ball safely to ground level. Both the publicity images of the wrecking ball and its appearance within the film powerfully collapse police fiction into the contemporary realities of urban renewal, once again mixing cartoonish exaggeration with topicality.

The popular vernacular in which the super-cop films portrayed the actuality of urban crisis establishes the cycles bond with Blaxploitation, which likewise couched generic narratives and broadly drawn characters within inner-city landscapes. As Peter Stanfield has shown, one of the signature features of the black gangster subgenre of the Blaxploitation cycle is the scene of stylish and self-possessed black males confidently striding through the streets of the ghetto. "In just about all of the films in the cycle with an urban setting there is at least one lengthy scene of the hero tramping the city's sidewalks," Stanfield writes, ". . . sequences that attempt to enunciate poetically everyday black street life" (Stanfield 290). The masterful negotiation of the inner-city streets that recurs in these films, Stanfield argues, underscores an emergent black urban experience, one defined by the racialized segregation of cities and suburbs, and by the limitations placed on black freedom by the invisible boundaries of the ghetto. Though the black gangster films of this era most often feature tragic endings on these very streets, these initial scenes of street mastery, scored with funky arrangements by soul artists like Isaac Hayes and Curtis Mayfield, are engineered to induce visual pleasure. Paula Massood makes a similar point about Blaxploitation, writing that these "tours" of the streets of the ghetto "offered their audiences undeniable voyeuristic . . . pleasure, either acting as anthropological documents for audiences unfamiliar with the ghetto, or sources of identification for those who were familiar with it" (Massood 85).

In the super-cop film, similar images of ghetto life are motivated by sequences of routine patrol and the rolling view of inner-city streets through the window of a squad car is a recurring motif. But while in the Blaxploitation film this display often provides the opportunity to vivify ghetto life and culture, the same image in the cop film is often the mechanism for framing a pious lament about the transformation of the inner city. In *The Super Cops*, the camera captures passing storefronts, groups of men, and children playing on the sidewalk as Greenberg and Hantz drive toward their new precinct. Both cops comment on the surroundings: "Oh man . . ."; "What a place to have to live, huh?"; "Ain't gonna be no picnic working here"; "No wonder them cats laughed when we got this assignment." The funk score that accompanies their short journey and its running commentary reverses the conventional valence of the Blaxploitation soundtrack. Whereas in the Blaxploitation films, rhythmic funk is associated with the ebullient energy of street life, here it serves to differentiate the principal characters from the environment they find themselves in and to mark the deprivation of the surroundings.

As much as super cops were external to the fecund culture of the inner city, they were also perniciously linked to it in many ways. Through the 1960s, the images of cops that proliferated in the mass media were within scenes of urban revolt and violent political demonstration wherein they could be found astride horses or wielding batons. Police, that is, were a significant part of the visual panorama of social disorder, constituents as much as agents of the transforming urban milieu. It is perhaps no coincidence that William Parker, following the Los Angeles riots, popularized the term "thin blue line" during this time. As an abstract chromatic figure for the distinction between order and disorder, the expression in fact places police in a liminal zone. In light of their falling cultural capital within liberal America, the super-cop phenomenon can be seen as a rearguard attempt to resuscitate the police image. The *New York* piece on Hantz and Greenberg and its accompanying images illustrate the attempt to graft police minorityism onto the appurtenances of a rapidly diffusing counterculture. Hantz and Greenberg, Frank Serpico, and the youthful members of "The Mod Squad" (1968–1973) in fact are frequently labeled, both in publicity and within their diegetic worlds as "hippie cops." Part of this identity had to do with the stances they took against the willful traditionalism of the superiors. Yet, the modes of dress that culturally marked these cops as different from their colleagues also functioned to place them in liminal zones of identity. The beards, dungarees, and sneakers adopted by hippie cops wavered between personal expression and the cop's search for identity within modes of disguise.

Serpico's Masquerade

More so than in earlier Hollywood cop cycles, plots involving disguise and undercover work pervade the super-cop cycle. If Blaxploitation films, and specifically black gangster films introduce urban subjects both in command of, and confined by their environment, the super-cop films engage the subjectively destabilizing nature of law enforcement—often thematized as the line between morality and corruption—by playing on the visibility of police figures within urban milieus. The prominence of disguise in *Serpico*, *The Seven-Ups*, *Badge 373*, *The New Centurions*, *Busting*, and *Report to the Commissioner* serves drama that oscillates police figures between visibility and invisibility within the urban environment. The now-you-see-them-now-you-don't aspects of these films position the white super cop as a figure that stands out from and seeks to disappear into the city.

Serpico is a key film working in this mode. Just as Frank Serpico's long hair, beads, and dashiki mark him off against other plainclothes officers (whose dress sense is more redolent of suburban leisure wear) and as a hippie cop to his superiors, so too do they help him integrate into his adopted bohemian Greenwich Village lifestyle. Reticent to reveal his cop identity socially, Serpico asks his new friends to call him "Paco." While remaining tied to his ethnic roots (in one scene he takes his shoes to be repaired by his brother Pasquale at the family shop) Serpico as Paco is also upwardly mobile: he sits in on Spanish literature classes at NYU, goes to the ballet, and attends happenings in artist's lofts. While he remains somewhat embarrassed about his career amongst his friends, at the precinct he is unabashed about his nonconformist tastes, dressing against the grain, carrying around Isadora Duncan's biography (an interest in dance courting questions of his sexuality from his superiors), and even adopting a pet mouse. His preference for social disguise aligns with his professional life, where he frequently dons elaborate costumes to blend into the environs he patrols—a train engineer's outfit at a subway station, the white apron of a butcher in the meat packing district—to better observe and collar criminals.

Although he integrates them into his police work, Serpico's disguises produce a distance between him and the other police. In one of the film's undercover scenes Serpico has embedded himself on a subway platform in his engineer guise and spots a man burglarizing a neighboring apartment. Giving chase, Serpico tackles the burglar in an alley as two uniformed cops come upon the scene and open fire on both men. After scrambling to safety and holding the burglar while also loudly identifying himself, the uniformed cops relent and Serpico angrily tears into them. "Jesus, Frank," one of the offending cops says, "how was I supposed to recognize you? . . . Frank, I didn't know you." The implications of this line go beyond just this scene. Serpico's multiple identities and disguises frustrate the ability of others to know him, just as his incorruptibility renders him in some way illegible, and possibly dangerous, to other officers who are "on the pad" (taking bribes).

In Peter Maas's book version of Frank Serpico's story the differences between mainline cops and Serpico are as defined by morality as they are by taste and place of residence:

> Perhaps it would have been easier for them if Serpico fitted a recognizable puritanical mold. But he dressed like a hippie and sported a beard and long hair, and he lived in a bachelor pad in Greenwich Village doing, in their minds, god knows what. In the suburban tract houses with tiny neatly trimmed lawns where most of the city's policemen lived, in the saloons where they gathered, in the precinct houses and the radio cars, Serpico became the prime topic of conversation. (23)

Thus, just as his undercover disguises and his hippie attire become emblems of an authentic ethos so too does his revulsion to mainstream policing become linked to a politics of taste.

For Wilson, even though Serpico's lone wolf status and entrepreneurial approach jibe with higher-level transformations within big city policing, his predilection for disguise and undercover work "inaugurate complex psychic investments" that take on a destabilizing life of their own. "Removed from aldermanic visibility, Serpico's investments involve more than standing for the law," writes Wilson, "Curiously, they allow him to stand in for the public or victim and yet stand outside cop (civic) authority itself" (363–64). This fluidity coheres with the contemporary culture of self-actualization embodied by the film's depiction of Greenwich Village; with a girlfriend who is "an actress, a singer, a dancer, and a Buddhist," and her friends who, between the jobs they perform and the callings they identify with (a poet who works for an ad agency, a novelist who works for an insurance company), are, as Serpico puts it, "all . . . on their way to being somebody else." Though this comment seems at first Serpico's way of questioning their authenticity, it is clear that he too, by playing with the visibility of his office, is on his way somewhere. If this somewhere is closer or further away from cop-ness, however, is unclear.

As Wilson points out, the flux of identity that Serpico finds himself within induces strange effects of doubling and inversion. In the book, he meets a Mafia member, also named Frank Serpico, who unsuccessfully attempts to bribe him. A rebuffed mafia Serpico reminds cop Serpico of their shared ethnic background, shared neighborhoods, and, with startling closeness, informs him also that he knows where cop Serpico's parents still live. A return of the repressed, this figure reminds Serpico of the more illegitimate path not taken. In a similar parallel universe scenario, Maas relates a dream Serpico has in which a long-haired and bearded police force pull over businessmen for appearing suspicious. In this dream world, the markers of respectability that Serpico militates against are inverted, and yet, significantly, an idea of the world in which appearance remains tied to essence remains in place.

Although not always to such topsy-turvy effect, the prevalence of disguise in the super-cop cycle indexes a cultural moment in which the meanings associated with the identity, visibility, and presence of police came to be invested with a range of conflicting meanings. In neo-conservative rhetoric, police became emblems of a wish for the restoration of a social order in which the groups grasping toward political presence (blacks, youth, women, gays, and lesbians) throughout the 1960s quietly reassumed their proper place out of sight. A deep mistrust of policing emanating from more liberal and progressive quarters came to recognize individual cops as ciphers of brute authoritarian power, a power that police seem to willfully self-expose. Within cities dealing with rising crime in addition to social disorder, police presence created new forms of paranoia and discomfort. It is difficult not to see the phenomenon of police disguise as a path through these tensions. As countercultural lifestyles moved closer to convention, civilian drag was not just a method of infiltration, a way to get closer to criminals, it was also a way to, like

Serpico, lean away from the social shame of being a cop, a way for cops to play at being, for once, cool.

Street Sensation

As a public relations exercise to rehabilitate law enforcement's tarnished image, super-cop culture was disingenuous and ersatz, and yet when pressed its charms could be acknowledged within liberal discourse. After sifting through 1973's stack of mass-market, super-cop, non-fiction titles (Maas's *Serpico*, Whittemore's *The Super Cops*, Robert Daley's *Target Blue: An Insider's View of the NYPD*, *Law and Order* by Dorothy Uhnak, *Rizzo* by Frank Hamilton), Richard Reeves at *The Washington Post* admitted to super-cop fatigue. Every New Yorker who had been mugged or lived with the fear of being mugged, noted Reeves, was abundantly familiar with the inadequacies of law enforcement so it was silly to imply that the ingenuity or moral integrity of individual cops had relevance to New York's crime problems. Moreover, he argued, books like *Serpico* and *The Super Cops* were "lousy journalism." "In both books," Reeves complained, "the authors have apparently done nothing but tape record the self-serving reminisces of their larger-than-life subjects." Yet as much as they were bad journalism, Reeves confessed that they were fun. "I may have had it with the books," he concluded, "but I'll go to see the movies being made of them."

Reeves's apparent pleasure in the super-cop cycle despite his liberal ambivalence toward new forms of cop populism exemplifies the sense that their appeal extended beyond a resonance with law and order rhetoric or as factually based narratives. What super-cop films specifically offered, that other media did not, were location-shot sequences involving the peregrinations of disguised agents through a contemporary urban terrain. Like Blaxploitation, police genres offered forms of urban tourism in which spectators were invited to watch cop avatars negotiate the modern city territories being left behind by the white middle class. In this sense, as much as the city of this time may have been posited as "lost" to a concatenation of social others (hippies, black revolutionaries, sexual hedonists), so too and for these very reasons did it become an explorable terrain of heterosocial sensation, a stage, unlike the suburbs, in which identity was public and fluid rather than fixed within increasingly privatized, and homogenized, configurations. Police themselves become figures through which a suburbanizing society comes to reacquaint itself with the phenomenological vicissitudes of the street. The motif of disguise allegorizes these impulses for Serpico: the city is not only a place to see and do new things, it is a place to be someone else. However, within thriller narratives, the trope of disguise matches the appeal of invisibility with the anticipation of its opposite: the exciting possibility of becoming unmasked. The deep and destabilizing involvements with disguise threaded within super-cop media therefore constitute a reflexive sensorial dimension, the suspenseful effects of which acknowledged urban tourism to carry the tariff of exposure for its protagonists. Part of the fun of watching these street games unfold centers on participating in the visual uncertainty they put into play between identity and disguise.

To take a mild example, the opening sequence of *The Seven-Ups* involves a complexly staged operation to take down a counterfeiting ring. Posing variously as a customer, a water deliveryman, and a sign painter, a police unit converges on an antique store the counterfeiters are operating out of, producing a diversion through a staged altercation that involves the somewhat excessive (and therefore pleasurable to watch) destruction of the store's upscale merchandise. The men coolly break character as uniformed police arrive, and it is revealed that their distraction has allowed the sign painter to climb through a window to snatch an incriminating box of counterfeit bills. Though as viewers we are given enough visual information to suspect the orchestration of an undercover police operation, the nature and target of the operation remain obscure. Playing detective by parsing the visual information provided momentarily, and thrillingly, suspends us between the legible and the illegible.

Of course, the illegibility of city streets has, since at least the nineteenth century, been consistently engaged with through popular forms of virtual urban spectatorship such as the detective story and it is useful to acknowledge the way these films sustain and update older formulas. Walter Benjamin famously suggested that the figure of the detective was forged from repurposed elements of the flâneur, an urban type whose modes of street observation had become obsolete. The flâneur's florid sketches of street life were originally found in *feuilletons*, serial sections of French newspapers, or in small books devoted to such topics, called *physiologies*. Yet the geniality of these forms was soon found to be inappropriate to a bourgeois experience of city life that contended daily with class friction and the possibility of social eruption. In the face of urban revolution the flâneur's good-humored caricature was simply untenable and "the soothing little remedies that the physiologists offered for sale," Benjamin wrote, "were soon outmoded" (*SW* 4: 21). Detective stories, however, could reverberate the shocks of urban life, sustaining their anxieties across the breadth of a narrative before allaying them through the canny investigator's final ratiocinative solution. Thus, the detective story became a more durable frame on which to hang varieties of urban spectatorship. As Dana Brand points out, Edgar Allan Poe's early detective stories "exploit the aesthetic appeal of the shock" (92) in their very form. Where "in the literature of the flâneur, the reader is shielded from all potential sources of anxiety at the moment he or she first encounters them," in Poe resolution to a mystery is "achieved only after some effort and some time" and thus "the structure of the detective story permits the reader to experience both the thrill of epistemological and physical anxiety in the city and the pleasure of its resolution" (92).

In some ways, the endurance of the detective story through the twentieth century attests to a mass audience receptive to consuming aesthetic forms as a way of both confronting and alleviating anxieties endemic to modern urban experience. As great as the historical differences between the nineteenth-century city and the city of the 1970s are, both were undergoing social transformations that disrupted the established bourgeois frames of understanding that had for some time held things in a legible, if invisibly repressive, order. But did the various cultural productions representing urban spectatorship in the 1970s fulfill a similar role in *containing* the visual uncertainty of urban spectacle? I would claim that they did not. The recurrent motif of destabilized identity and vision within the super-cop cycle indicate fissures of anxiety that rippled within middle-class culture and enabled new forms of urban sensation.

Games of urban legibility, similar to the games of sensation and legibility played out in the nineteenth-century detective story, appear in 1970s visual media, suggesting that the anxiety of the streets had reemerged as a pressing concern. In January of 1972, *LIFE* published a feature on mugging and street crime. Included amongst the grim statistics, stories from muggers and victims, and advice on how to avoid being mugged was a two-page photo-spread headlined: "The Police Counterattack: Everyone Here Is a Cop" (figure 2.2). The photograph depicts a wide, high-angle view of a street scene bustling with a spectrum of quotidian activity. We see a jogger, a delivery boy, a man in a wheelchair, businessmen, a blind man, and a number of workmen (indeed, the scene is mostly men) all seemingly engaged in everyday business. The caption to the photo informs us that everyone depicted within this everyday image is part of the New York Police Department's newly formed Street Crime Unit. In other words, this image is staged by police and composed entirely of undercover officers.

Beginning in 1971, the Street Crime Unit employed 200 officers to conduct surveillance and decoy operations in high-crime areas. Donning civilian garb, members of the unit would anonymously position themselves and then hope to spot, or become targets of, criminal acts so that they could spring on the perpetrators and make an arrest. Much like the super-cop films, these units themselves became somewhat of a fad within

THE POLICE COUNTERATTACK: EVERYBODY HERE IS A COP

Figure 2.2. Photograph of NYPD's Street Crimes Unit in *LIFE.*

urban law enforcement. Similarly styled surveillance teams emerged in a number of other major cities in the 1970s, including Detroit, Boston, and San Francisco. So too did these departments encourage publicity of their efforts by allowing news coverage—coverage which mirrored the content of the *LIFE* feature. An article for *Ebony* entitled "You Can't Tell the Cops from the Robbers," profiled the New York anticrime team in action, even providing photos of the unit disguised within different street settings and providing vivid descriptions of the team—with a focus placed on its black members—in action. Spotting a man who looks to be carrying a concealed weapon from the unit's unmarked patrol van,

> Ford, Glaspie and Niles (the only black woman in the street crime unit) jump out of the van and glide smoothly down the street, blending into the crowd, their eyes never losing sight of the man on whom they are swiftly gaining. When they catch up with him, quietly, unobtrusively, they identify themselves and tell him their purpose. A quick check reveals that he is "clean." . . . They apologize and he's on his way. Except for perhaps two or three people nearby, none of the passers-by knows what is happening. The response to a uniformed cop in such a situation probably would have been different, both from the man and the people on the streets. (Bailey 116)

While the writer here chooses to emphasize the stealthy efficiency of the team, other articles played up the campy nature of undercover strategies, telling stories of uniformed cops arresting bearded undercover agents, of police hobbling down the street dressed as old women, and making sly reference to the affinity of these practices to the cops and robbers of the screen by underscoring their backstage efforts to create authentic costumes.[5]

In many ways, it seemed as if the undercover work undertaken by actual police was mimicking the screen exploits of super cops, building even more feedback into an already recursive loop. *New York Street Crime Unit: An Exemplary Project* (Halper 1975), the first official report outlining the development, operations, and progress of the program, includes a variety of photographs of the unit in their undercover gear, either in character or posing for the camera (figure 2.3). One wears roller skates and loud clothing emblazoned with Coca-Cola logos. Another is shown on a street dressed as a junkie. Two men dressed in women's clothing chat casually on some outdoor steps. The pictures create a difficult-to-ignore clownishness that contrasts with the bland institutional prose and the spectacle of grown-up men in dress-up unravels the sobriety of crime-fighting in much the same way that the invocation of Keystone cops undercuts the portentousness of super-cop films in the *Times*'s "Cheezit—Here Comes the Cops" piece.

So too does the photo spread of undercover police populating an urban scene in *LIFE* seem to subvert the tone of the surrounding pages, which are dedicated to reporting the various ways that street crime has affected the lives of everyday people. The image itself is a hyperbolic representation of the unit's actual operations—the street crime unit usually worked in teams of two or three, it never took over an entire street corner—so in fact the photo hardly serves a documentary purpose. There is an overtly polysemic quality to the picture as well. Depending on one's view of the police one might gain comfort from the fact that any innocent-looking civilian could be a protective agent in disguise, or one could tense with panoptic insecurity, the photo echoing the paranoid feeling that agents of authority lurked everywhere. But the caption to the photo also introduces a layer of counter-surveillance that overturns its panoptic aesthetic. "Bobby" a mugger interviewed for the feature is unconvinced by police disguise, saying that he "can always spot a policeman by watching eyes." "Coppers are always looking around," Bobby says, "just like criminals do." One message the photo sends is less that the police *see* everything, than that they *are* everywhere, in a position to both see and be seen.

If *LIFE* participates in the culture of detection inaugurated through Poe's stories, it updates by way of a paranoid, though not un-humorous, aesthetic. The game this image asks us to play becomes particularly

Figure 2.3. Members of NYPD Street Crime Unit depicted in *New York City Police Street Crime Unit: An Exemplary Project* (1975).

charged in the context of undercover agents' ongoing infiltration of college campuses and radical political groups. Just who are these agents taking cover within these ordinary scenes? Are they looking for us or *at us*? Even if we were the target middle-American audiences that constituted *LIFE*'s core readership, could the nervous energy induced by this game truly be assuaged by the instantaneous assurance that nothing that we were being presented was as it seemed? On what perceptual grounds, if any, did we stand when navigating city streets? More and more we seem to be in the realm of Serpico's dream where identity's appearances and valences have become inverted. Except here we move even further—it is not just that appearance and identity have become reversed, the grounds on which we might have a perspective on either have inalterably shifted.

Unusual Energies: *The French Connection*

A closer examination of *LIFE*'s "Everyone Here Is a Cop" feature, reveals that the well-publicized activities of New York's anti-street crime unit form only one half of its DNA. The other half of the photo feature's provenance is encoded in the caption to a photo of a portly long-haired hippie that appears in the top-left corner of the same page. The caption reads: "Under his disguise he is a crew cut cop. He has also played Santa Claus." The caption is a winking reference to the opening scene of *The French Connection*, in which Popeye Doyle (Gene Hackman) stakes out a Brooklyn bar disguised as a Salvation Army Santa with his partner, Buddy Russo (Roy Schieder), who is dressed as a hot dog vendor (figure 2.4). Naturally, the larger *LIFE* photo also depicts a Santa and a hot dog vendor, solidifying that reference even further. The presence of these figures nods to the film and to its characterization of police detective Eddie Egan, both of which had been featured in the magazine's pages only a few months earlier. The *LIFE* photo therefore captures not only the growing fears of city streets, it is also an intertextual promotion that participates in the super-cop cycle's ongoing elision of the boundaries between the facts and fictions of urban policing, an elision that made it possible to conceive the realm of the city streets as both a zone of peril and an object of fascination for movie audiences. The roots of this conflicted investment can be tracked to the aesthetic experience of *The French Connection* itself.

The French Connection is concerned almost exclusively with movement and observation in public spaces. Perhaps more so than the super-cop films that preceded it, and the many that have succeeded it, it is a film that closely aligns with the street-based origins of the detective story as developed by Poe. The film also plumbs the realms of action and sensation that developed in detective film and popular literature, rather than the rarified spheres of ratiocination that emerged within the works of Agatha Christie. As Benjamin writes, Poe's "Man of the Crowd" (written just before the Dupin stories that would formalize the detective figure) is "something like an x-ray of a detective story" because it "does away

Figure 2.4. Popeye Doyle (Gene Hackman) undercover in *The French Connection.*

with all the drapery that a crime represents," leaving only "the pursuer, the crowd, and an unknown man who manages to walk through London in such a way that he always remains in the middle of the crowd" (*SW* 4, 27). Like "Man of the Crowd," Popeye and Russo's investigation in *The French Connection* begins with an inscrutable scene that prompts an all-night pursuit leading to the suspicion of deeper crimes. Spotting a man unknown to them (Sal Boca/Tony Lo Bianco) spending wads of cash with underworld figures in a nightclub, Popeye and Russo trail him through the night from Manhattan into Brooklyn. By early morning they observe him—incongruously, given the toney environs from which he had disembarked—opening a dingy snack bar. In this scene and many others the film exuberantly sidelines much of the drapery that seems to clutter the police genre—the morality of police practices, semi-factual depictions of broken institutional structures, the psychological and personal tolls of police work, and, most significantly, the positivist alignment of police point-of-view with objective truth—to get at the genre's street level armature.

Its well-remembered car chase sequence notwithstanding, *The French Connection* is structured around a series of street surveillance and foot pursuit scenes that press notions of legibility and, indeed, of urban spectatorship as a cinematic aesthetic, into the foreground. In different ways than *Dirty Harry* or *Serpico*, *The French Connection* is interested in conveying the street as a field of perceptual uncertainty and opacity. Although the viewer is often yoked to the point-of-view of the detectives in the conventional manner of a detective film, so too are we shown what an investigating figure looks like within an urban scene. We are frequently placed, that is, to behold and judge how watching detectives look within urban settings, just as in *LIFE*'s "Everyone Here is a Cop" feature. To accomplish this, director William Friedkin adapts visual codes that depart markedly from conventional Hollywood techniques predicated on producing narrative clarity.

An opening sequence set in Marseilles quickly initiates the viewer into the film's atypical observational style. The first shot of the film zooms out from the Notre Dame de la Garde to settle on a wide view of a port scene. Moving closer, we are shown a man in a brown leather jacket (André Ernotte) watching an American car. Men exit a restaurant and drive away and the watching man dips into the darkness of an alcove to avoid being spotted as they drive by. A quick cut, again to a very long-shot, establishes a different setting: a busy street corner outside the café *La Samaritaine*. The camera zooms to pick out the watching man from the previous scene sitting at a café table, this time wearing a tan mackintosh. After cutting to a medium-shot of the man, the camera pans quickly following his gaze to the same American car. The scene cuts again to a different setting, this time showing the man, now in a navy overcoat, strolling through a series of small neighborhood passages. He is now more relaxed, no longer in surveillance mode. As the man checks his mail in a secluded hallway, he is surprised by an assassin who abruptly shoots him in the face. The next scene shifts the setting to Brooklyn.

Who is this man? Why has he been shot and by whom? Why was he watching this car? These are questions that the film that follows will slowly, and only obliquely disclose but for which it will never supply firm answers. It becomes quickly apparent that this is a film that has adopted a peculiar style of address to the spectator: although it has set a scene and directed us toward relevant details, its rapidity challenges a firm grasp of what is happening. Rapid pacing and elliptical editing confuse stable spatial and temporal continuity. Even careful attention to the unfolding events will not provide access to clear knowledge, and even attentive viewers will be made to feel that they have been inattentive. Just as much as this sequence motivates a series of questions that will animate narrative involvement, so too does it initiate viewers into the dynamics of space, movement, and observation that will dominate the balance of the film.

Close examination reveals that there is a method and a logic to the assembly of these images. Many of the scenes within this opening sequence are captured through conventional framings, and a general adherence to the 180-degree rule ensures a semblance of orientation during brief-shot/reverse-shot moments. But there is also a palpable sense of *verité* style immediacy that is produced through unsteady zoom reframings, handheld shots, and, in one instance, a whip pan that momentarily blurs the visual field. The sense of visual presence these techniques convey also create a perceptual environment of uncertainty. Friedkin claims that he would often abstain from providing camera operator Enrique Bravo information about blocking and movement, letting him instead "find the scene" as it was being acted out (DVD commentary, 2001). This statement rings true to the sense that the camera is co-present to the action, often half a step behind. The questions that the Marseilles sequence immediately raises and its seeming disinterest in conventional modes of exposition cue viewers to watch closely and to expect, in the film that follows, that what is being shown (a watching man, a car, a murder) will not necessarily be conjoined to knowledge.

The French Connection bears marks throughout of a director and crew interested in pressing the visual possibilities of conventional crime filmmaking. Friedkin and cinematographer Owen Roizman experimented in early stages of production with a plan to shoot the film entirely over the shoulder of Doyle and Russo. They abandoned the idea after several tests proved it would be too tedious to watch.[6] The visual design that was settled on, however, did adapt similar techniques from observational documentary, and likewise drew on the ways that European New Wave filmmaking had taken advantage of lightweight camera equipment for location production.

Friedkin himself had in fact begun his filmmaking career, after working as a director of live television, in documentary. In Chicago he made *The People vs. Paul Crump* (1962), about a death row inmate believed to be innocent. On the strength of that film he was hired to work for David Wolper Productions in Los Angeles, where he made a number of television documentaries including *The Thin Blue Line* (1966), about modern policing. Around this time, *verité* and direct cinema techniques were coming to be incorporated into fictional features. In Haskell Wexler's *Medium Cool* (1969), for instance, which was shot in and around the violence surrounding the 1968 Democratic Convention in Chicago; and the work of British BBC director Peter Watkins (for example, *War Game* [1965], *Privilege* [1967]). Friedkin specifically acknowledges the influence of Costa-Gavras's *verité*-styled political thriller "Z" (1969), on the visual design of *The French Connection.* "Z," notably, was shot by Raoul Coutard, the cinematographer responsible for bringing a *verité* style into the 1960s nouvelle vague films of Jean-Luc Godard. Although his first few features, such as *The Night They Raided Minsky's* (1968) and *The Boys in the Band* (1970), dealt with urban themes, *The French Connection* would be

Friedkin's first thriller, and the first film in which he applied the techniques of *verité* and the European New Wave to a fictional film narrative.

The importation of the techniques of observational documentary allowed *The French Connection* to convey apparent immediacy within narrative action. Within the film's scenes of street observation, as I've mentioned above, Friedkin retains the method of shot/reverse-shot construction familiar from Hollywood continuity editing. Yet for reverse angles, he frequently employs handheld camera shots, emphasizing an embodied viewpoint within the flux of the action, not outside of it. Thus, it is clear that *verité* elements are strategically annexed within conventional structures. As much as the effect of this fusion is the impression of authenticity one also gains the feeling of the visual uncertainty that surrounds being "in the moment." The unsteady, mobile frame indicates that looking in the moment is often a frenetic search for detail rather than simply a gathering of truth. The language of observational cinema is used to tell us that this is, perceptually, how observation sees within the unfolding diegesis.

For instance, following the Marseilles opening, we are whisked into Brooklyn and presented with the scene that is referenced by the *LIFE* photo, a scene that serves to introduce Popeye and Russo and their methods of policing. The scene is set by a wide establishing shot of a sidewalk outside a bar—onscreen text informs us that this is Brooklyn—underneath elevated subway tracks. We see a hot dog vendor and a crowd of children circled around a Santa Claus ringing a bell. Santa is interested in what's going on in the bar and the film cuts to his point of view as he peers through the bar's window. Seeing two men brush up against one another at the jukebox, he rings the bell more loudly. The hot dog vendor leaves his post and enters the crowded, noisy bar, and scans the surroundings. As he is moving through the crowd, a man peals behind the bar for the door and now the hot dog vendor and Santa Claus give chase. This short surveillance scene occasions a number of point-of-view shots. Those attributed to Santa/Popeye are steady, likely shot using a mounted camera. Russo's point of view, inside the bar, is shakier and handheld looking. Where Popeye's gaze isolates a particular moment within a larger field, Russo enters into that field and his fervent search for what Popeye sees is transmitted both through his placement within the crowded mise-en-scène of the bar interior and the tremulous way in which the camera embodies his look. This small strip of action epitomizes the style that will pervade the film: a back-and-forth between watching police look and seeing what, and how, they see.

The suspense in this particular scene is amplified, of course, by the fact that this is a black cultural space, one understood to be hostile to the presence of police interlopers. Thus, as Russo moves to enter the bar he pulls out his police ID, the only authority—a token that says any resistant response will be revisited by more police force—under which he may enter the space and violently accost people within it (a policing pattern that is repeated in the film). As Popeye and Russo follow on the heels of the man who races from the bar, the streets that they move through in the Bedford-Stuyvesant area of Brooklyn are marked by an iconography of blight. The moving camera, following the running men (operated by Bravo using a wheelchair [Friedkin 163]), stops short at the edge of an expansive dirt lot strewn with garbage. Moving further into this landscape and away from the camera the detectives catch up with their quarry after he trips and begin to beat him. The motion of the men and the red Santa Claus suit generate a small speck of action against a drab landscape of urban renewal, caught by the camera as it would occur to a passerby. Just as in the film's opening shot of Notre Dame de la Garde in Marseilles, this landscape of urban decay also features a church in the distance. But where in the opening scene, the church on the hill provides an iconic reference establishing a European location, here it signifies the absurd and abject dimension of American urban life, both its landscape and its social potential.

In certain ways, *The French Connection* aligns with super-cop films that treat the problems of the city as beyond comprehensibility, and thus also beyond white suburban blame. In *Film Quarterly*, Michael Shedlin provided a representative take on the film along these lines:

> By playing on the confused fantasies of a frightened and schizophrenic culture, the makers of *The French Connection* have built a product that addresses itself directly to the major issues of our society—racism, corrupt power, brutality, drugs—and yet manages to subsume all social significance beneath an explosion of gaudy adventurism that ultimately reinforces the heroism of the authorities it seems to be criticizing. (3)

It is a familiar critique of Hollywood: a film cloaks itself in the markers of contemporaneity, but codes them into adventure and heroism, thereby solving at a formal level what remains unsolved at the level of society. The critique is sound, and applies well to the gaudy adventurism that pervades a number of the super-cop films. Shedlin's refusal to countenance the immersive, environmental experience offered by the film, the ways that it is formally attuned to the tactical negotiations of walking and looking in the city, however, prevents us from grasping the particularity of these "confused fantasies," and the way they connect to longer traditions in the aesthetics of urban anxiety.

That *The French Connection*, with its kinetic narrative style and hangnail ending, left many contemporary viewers unseated, was undeniable. Jonas Mekas's short review reverberates such feelings:

> Every second of this film is packed with action, in sound and image. You walk out of it like from a Rolling Stones concert, with every cell of your body shaken. After one viewing I am not too sure about its ultimate values, but it's clear that it contains very unusual visual and sound energies. The story itself (drugs, detectives) is of no interest. The good things are beyond the plot—in the visual richness, in the streams of energies, in its pace, its dynamics.

Charles W. Stroud, a friend of Friedkin from Chicago, wrote the director to say that he was similarly shaken after a viewing:

> I couldn't sleep that night. The elevated chase kept haunting me, reminding me of a sequence you had Bill Butler shoot for a documentary you did years ago . . . You somehow turned New York into Chicago . . . you were getting inside people with the lens. (Personal correspondence between Stround and Friedkin)[7]

For Mekas and Stroud, *The French Connection*'s streams of energies registered at volumes that seemed to drown out the plot. Yet what these responses have in common with Shedlin is the sense of being overwhelmed by a spectacle—the sense, in other words, of consuming visual materials without always being provided routes toward meaning.

Here, again, *The French Connection* links with longer traditions of detection and urban sensation. Both the body of literature associated with the figure of the flâneur and the subsequent development of the detective story imply a modern urban experience that is marked by inscrutability and opacity, qualities that, especially in the case of the detective, could be combatted through a fierce observational intelligence. The other, less well-known urban type important to this history is the *badaud*, or gawker; the individual who is fully absorbed by urban spectacle and immersed in the sparkling appearances of consumer culture. In Benjamin's schematization of these types, the detective is an evolution of the flâneur who converts the former's joy of watching into purposive activity. The flâneur's joy, however, always threatens to "stagnate in the rubbernecker, then the flâneur has turned into the *badaud*" (*SW* 4, 41). In thrall to the visuality of the city rather than a master of it, the gawker is the opposite of the detective. The recurrent dangers faced by the detective in labyrinthine passages, spectacular machinations of master criminals, feminine seductions, and other border areas of intellectual consciousness threaten to convert the detective into a mere gawker.

As Tom Gunning has convincingly argued in his essay "From the Kaleidoscope to the X-Ray: Urban Spectatorship, Poe, Benjamin, and *Traffic in Souls* (1913)," modes of urban spectatorship forged within the visual culture of the nineteenth century were folded into the visual techniques of early film to form the basis for the cinema spectator. The optical corollaries of the detective and the gawker are the penetrating gaze of the X-ray and the dazzling abstraction of the kaleidoscope, technologies of sight that can, in turn be seen to correspond with cinema's formalization of spectacle and narrative around the turn of the twentieth century. In the cinema, Gunning argues, we are both detective and gawker: just as much as we put together clues and decipher complex visual information through close-up and montage, so too is it possible to become passively absorbed within a brilliant parade of images.

The integration of modes of urban spectatorship and representation into modes of cinema underscores the deep connection and shared cultural optics of cinema and urban modernity near the beginning of the twentieth century. *The French Connection* demonstrates how this relationship was being extended by New Hollywood into the modern terrain of urban crisis. Within the cinema of narrative integration embodied by Classical Hollywood, spectators are dutiful detectives provided a highly standardized array of visual information that, with brilliant hiccups here and there, delivers a conclusive (re)solution. By contrast, New Hollywood questioned the values of action, motivation, and resolution that it inherited, creating instead unmotivated heroes and storylines that seemed to disperse rather than resolve through meaningful action (see Elsaesser). As in early cinema, detectives were employed within popular film as avatars of an urban terrain defined by incomprehensibility, the difference being that solutions were not conjoined to resolution. The exemplary figure here of course is Jake Gittes (Jack Nicholson) in *Chinatown* (1974), who, after finally piecing together clues to unravel a crime that weaves through both urban and family history, is told: "Forget it Jake. It's Chinatown."

Though *The French Connection* works in a similar vein as *Chinatown* and other frustrated detective films of the 1970s like *The Long Goodbye* (1973), *The Conversation*, (1974), and *Night Moves* (1975), it distinguishes itself in the way it zeroes in on the micrological dimensions of urban experience. The Chinatown of *Chinatown* is an apt metaphor for the deterritorialized spatial experience endemic to an increasingly decentralized metropolitan environment. By contrast, *The French Connection* is concerned with mimetically reproducing the actual perceptual experience of being within this environment. Like the city symphonies of the 1920s and 1930s, the adoption of the *verité* camera and the elliptical cutting style of the New Wave was one way of bringing the audience into the strange energies that could be felt while walking the streets of the postindustrial city.

The car-chase sequence that made the film famous provides a particularly intense example of an observing body hurtling through city streets. This intensity, however, is matched by the—initially quotidian-seeming—scenes of pedestrian observation and pursuit. An early example is a sequence involving a surveillance team led by Popeye and Russo that tracks Boca (the man who had led them from a nightclub to a snack bar) through downtown streets, the team hoping that he will lead them to a connection higher up the chain. Momentarily losing Boca's car in bridge traffic, the target is picked up on again by Klein (played by Sonny Grosso) after he emerges from an underground parking garage in Manhattan. Here, a problem arises. As Boca stops at a street corner, he scans the surroundings. Klein is in the background, looking into a shop window. A brief cut to a close-up of Klein catches him furtively raising his eyes to look in Boca's direction but unfortunately catching Boca's glance as he does. Cutting back, we see Boca look ahead, and then back to Klein, who now, knowing that his cover is blown, walks casually away. Just as in the *LIFE* article: "coppers are always looking around, just like criminals do."

The trailing of Boca continues, involving more complex choreographies. Boca proceeds down the street and, it seems, is going to slip away once again. But just as he is receding from view, Popeye emerges from behind a concrete column, picking up the tail. As soon becomes clear, Popeye is the lead follower, along with Russo and Mulderig (Bill Hickman), in a three-person "parallel pursuit formation" (see Moore, 88). The operation involves two agents trailing behind a quarry, and one walking parallel to him, but across the street, each trading positions every few blocks. As in previous scenes, Friedkin orchestrates this observational pattern with a likewise observational camera that seems to find the scene as it unfolds. Using long lenses that allow the camera to be positioned back and away from the action, an oscillating visual attention is mimicked through focus pulls alternating between the agents and Boca in eye-level shots pointing along the length of the street, and through high-angle views that whip pan back and forth from sidewalk to sidewalk. Sorting out the mode of surveillance employed by the detectives, keeping up with their mobile and clandestine tradecraft, requires a parsing, interpreting spectator. If we are detectives or merely gawkers depends on how well we can keep up with the moving camera and shifting points of view.

These scenes explore and reveal how maintaining anonymity within surveillance operations involves forms of observation that can gather information while performing inattentiveness—to look, in other words, without making eye contact. The mistake that reveals Klein is a directed look to Boca that produces a charge that neither man can ignore. A similar moment happens a few shots later, as Popeye is once again Boca's lead tail. Boca has stopped to look into the window of a perfumery and Popeye walks past him. Likewise pretending that something in the perfumery has caught his eye, Popeye stops at a facing window around the corner. Cutting to a closer view, a single shot captures Boca raising his head to look directly through the glass toward Popeye. Popeye's gaze is caught by the camera as it is reflected in the store's window (figure 2.5). For a moment it becomes possible to see the men catch each other's gaze within a single frame—an eye line match that works through a practical superimposition rather than a cut.

This brief moment, and the scenes that precede it, demonstrate the ways that an urban landscape can both bestow anonymity and endow vision. The commercial architecture of Midtown Manhattan performs multiple functions for both the pursuers and the pursued: an excuse to stop and peruse store windows that forces potential stalkers to do the same, revealing themselves against streams of downtown foot traffic; a variety of corners to conceal oneself in wait; or an optical device to look indirectly at another person. In order to maintain the appearance

Figure 2.5. Sal Boca (Tony Lo Bianco) catches Popeye's gaze in *The French Connection*.

of disinterested urban strollers, both the police and the criminals feign the passive discernment of a consumer, using the window displays as an adjunct to their disguise. The moment in which both Boca and Popeye catch each other in a look through glass recalls the photography of Lee Friedlander and the work of photorealist painter Richard Estes, both of whom represented the kaleidoscopic visuality that plate glass storefronts generate. In the work of these artists—roughly contemporaneous to the release of *The French Connection*—pocketed explosions of buildings, automobiles, and streets that become refracted and superimposed on plate glass screens destabilizing perspectival space. Popeye and Boca's eye contact demonstrates the way that a look can pierce this phantasmagoric space, revealing detectives amongst shoppers. Friedkin, who had previously adapted the gay stage drama *The Boys in the Band* and would go on to direct *Cruising* was also well aware that male looking in public places invoked patterns of gay seduction and solicitation. The affinity of the exchange of male gazes in *The French Connection* to cruising practices supplies a relational insight into the overlapping social techniques of the consumer economy and sexual economy. More significantly, however, the allusion helps to suggest how the city's public spaces could be sites of stimulating social possibility.

This trope of walking and looking, of disguise donned and uncovered, is pushed to its limit in a subsequent sequence, in which Popeye struggles to follow Charnier/"Frog One" (Fernando Rey) without the aid of his unit. As in the previous sequence, both men use the street and its consumer attractions as a disguise. Popeye is shown to be a talented surveillant in the previous sequence, but here it is Charnier who is the more skillful tactician, consistently eluding his pursuer and straining his abilities. Abruptly changing direction, disappearing into a flower store, dipping down into subway stations and out again, and, finally, bobbing in and out of a crowded subway car, Charnier's movement is calculated to force Popeye to reveal his intentions. For his part, Popeye walks, occasionally runs, and spins around erratically, losing sight of Charnier then picking him up again. The camera in this sequence becomes less of an observational bystander, as in the previous pursuit scene, than yoked to Popeye's point of view. As he breathlessly scans avenues of potential flight in all directions, so do we search the screen for a trace of Charnier. This trace takes the form of Charnier's walking stick, an accessory that also marks a European-seeming gait. Picking up this trace and holding it is the only way that Popeye, and we too, can continue the breathless pursuit.

Despite his struggle to keep up, Popeye relentlessly applies a number of improvisational disguise techniques. When Charnier leads him down into the subway, he removes his coat and hat to effect a quasi-costume change. When loitering on a subway platform brings him into an uncomfortable proximity with his quarry, Popeye dissimulates his presence by accosting a woman and pretending to argue with her, and, later, arguing over a bar shift on a payphone. Yet while Popeye's fluency with the streets is abundantly clear, for mysterious reasons Charnier outplays him at every turn. This leg of the film's ongoing pursuit culminates with the iconic moment in which Charnier waves smugly from inside a subway car that leaves an apoplectic Popeye on the platform. The punctuating force of this little wave is that it openly acknowledges the victory of a secret game that both men strove to keep invisible.

We eventually come to know that Charnier has been actively attempting to lose Popeye's tail but, until the wave, the gentleman never breaks the veil of disinterest. In many ways, Charnier fulfills Popeye's derogatory nickname—Frog One. He wears a goatee, dresses in a genteel manner, and dines at upscale French restaurants (because why would a Frenchman in New York want to eat anywhere else?). This appearance of refinement extends into the performance of a discriminating taste. When Charnier stops to look into a window, he never lifts his gaze like Boca and Popeye but he will touch his finger to his lips in a gesture of contemplation that says "I might buy this. Perhaps later." In his European comportment, Charnier is somewhat of an echo of Poe's figuration of the stranger in "Man of the Crowd." Like that character, Charnier seeks out a city crowd in order to elude grasp. But he's less frenetic than Poe's wanderer, less apparently in need of stimulation. The obsessive character in search of stimulation in the *French Connection* is instead Popeye, who moves through city around the clock, ardently scanning the streets for signs of crime.

The unusual energies of *The French Connection* cannot be limited to its vehicular sensations, they are sustained as well within kinetic sequences of motion and observation less immediately violent but no less visceral. They are located in the ability of Friedkin, as Stroud comments, to get inside people with the lens. What is so compelling about these street charades that could leave spectators reeling, and inspire copies in film and magazines? To what does this suspenseful detective armature appeal? The answer to these questions lies in that way that stylistic effects mobilized latent feelings about the public realm of the street in the time of crisis, a topos in which everyone, as Benjamin surmised, was a potential conspirator.

The first clue to this connection is the undeniable influence of *The French Connection* on the subsequent street crime feature in *LIFE*. The fact that everyone in the image is a cop, alludes to the way, within the film, police and criminals alike take on the guise of everyday strollers in order to carry out crime fighting surveillance activities. While the film is much more dynamic in the portrayal of these activities, both are invested in the idea that, within a moment, what seemed to be an unremarkable scene could be revealed to contain a variety of schemes and sightlines. This synchronic, vacillating moment, one could say, plays in the in-between territory that lies between the interpretive activity of the detective and the dazzled enthusiasm of the gawker. Despite the sobering engagement with the problem of street crime, both texts tag viewers in on an anxious game of appearances.

The shape of this anxious game forms within a renewed, yet circumscribed, enthusiasm for street life in New York City and other towns seeking to reinvigorate their downtown cores. Through the 1960s, as opposition to suburbanization and automobile-centered urban design swelled, a new appreciation for the vitality of pedestrian activity arose, evident in the influential work of Jane Jacobs's *Death and Life of Great American Cities*, Kevin Lynch's *Image of the City*, William H. Whyte's research leading into *The Social Life of Small Urban Spaces*, Bernard Rudofsky's *Streets are for People*, and Jan Gehl's *Life Between Buildings*. Under the leadership of John Lindsay, New York was at the forefront of fostering the development of vibrant public space, much of it through programs in recreation and culture that attempted to make increased use of the city's streets and parks (Mogilevich 241–44). Yet, despite the vaunted egalitarianism of Lindsay—who had famously conjoined pedestrianism with the ideals of racial harmony by walking through the streets of Harlem on the night of Martin Luther King's assassination—the growth of street life in the city was unevenly sponsored. As urban historian Mariana Mogilevich shows, the *Plan for New York* that was released in 1969 featured a vision for Midtown Manhattan that was distinct from the rest of the city. Its vision was to expand the appeal of the area as a space for the location of corporate offices. Part of making Midtown into an attractive corporate base involved creating a particular type of public realm, one which provided the cultural, commercial, and design amenities that aesthetically appealed to office workers and out-of-town travelers. This group, Moglivech argues, constituted a revised understanding of the figure of the pedestrian, the parameters of which would exclude a large class of the city's population. Conjoined to this new pedestrian was a vision for a "limited convivial public realm" (247) amenable to lunch-break sociality, an ersatz café society, and window-shopping. Over the course of the 1970s, Midtown would benefit from continued public/private partnerships that sought to make parts of New York attractive to the white-collar workers and tourists who were in increasing numbers visitors to, rather than residents of, the city.

The pedestrian-centered urban landscapes constructed in New York and the downtown areas of other major American cities through the 1970s and 1980s portended a new city center predicated on consumer spectacle and secured division from areas marked by race, poverty, disorder, and, increasingly, drug economies. The detectives of *The French Connection* map the relations between these emergent spaces, moving through a supply chain that flows from France all the way to Bedford-Stuyvesant. The source—or rather, connection—that makes this possible is a rather anonymous European gentleman who moves fluidly through New York streets, and, eventually, slips through Popeye's grasp. In tracing out these connections and refusing to show an inner city disconnected from the rest of the world, *The French Connection* posited an implicit challenge to the contemporary discourse that pathologized the social and economic problems of the inner city.[8]

On a more microscopic level, *The French Connection* imagined a street world gripped by an anxious fascination with the thin line that separated everyday civility from a roiling sea of disorder *within* spaces of putative order. In many super-cop films, in *LIFE*, and in the publicity surrounding the NYPD's undercover street crime unit, what lay beyond this line were covert armies of guards, ready to spring into action. Yet, these representations of deceptive appearances also inevitably invoked their opposite—a street scene filled with nefarious agents. Regardless of what one thought about the police, it mattered less who people really were than that any street scene required circumspect caution and careful interpretation. Police or criminal, both become ciphers for a public realm pervaded by visual uncertainty.

The boundary between civility and disorder that the *theatrum mundi* of the 1970s street could both cover and disclose was also determined within the sociological thought of Erving Goffman and Richard Sennett, who assiduously studied the codes that governed conduct and performance in the public realm. Goffman explicitly situates his book *Relations in Public: Microstudies of the Public Order*, published in 1971, within a public urban realm defined by the miasma of 1960s incivility. He was less interested in positing the conditions for a normative restoration of social order than in describing the ways that individuals commenced with everyday activities in a public realm that was broadly understood to conceal a panoply of threats. In "Normal Appearances" he draws on journalism, popular fiction, and true crime narratives to probe the mediating factors that individuals employed to make judgments about the relative security of their surroundings—the capacity, in other words, for normal appearances to conceal threat, and the perceptual techniques used to detect such threats. The public realm, Goffman illustrates, is, like the world of animals, divided between moments of relative calm and intense alarm. Because potential predators relied on the appearance of normalcy until the last second, potential prey are alert to signs within their immediate environment (Goffman employs the German word for an individual's surround: "ümwelt") that betray nefarious designs. While prey in this scenario are akin to detectives, criminal predators are like sociologists, they study the behavior of humans to better author themselves into normal appearances.

In tracing the vulnerabilities contained in everyday situations, Goffman points out that it is precisely scenes that seem most innocent of which one should be most suspicious. Scenes that seem the most "normal" should be carefully inspected for signs of alarm. In contrast to ways in which forms of "by-stander apathy" (a phenomenon explored in more detail in chapter 4) were seen to be symptomatic of a general disregard for others, Goffman writes:

> The forms of civil inattention, of persons circumspectly treating one another with polite and glancing concern while each goes about his own separate business may be maintained, but behind these normal appearances, individuals can come to be at the ready, poised to flee or fight back if necessary. And in place of unconcern there can be alarm—until, that is, the streets are redefined as naturally precarious places, and a high level of risk becomes routine. (331–32)

In fact, this is an apt description of an urban thriller, a narrative in which epistemological pursuits are often bound up in, and give way to, physical pursuit and sensational action. Likewise, the oft-spoken clichés of characters in genre films like "something's up" or "things are quiet . . . too quiet" are coded expressions for what Goffman calls the "classical dynamics of suspicion" (326) that power the perceptual mechanics applied in the public realm.

The preponderance of disguise in super-cop films, not to mention the popular culture of policing more generally, mobilizes the suspicion of normal appearances for a variety of ends. In a certain sense, the films, aimed in the general direction of white audiences, exploited anxiety over public space and thus played a role in the rise of conservative law and order rhetoric. Yet in *The French Connection*, arguably the ur-text for super-cop film and for trends in law enforcement drag more generally, it is possible to see a portrayal of urban spectatorship that is invested in prying open the moment between the ordinary and the extraordinary, vision and knowledge, disguise and what lies beneath, to get at the fundamental alterity of modern urban experience that results from being in situations of close contact with strangers. Georg Simmel recognized the tendency of city dwellers to maintain a stimulus shield of impersonality that would protect the psyche from all the variety of shocks subtended by urban modernity. Goffman's "normal appearances" is an evolution of this tendency; it names the eerie sense of beholding the crowd and moving, as Gunning has it, between the optics of the kaleidoscope and the X-ray; that is, between the entrancing flow of bodies in space, and the details within them that may become the basis of some kind of social knowledge. In Poe's "Man of the Crowd," this detail is the fleeting and ambiguous flash of steel spotted by the narrator in the flux of pursuit. In *The French Connection* this detail becomes eyes—flashing signals of attention within a field where the performance of inattentiveness has become a normative mode of social survival.

In the sophisticated cultural optics of urban observation explored by *The French Connection*, city streets are a medium for looking and for being seen. In the film's foot pursuit sequences, the detail that both cops and criminals seek out and conceal on the street is eye contact itself. The looking behaviors dramatized in the film's many scenes of foot pursuit demonstrate a curious principle known to both criminals and perceptual psychologists alike: looking is not just a way of perceiving the world, but a way of signaling oneself as engaged in focused perceptual activity.[9] In other words, in looking we also mark ourselves within the crowd, and open ourselves to being seen. Whatever disguise one may be wearing, looking signals an interest that moves beyond impersonality toward something else. What is this something else? Outside of detective plots and criminal intrigues, to where can the connection of eye contact lead?

Sennett names the diffuse stimulation that is possible when strangers share a public space "the art of exposure" (1990, 138). For Sennett, the street is a significant topos of public-ness because it is the site where strangers mutually arouse the sense of difference in each other that underpins the dynamism of public life. This sensing of difference in others is coeval with the sense, endemic to modern experience, that one's self is puzzlingly incomplete:

> A man or a woman can become in the course of a lifetime like a foreigner to him or herself, by doing things or entering into feelings that do not fit the familiar framework of identity, the seemingly social fixities of class, age, gender, or ethnicity. (1990, 148)

This quintessentially modern experience of incompleteness is productively dealt with, Sennett argues, by turning outward, and undergoing a subjective transformation in which the differences of strangers do not need to be overcome (or aggressively dispatched) in order to guard self-definition, but help to define forms of life in which difference and disorder are positive ideals.

When trading on the precariousness associated with looking in public places, *The French Connection* elicits the allure and fascination with the dynamics of urban encounter, bringing the art of exposure into visibility through the investigative form. The film constructs not a panoptic aesthetic in which watching agents remain in the shadows but, through a complex choreography of appearance and disappearance, scenarios in which surveillance is itself tinged with the thrill of its opposite, a site of potential initiation into a realm of heterogeneous stimulation. Today's streets are much different than the streets of urban modernity discerned by Poe, Simmel, Benjamin, and Baudelaire. In the socially homogenized, fortified, and consumerist cities of the present, the problem is not over-stimulation but under-stimulation (Sennett 2011, 397). The super-cop films of the 1970s stand on the precipice of this transformation. Their white police avatars and urban tourism demonstrate an enduring interest in the city as a social location. If *The French Connection* rises above the rest to remain a compelling film today, however, it is because its strange energies of urban stimulation still speak to us, beckoning us around corners, down streets, and through strange passages.

3

Detroit 9000 and Hollywood's Midwest

DETROIT 9000 PREMIERED AT THE Madison Theater in downtown Detroit in August of 1973. The Sunday afternoon screening of the locally shot crime film was followed by a champagne brunch attended by the film's stars Alex Rocco and Vonetta McGee, director/producer Arthur Marks, and a number of local celebrities who had played small roles. For a short time, *Detroit 9000* was a local blockbuster. The Madison, one of a handful of Detroit-area cinemas exhibiting the film, posted record grosses, exceeding its previous box-office record holder, *Lady Sings the Blues* (1972). Local critics, however, cared little for the police thriller made in the new Blaxploitation style, finding its plotting stale and its depictions of violence and sex unsavory. The countercultural magazine, *The Fifth Estate*, was typical of the critical consensus, its critic Neil Rutledge writing that the film was "about as good as an episode of 'Mannix' with less commercials and more sex and violence" ("Detroit 9000" [1–14 September 1973] 17).

The withering review was embedded in a larger story that also included coverage of the premiere and an interview with Arthur Marks. Rutledge attempted to elevate his sense of disillusionment by sketching in the sleazy mise-en-scène of the Hollywood director's hotel room prior to show time:

> A small tire of fat rolled softly over the belt of [his] swimsuit as he sat forward on the bed. Sipping slowly on his coffee, he gazed disgustedly out the window at the hotel pool. "We

> were looking for the right city to film it in. It had to be a good size near the Canadian border, with a high concentration of blacks. We looked at Cleveland, Buffalo, we even thought about Chicago, but Detroit just seemed to fit our requirements best." (17)

The admission by Marks—both the film's director and the head of the production company, General Films Corporation, behind the making of *Detroit 9000*—that other cities were considered for the production was somewhat surprising. In the weeks leading up to the premiere local publicity had heightened anticipation through ads that promoted the film's roster of local cameos, which included police commissioner-cum-mayoral candidate John Nichols, radio personality Martha Jean "The Queen" Steinberg, soul vocalist Laura Lee, Detroit Tigers linebacker Mike Lucci, and a host of others, and pronouncements of the first film "made in Detroit . . . *about* Detroit." *The Fifth Estate*, however, catches Marks betraying the spirit of this boosterism by allowing that Detroit was chosen rather incidentally for a film that might just as well have been set in a number of other rust-belt cities. While the title of the film promised a focused urban exposé, the article revealed the film's primary commodity was much more generic. "That's where the exploitation comes in: the violence, the sex," Marks explained, "We have to make sure people come to see it" (17).

Given the film's title and the effort put into local publicity, it was odd to hear Marks admit that *Detroit 9000* might have just as easily ended up as *Cleveland 9000*. But the cynicism on display here is slightly overplayed. *Detroit 9000* makes significant efforts to integrate the specificity of the city into its narrative and mise-en-scène: crime scenes are investigated on the waterfront in front of the city's skyline; sites like Cobo Hall, Belle Isle, the Ambassador Bridge, and the Elmwood Cemetery figure prominently. One scene even incorporates an iconic White Tower hamburgers restaurant—a Midwestern imitator of White Castle with deco-style franchises designed by modernist architect Charles Johnson. There is even a fictional staging of "Buzz the Fuzz," a Detroit area radio call-in program on WJLB-FM hosted by Martha Jean Steinberg, an important media figure during the 1967 riots (she famously stayed on air for 48 hours attempting to quell tensions).

But without the title of the film, or the pointed references made to the city in the film's dialogue, a spectator without an intimate knowledge of the city would be forgiven for missing the film's narrative setting. Scant reference is made to the automobile industry, then, as now, the definitive metonym for the city. Detroit's skyline was hardly as recognizable as New York's, San Francisco's, or even Seattle's. The institutional corridors of police headquarters, streets, and, most importantly, the topographies of urban blight that figure so highly in the film are largely indistinguishable from any other city. Visually, the Detroit of *Detroit 9000* looks utterly generic.

Detroit 9000's oscillation between specificity and indistinguishability reflected the broader status of the city within the national imagination. As much as the film's publicity and mode of representation were designed to capture as large a swath of contemporary moviegoers as possible, so too did it exploit cultural energies that were working through the tensions manifested by urban riots through the 1960s and a variety of other struggles, including unemployment and rapidly receding social services. Early 1970s Detroit, still recovering from the riots and revolts of 1967, exemplified the tensions and the problems faced by many American cities at the time. Historian Sidney J. Fine points out that even at the beginning of the 1960s, the Detroit of liberal Mayor Jerome Cavanaugh was widely considered to be a paragon of race relations (1). Those who lived in Detroit, however—downtown particularly—knew otherwise. After the riot left forty-three dead, many more injured, and a burnt swath of buildings downtown, the national image of Detroit changed. No longer a model city, Detroit was more likely a "representative" city: a city, that is, against which other cities could measure their relative success or failure against rather than aspire to. A 1973 cover feature in *The Washington Post*, for example, was titled: "Detroit 'Everycity USA' Looks to Future—And Hopes" ([20 February 1973] A1, A12]. Detroit, in effect, became the litmus test for the future of American cities.

Between the end of World War II and 1967, Detroit had lost close to 130,000 manufacturing jobs and the numbers continued to decline into the 1970s (after a short spike from 1964 to 1969) (Sugrue 143). As the cradle of the American auto industry, Detroit had always been, as Thomas Sugrue terms it, the "avant-garde of industrialization"; and up until the 1950s the city's economy was robust, "dynamic and unstoppable, insatiable in its demand for labor" (143). The forces unleashed by Detroit's automobile production helped to reshape the American landscape into highways, suburbs, and car-centered commercial architecture. The effects of this reshaping, likewise, were acutely felt in Detroit itself. Like other cities, Detroit saw its white middle classes pulled into the suburbs. As Sugrue demonstrates, these real estate territories were rabidly guarded by homeowners, who found a variety of methods to exclude people of color from their neighborhoods. Battles against school bussing were as pitched in Detroit and its suburban rings as in the Southern states, underscoring an opposition to integration that seemed to be fundamental to America as a whole.

In the face of the American automobile industry's decreasing returns, Detroit was poised to be the foremost symbol of the deindustrialization that was sweeping through Midwestern and Northeastern states, a geographic phenomenon that would come to be called the rust belt. Among the hardest hit by this decline in Detroit were black workers. African Americans had faced continual barriers to employment within the auto industry and, because they primarily occupied unskilled positions, were disproportionately affected by the auto industry's automation. Although deindustrialization afflicted Detroit as a whole the effects were multiplied for black workers who were chronically underemployed and trapped by suburban discrimination within the declining inner city (Sugrue 143–45).

As with other cities, urban blight became the palpable face of Detroit's precipitous fall. As part of the "model cities" program, Detroit in the 1970s was the location of ongoing urban renewal projects that involved the bulldozing of old neighborhoods—an outgrowth of federal initiatives that were beginning to face stiff opposition in other cities. The construction of the Lodge Expressway, an additional annex to downtown from the Fisher Freeway, likewise cut through a number of historically black neighborhoods, displacing residents in the process. With its combination of urban renewal and deindustrialization, Detroit's downtown landscape was similar to many cities facing decline in the 1970. But though subject to a complex of governmental and economic forces, the problem also lay with an ambiguous national vision for what cities could be or should be. As one Detroit official put it in *The Washington Post* feature on Detroit as America's "Everycity":

> The American people haven't made up their minds what they want cities to be. They don't know how much agony they want cities to go through. They have to ask themselves: do cities represent an important national resource? And if so, they have to support them. ("Detroit 'Everycity USA'" A12)

If Detroit was representative then, it was representative of a city held in suspense by national ambivalence.

The specific but exemplary nature of Detroit made it an ideal setting for popular film. If Detroit was indeed Everycity, USA, stories set there could have wide appeal. Yet the commercial imperatives driving *Detroit 9000*'s production undercut the ways that the film could be said to have been made wholly in Detroit, wholly about Detroit. The narrative was based on a script entitled "The Holly Hill Caper," written by genre veteran Orville H. Hampton. The title of the script is a reference to a fictional site in the story rather than an actual site in Detroit, and it was presumably written without being tied to a specific city. Hampton, in fact, had previously written screenplays for *New Orleans Uncensored* (1955) and *Hong Kong Confidential* (1958), films which made up the briefly popular urban exposé cycle of the 1950s (see Straw 2005), as well as *Riot on Sunset Strip* and a number of other location-centric scripts for B-films through the 1950s and 1960s. The name of the film was *Motown 9000* before being switched to *Detroit 9000* (more on this below), a reference to a police radio signal for "officer in trouble." This title also sustains a connection to crime procedurals like *Call Northside* 777 (1948) and *Southside 1-1000* (1950). Hampton's plot was very much modeled on the 1950's urban exposé, but updated for the burgeoning market in black-oriented cinema: two detectives, one black (Sgt. Jesse Williams, played by Hari Rhodes), one white (Lt. Danny Bassett/Alex Rocco), are assigned to investigate the jewelry heist of a fundraising effort for a black politician, their investigation leading them to all corners of the city to uncover a variety of personages. As in the urban exposé, the places and people the detectives visit turn up forms of vice and corruption: a brothel popular with the city's convention-goers, an upstanding doctor who performs abortions for prostitutes, and the senator running for governor, Aubrey Clayton (Rudy Challenger), with questionable morals.

On a modest budget of $800,000, location production on *Detroit 9000* spanned a few weeks in the spring of 1973 with additional scenes shot in studios and locations in Los Angeles (a fact that belied the home-grown angle of the advertising and seems to have escaped local commentators). On such a tight shooting schedule and budget, time could not have been devoted to extensive location scouting or rewrites that would enable melding Detroit's specificity into the preexisting screenplay. As Marks makes clear, Detroit was required by the production to be a type of city; a city with a "high concentration of blacks, near the Canadian border." And yet, even if the story wasn't inspired by Detroit, we do see people and places specific to Detroit on screen. And, because Detroit's problems were also the problems of most other American cities, this was, by default, a film *about* Detroit.

In effect, *Detroit 9000* evokes a familiar parallax: it is at once a photographic document of urban specificity at a particular period of time and a fictional construction of a locale. This duality was perhaps even more acute for Detroiters, who watched real police mixed with recognizable actors playing detective roles carry out a pursuit of a fictional gang of criminals (a gang that included a well-known NFL football player) through familiar landscapes geographically reorganized through montage. For scenes of action and investigation, *Detroit 9000* established a rust-belt iconography, enlisting a series of marginal spaces adjacent, or with views toward, the downtown skyline. Many of these locations were run-down zones of urban blight or uninhabited, formerly industrial areas. For Detroiters, and for American audiences generally, images of urban blight were familiar both as commonplace territories of the modern landscape, and as an emergent metonym of racial conflict and decline. Yet these sites that in everyday experience inspired worry and anxiety were also vivified by the film's narrative energy, especially in its many scenes of pursuit. The story of the production, publicity, and reception of *Detroit 9000* is helpful for understanding how Hollywood's urban representation was coalescing not just around New York, but around the emergence of *generic* environments of de-industrialization and racial division.

The Ballyhoo of Urban Exploitation

Though it is not difficult to point to the ways that *Detroit 9000* exploits urban social issues for its narrative, it is perhaps more accurate to say that it appropriated the topicality of urban decline and disorder, a discourse that in the 1960s and 1970s unevenly threaded itself through the American public sphere and popular culture. In fact, *Detroit 9000* was joining a cohort of location-shot crime films that spun narratives out of urban crisis, including black-oriented films like *Sweet Sweetback's Baadasssss Song*, *Across 110th Street*, *Gordon's War*, and *The Spook Who Sat by the Door*; and police thrillers such as *The French Connection*, *The New Centurions*, and *The Seven-Ups*. Though thematically similar, the budgets and demographic aspirations of this cycle varied, as did their perspective on the nation's racial fissures.

Mainstream genre films are typically structured around repetition and variation, offering both familiar pleasures and surprising turns. Exploitation typically assures shock and sensation in publicity, but then thinly delivers on the promise across the duration of a loosely plotted narrative. In the end, the explosively bold-faced build-up of ballyhoo may only amount to one or two key moments of display surrounded by drab narratives. There are exceptions, of course, but *Detroit 9000* was generally not seen to be one of them. As one critic for the *New Amsterdam News* put it "If you can't imagine a police drama being dull and listless, take a look at 'Detroit 9000' " (James P. Murray "Reel Images, The Film Scene," (22 September 1973) D9).

But on the front-end, the publicity images and text for *Detroit 9000* implied a series of thrills—based in violent action and sex for the most part—discharged via a crime-centered narrative with a mainly black cast. General Films and JMG Films (a distributor) were keenly aware of the unique opportunities afforded by the genre categories and markets straddled by the film: it was a Blaxploitation film which might also appeal to white audiences due to its black and white principals; and a film with inherent appeal to Detroiters and Midwestern audiences familiar with the city. A potential obstacle lie in convincing audiences further afield, who thought little about this cinematically undistinctive city, that Detroit was intrinsically entertaining.

Detroit 9000's primary publicity tagline read: "It's the Murder Capital of the World, The Biggest Black Rip-Off of the Decade. It's Gonna Get Solved . . . Or the Town's Gonna Explode!" Another tagline, often placed below the title, simply read: "A City Torn Apart." Within the various forms of publicity using this tagline (see figure 3.1 on page 120 for another example), however, there were contrasts in copy and design that demonstrate a bifurcated marketing strategy. For example, there was a subtle variation in the primary poster design for the film. The predominant design featured an illustration of the black and white leads, Hari Rhodes and Alex Rocco, towering above a collage depicting characters and vignettes from the film; the collage itself seeming to erupt from the frame of a police light emblazoned with the metallic-looking words "DETROIT 9000" on its base. However, depending on the publicity context, the prominence given to Rhodes and Rocco was switched. In one design Rhodes stands, slightly larger, with a shoulder in front of Rocco, in the other design this configuration is reversed, giving the white detective pride of place. So too was the copy slightly different in each variation. The copy on the design giving prominence to Rhodes intimated that if the crime went unsolved the city would explode, a not-so-subtle allusion to the 1967 riots. But the copy on the design foregrounding Rocco replaces ". . . Or the town's gonna explode" with ". . . And a white cop squeezed in the middle," centralizing instead the storyline of Rocco's character rather than the diegetic fate of Detroit. Other promotion, presumably for black markets, amplified an alliance against white policing. An ad placed in the black-oriented *Atlanta Daily World* employed a different visual design that placed a large image of Rocco in the center, pointing a gun out toward the beholder. The copy in this instance boldly suggests mismanagement, asking: "Who Put a White Cop on the Biggest Black Rip-Off Of The Decade?"

These variations in publicity design underscore a key aspect of the marketing strategy employed for *Detroit 9000*: multiplying the film's box-office potential by promoting to both downtown Blaxploitation markets and suburban theaters and drive-ins. After the opening, JMG Films took out an ad in the exhibitor trade magazine box office to share how the film's diverse appeal translated into hard numbers:

Figure 3.1. Advertisement in *The Chicago Tribune*.

> Sunday, August 12: $13,882.00 at the Madison Theater, Detroit, a downtown "inner-city house. This beat the former record holder, "Lady Sings the Blues," by $5000.00.
>
> Sunday, August 12: $5,375.00 at Norwest Theater, Detroit, a Dick Sloan suburban house. This is a normal week's gross! (in just ONE day).
>
> Sunday, August 12: $3,532.00 at the Camelot Theater, Dearborn Michigan, a Nick George suburban house. This is phenomenal business! (*Box Office* [20 August 1973], ME3)

The selling of *Detroit 9000*'s cross-over appeal in this way was opportunistic, but not necessarily misleading. The film's racially divergent appeal was not wholly an empty promise, but in fact—as I discuss below—sustained on the level of story.

This "wide appeal," however, also aligned with general market trends. The Blaxploitation cycle was unique for the way it featured black protagonists and integrated contextual aspects of black culture, but it was also similar to other commercial genres of its time. Although the cycle would later envelop horror, espionage, musical, or western narratives, its early iterations were predominantly in the broader realm of action and crime, a genre in which cross-over appeal was fundamental, and which was familiar to downtown audiences. In the early 1970s, the downtown theaters that began to exhibit Blaxploitation films for black spectators were also showing action genres featuring white protagonists, including popular urban police thrillers like *The French Connection* and *The Seven-Ups*. Although rarer, it also wasn't inconceivable that the Blaxploitation films made for and marketed to black audiences could draw viewers in predominantly white suburban markets (Both *Cotton Comes to Harlem* [1970] and *Shaft*, for example, were shown on suburban screens in Chicago for many weeks.) This is not to suggest that there were not core differences in content between black action films and other action films. Where Blaxploitation bluntly caricatured a white racism to be vanquished by black heroes, cop thrillers trafficked in racial stereotypes and, frequently, a white view of urban disorder as a pathology of inner-city culture, with white cops acting as surrogates for a pitying suburban gaze. Dividing its story between two detectives, one black, one white, allowed *Detroit 9000* to ally itself with two predominant forms of action narrative for the price of one.

The extraordinary sales figures that JMG Films boasted of in *Box Office* were partially due to localized publicity efforts. In some sense, regardless of its critical reception, *Detroit 9000* had a built-in audience of locals who had been prepared by ongoing press coverage of the production and its ensuing controversies to anticipate a film made, as area publicity reminded them, "in Detroit . . . about Detroit." When negative local reviews were published, General Films' parried with a new string of ads in Detroit newspapers:

> DECIDE FOR YOURSELF!
>
> IS IT "Slam Bang Action . . . Shows the hazards and pressures of police duty with authenticity"?
>
> OR
>
> IS IT "Garbage, Garbage, Garbage!"
>
> The most controversial movie to hit the screens of Detroit theaters has been roundly applauded and condemned by critics and headlines throughout the U.S. . . . DECIDE FOR YOURSELF WHO'S RIGHT!

In imploring audiences to pay for a ticket in order to make up their own minds about the film, the publicists were adopting a tactic with a long history in American exploitation culture. In *Humbug: The Art of P.T. Barnum*, Neil Harris names this "the operational aesthetic" (59–89), a technique in which exhibitors acknowledged the existence of skepticism—toward, for example, the authenticity of a mermaid cadaver (62–63)—before asking the public to take it upon themselves to decide upon an exhibition's veracity. Publicity for the mermaid exhibit in 1843 pointedly referenced public reservations by scientists, asking: "Who is to decide . . . when doctor's disagree?" (65). The operational aesthetic allowed Barnum to capitalize on a tendency latent in America's democratic culture: audiences, wrote Harris, "did not mind cries of trickery; in fact, they delighted in debate" (62).

The operational aesthetic adopted by the publicity for *Detroit 9000* pushes the film's admixture of actual Detroit and fictional Detroit into focus: reading these ads, audiences are interpellated as judicious, able to separate cinematic garbage from honest filmmaking, the real city, from the city of low grade filmmaking. Deliberating the realism of the film, its connection to the travails of Detroit's police department, could be part of the experience of the film itself. Ingeniously, the ad's copy also suggests that the controversy is a national one, implying that watching this film and making this decision places spectators within an important nationwide debate about their city. As we know now, the box-office figures that indicated the film's racially diverse appeal within Detroit and its suburbs could, in turn, be used to sell the film within other markets where audiences for popular films were increasingly segregated.[1]

This subtle scaling up of the controversy—the full substance of which will be discussed below—to a national level is also interesting because it alludes directly to the marketing issues facing a production made in a city that was somewhat lacking in a history of cinematic representation. Though location filmmaking was burgeoning in the early 1970s, urban settings had primarily been situated in New York, Los Angeles, and San Francisco; cities that enjoyed significant cinematic and cultural histories, a cachet of familiar landmarks, skylines, and recognizably specific architectural backgrounds. Prior to the late 1970s and 1980s, when films set partially or wholly in Detroit would dramatically increase (see, for example, *Blue Collar* [1978], *The Betsy* [1978], *Beverly Hills Cop*, *Robocop*, *Collision Course* [1989]), the motor city lacked the iconicity enjoyed by other cities. Selling a film set and shot in Detroit would necessitate mobilizing signs and settings familiar to national audiences with only a cursory sense of the city, and, unlike other cities, Detroit in the early 1970s lacked a familiar skyline, or even a set of readily recognizable landmarks.

From Motown to Murder Capital

Despite its lack of cinematic identity, Detroit, as Marks put it, "fit the requirements" of a major city, close the Canadian border, with a large black population. Additionally, General Films initialized their project with plans to take advantage of the city's stake in the landscape of pop music. The film to be based on Hampton's generically titled "The Holly Hill Caper," was initially named *Motown 9000*. An association with Detroit's most well-known sobriquet and successful musical export was sure to have been a boon to national ticket sales. Additionally, General Films retained the songwriting team heavily responsible for Motown's signature sound, Holland-Dozier-Holland (Brian Holland, Lamont Dozier, Eddie Holland) to compose a soulful score and lend a recognizable name (just as Isaac Hayes had done for *Shaft*, Marvin Gaye had done for *Trouble Man*, and Curtis Mayfield had done for *Super Fly*). Shortly afterward, it was arranged that Motown Records would release the soundtrack, further extending the film's cross-promotional potential and mass cultural appeal. But, just months before *Motown 9000*'s scheduled release, Motown Records reneged, threatening legal action against General Films if they continued to use "their" brand name in the title. Because Holland-Dozier-Holland had recently become legally reattached to Motown after a period of separation (they had cut ties with the label in 1968 over royalty disputes), the record company was subsequently also able to prevent the use of their music in the film or sales of a soundtrack album. Thus, *Motown 9000* was deprived of a both title and a score in short order. The circumstances for Motown's actions are unclear, but it is telling that the company was in the process of migrating its operations from Detroit to Los Angeles.[2] Having made a foray into film production with the successful Billie Holliday biopic *Lady Sings the Blues*, starring Diana Ross, the year before, the record company was in the process of diversifying its media output. In 1971, the company launched MoWest, a subsidiary label specializing in a coastal soul sound. Motown also released a number of Blaxploitation soundtracks—including releases for *Trouble Man*, *The Mack* (1973), *Hell Up in Harlem* (1973), and others—so it was unlikely that this was a matter of Blaxploitation's respectability. The concern over *Detroit 9000* for Motown, therefore, was possibly its obdurate association with the city the label was leaving behind. In seeking to develop a more diverse, cosmopolitan, and nationally recognizable brand, it is likely that Motown was disinclined to be re-linked to a city it was now attempting to transcend.

General Films' *Motown 9000* tracked in the opposite direction of the record label that bore its name, tying their production narratively and materially to Detroit in a number of ways. The film was partially financed by Edward Bell, a Wayne County judge who was also given a small screen role, and a group of local black businessmen. Additionally, the production was given access to the facilities, equipment, and personnel of the Detroit Police Department, and demonstrable use was made of the headquarters facility, cars, helicopters, boats, and even horses. Herein lies one possible explanation for the choice of Detroit over Buffalo and Cleveland: Detroit fit the "requirements" best not because of territorial uniqueness, but because of material incentive. Like other regions around the United States that had developed film offices and commissions to attract Hollywood productions, Detroit offered the use of its streets and public offices as shooting locations. Moreover, General Films was able to secure investment in the production from a consortium of local business people.

Over and above the various forms of support provided by the city, the film's producers clearly saw the film's namesake and location as an intrinsic draw (perhaps after funding and local support were already in place). In April of 1973, JMG Films invited exhibitors from across the country to witness the shooting of the opening sequence of the film at the Sheraton Book-Cadillac Hotel. The junket was covered in *Box Office* (notices appeared in in three separate issues) and photos featured exhibitors inspecting the film's Panavision cameras and posing with star Vonetta McGee, Marks, and producer Don Gottlieb. The scene the exhibitors observed being shot featured a large and glamorous black crowd at the banquet that opens the film, music by Laura Lee (performing songs written by Holland-Dozier-Holland, one of the few vestiges of their involvement with the film), and an elaborate heist sequence. This scene, in fact, was of a notably higher production value than the rest of the film, so the timing of the junket had clearly been carefully chosen to boost exhibitor anticipation. It served, that is, a double purpose: it was lavishly staged both for the film and for the exhibitors. The hosting of exhibitors from around the country demonstrates that it was understood that publicity was a consideration even as the film was being shot, and that the location of the production itself was an aspect of this publicity.

Without Motown's cooperation, however, General Films was bereft of title and soundtrack mere weeks before its film was slated to open. (Blonston "'Detroit 9000' starring Detroit Finally Premiers" *Detroit Free Press* [12 August 1973] A3, A6]. The dire circumstances led to the late hiring of Luchi DeJesus to compose a score and of publicists for the film scrambling to come up with different promotional approaches. According to Gottlieb, last minute creative inspiration came via a recent report in *TIME* on Detroit's high homicide rate entitled "Murder City." ([16 April 1973], 17]. Henceforth, many of the taglines would employ the epithet: "Murder Capital of the World." Just as publicity had been differentiated according to genre's social geography (a Blaxploitation film for the inner city, a cop thriller suburban drive-ins), so too was it again geographically divided between local Detroit markets and markets further away.

The lurid tagline quickly came to the attention of Detroiters, and, in turn, prompted lame duck mayor Roman Gribbs to publicly declare his opposition to the film and its advertising. Gribbs found the promotion based on Detroit's homicide rate "scurrilous and scandalous," especially because, as *The Detroit Free Press* claimed, the advertising became more strident the further away from Detroit it appeared ["Filmmakers Tell Gribbs 'That's Life'" [19 September 1973] A3). Gribbs held the production company in violation of a "gentleman's agreement," claiming they agreed that "the crime problem would be represented truthfully and that there would be no inflammatory advertising" (ibid.). While outside of Detroit and Michigan, ads mainly capitalized on the "murder capital" copy, local advertising tended toward "The First Film Made Entirely in Detroit," and a film "made in Detroit, about Detroit" (subtly analogizing it to the motor city's more renowned industrial product). Responding to the charges made in the press in a letter to *Detroit News*, Arthur Marks asserted that the taglines that Gribbs objected to appeared on the posters at the Madison Theater at the film's premiere ("GFC Prexy Marks Answers News Editorial" *Box Office* [5 November 1973], ME-2, ME-8). In fact, ads featuring "murder capital" did appear around Detroit, but primarily around downtown theaters, not the suburbs.

This strategy aligned with General Films' position on the content and promotion of the film, which maintained that its draw for inner-city audiences and police alike was that it "told it like it is." It was at this point that ads for *Detroit 9000* began to ask audiences to decide for themselves whether what people were saying about the film was true. Gottlieb also used the opportunity to underscore the film's topical position on Detroit's racial geography: "As long as blacks are confined to the inner city, and whites are restricted to the suburbs, we will also continue claiming that in Detroit, honkies are in the minority. Our ads reflect today's Detroit" ("Filmmakers tell Gribbs" A3).

In responding to the mayor's complaints in *Detroit News*, however, Gottlieb also took a slightly different approach, one that was more open about General Films' commercial motivations:

> I don't think the advertising is necessarily in bad taste. You couldn't expect us to use the same approach in the rest of the country that we used in Detroit. The farther away from Michigan you go, the tougher it is to sell Detroit as a glamorous movie site. When you bill it as the 'murder capital of the world' you start drawing customers. And we made the film to make a profit. ("Gribbs fights film's ad on 'Detroit-murder capital,'" *Detroit News* [16 September 1973] 1)

Beyond the candid lesson on the bottom line of exploitation filmmaking, this statement underscores some of the difficulties incurred in mobilizing a film made in and about Detroit, and, relatedly, how expansive the cinematic concept of glamour could be. Lacking the immediate alliance, via the Motown moniker, to the productive energy of the automobile industry and the syncopated beat of its emergent cultural institution, a tie to a nationally recognized homicide rate slips in as an equivalent. Chipping in to scoff at the naiveté of the mayor and other Detroiters who thought the film would be a boon for the city, *Detroit Free Press* columnist Bob Talbert pointedly asked his readers: "Why else would they wish to film a black exploitation cops-and-crooks film in Detroit if they didn't want to play up our murder rep? Motown is not exactly your

Scenic City or Garden Spot of the U.S.A., now is it?"("If It's a Rip-Off Special, It Must Be Best" *Detroit Free Press* [20 September 1973] 19A).

It is useful to briefly refer back to the cinematic context within which these judgments about positive or negative urban depiction are taking place. The most well-known urban setting for American film in the early 1970s was New York City, and the spike in New York-based production was due to John Lindsay's establishment of the Mayor's Office of Film and Television in 1966. Architectural historian McLain Clutter has convincingly shown that the gritty depictions of vice and crime in these films mattered little to Lindsay, who was primarily preoccupied with establishing a mediatized—rather than merely favorable—identity for the city (58–89). As Lindsay seemed to recognize, Clutter shows, a desire for travelogue urban views or "positive" images misunderstands the power of film to give presence to a city within the cultural imagination. Lindsay's lack of concern with the nature of a specific film's portrayal of New York hints at an understanding of cinematic representation that moved beyond the polarities of "positive" or "negative."

Leaders in other American cities, however, retained a less nuanced vision. In Chicago, for example, Mayor Richard J. Daley was said to staunchly oppose film and television production through the 1970s, worried that the city's incessant association with crime and police corruption was harmful (Bernstein 189).[3] Cities facing economic hardship, however, would need to weigh the short-term economic influx offered by feature film and television production against the more intangible, and potentially longer lasting consequences of filmic depiction. Unlike New York, which retained enough cultural currency to offset negative portrayals and could afford to experiment with the possible beneficial outcomes of such portrayals, Detroit had little such currency with which to gamble. Of course, in the short game of city politics, fleeting economic upswings are often preferable to long-term investments. As Bob Talbert seems to surmise, Gribb's complaint may have been a rearguard attempt to save face. Whatever Talbert's views, *The Detroit News* promulgated the view that *Detroit 9000* was indeed bad for the city's image, featuring a quote from a Washington, DC, audience member who said after watching the film that "Detroit must be the baddest place there is, you know, these dudes getting ripped off all the time." The controversy, such as it was, was converted to an advantage by General Films through their "You decide" advertising. Ads for *Detroit 9000* in Chicago, meanwhile, now proudly, if untruthfully, proclaimed: "The Film that Detroit Tried to Stop" (figure 3.1).

Although Gottlieb's defense of the company's publicity may read as offensive, the suggestion that "murder capital of the world" is connected to movie glamour bears reflection. In invoking the city's morbid nickname, publicity for *Detroit 9000* was bolstering the film's topicality, promising a film that was literally "ripped from the headlines." Indeed, *Box Office*'s "Exploitips" capsule on the film advised exhibitors to invite local sociologists to discuss the film with patrons ([16 July 1973] B12). Not only was General Films' publicity convincing Detroit audiences of its topicality, so too were commentators. An editorial in the *Los Angeles Sentinel* published while *Detroit 9000* was still in production made a connection between its interracial detectives pursuing a crime ring and a report that, at the same time, twenty white Detroit Police officers had brutally beaten a handcuffed black prisoner as well as two black police officers who came to his aid. "What is more true to life?" the writer asks (Lane "Black Movies Today & Tomorrow," *Los Angeles Sentinel* [19 April 1973] C13). Without full knowledge of the film's representation of the Detroit Police (which could be quite favorable), the editorial assumes that *Detroit 9000*'s diegetic milieu and crime-based themes will, like other Blaxploitation films, directly connect with the modern urban conditions of black Americans. The writer, arguing against critics who objected to Blaxploitation on moral grounds, points out that the commercialized black-cast filmmaking represented by films like *Sweet Sweetback's Baadasssss Song* and *The Mack* offered an opportunity to make inroads into an entertainment industry pervaded by upright Sidney Poitier films, and tasteful productions like *One Potato, Two Potato* (1964) and *A Patch of Blue* (1965). Hopefully, Lane writes, there will be an opportunity for plurality within black entertainment: "Like life, it is a natural corollary that there will soon be many movies depicting the highest ideals of black people. It is hoped that they are equally successful as the films telling of dope traffic, super studs, and super sleuths" (C13). Thus, Lane too reproduces the tendency to couple the social realities of crime with its sensational presentation within crime genres.

"Hollywood Midwest"

The responses and controversy surrounding the publicity for *Detroit 9000* illustrate the desires and anxieties, particularly pronounced in crime genres, that surround an understood compact between film and social reality. It was precisely this connection that General Films recognized and was likely behind its requirement of both a type of city and a specific city. The bold words and the colorful images that accompanied this publicity promised a narrative expansion of contemporary urban issues, and access to an imaginative dimension endowed by film narrative: the detectives, towering over the city they will plunge into to solve crime; and the film's title itself, cryptically promising, not just a city, but a numeric code that might somehow unlock it. In the publicity alone, audiences were promised Detroit, but more. *Detroit 9000* was defined and built up by General Films as a production event, a publicity event, and, finally, a cinematic experience.

Much of the press surrounding *Detroit 9000* declared that it was itself the rip-off it claimed to dramatize, and some worried about the negative publicity the film would give the city. But in the local press covering the film, there is one telling exception. *The Michigan Chronicle*, a black-oriented weekly, downplayed the film's faults and, following cues and quotes from the audience, pointed out the variety of pleasures it offered. Highlights for reviewer Bill Black included recognizing the Detroiters with cameo roles in the film and the segment portraying the "Buzz the Fuzz" radio program that featured both Alex Rocco as fictional detective Jim Bassett and Detroit's actual police commissioner John Nichols. Audience members reportedly delighted in Rudy Challenger's portrayal of the sleazy Senator Aubrey Clayton, with one claiming it was a "too real imitation of a local pol." The review also listed most of the locations availed by the film, including Cobo Hall, The Fisher Freeway, and the Elmwood Cemetery. Most interestingly, however, was Black's perceptive understanding of the duality of *Detroit 9000*'s urban representation. Entitled, "'Detroit 9000,' Half Reel, Half Real," the review acknowledges the film's partial authenticity up front, going on to declare that "the movie is a contemporary (mid) western, featuring plenty of blood and guts, cursing, sex, and some out-of-sight chase scenes filmed on location in Detroit" (*Michigan Chronicle* [18 August 1973] B9)

Evident in the review—and specifically in the portmanteau "Mid-Western"—is the spectatorial practice of separating a film's documentary properties from its fictional constructs, the ability to parse fiction from document in order to enjoy the appearance of familiar sites. Shadowing this type of spectatorship however is another type of pleasure, evident in this review, one that inheres in giving up place to fictionalization. It is not the "real" that, detached from the "reel," supplies delight, but rather their dialectic. Unwittingly, and to a degree uncaringly, General Films' production and promotion of *Detroit 9000* revealed Detroit as a contested site of identity, with Marks claiming that his portrayal of the city was supported by locals who urged him to "please say it as it is." ("GFC Prexy Arthur Marks Answers News Editorial," *Box Office* [15 November 1973] ME 8) and Gottlieb admitting that the city needed to be glammed up to be sold to audiences. Indicated in the *Michigan Chronicle*'s review, and especially the term "Mid-Western," however, is the idea that as much as Detroit becomes Hollywood-ized by *Detroit 9000*, so too has Hollywood become midwestern-ized. In its yen for finding variegated locations further and further afield from southern California, American feature filmmaking became colder, flatter, grittier than before. In a way this reviewer's remark speaks volumes about popular American filmmaking's gravitation toward regions and locations, whether it be the booming production happening in the South (particularly around Atlanta) or in the way that New York's policies had introduced different urban forms into Hollywood's lexicon. More than a clever turn of phrase, "Hollywood Midwest" contains an insightful observation about the way that the iconography of the rust belt—abandoned manufacturing sites, rusting machinery, desolate streets—emerged in popular culture of this time *through* the action film, both in Blaxploitation and urban crime thrillers.

This is not to argue the realism of *Detroit 9000*, but it does imply, when added to the overall controversy and naming problems surrounding the film, that what "Detroit" meant was not only in a period of transition, but also connected to broader changes affecting other American environments. Conjoined with "blood, guts, cursing, sex and some out of sight chase scenes," ("Half Reel") the mundane and increasingly distressing aspects of Detroit's built environment were becoming newly invested with meaning. To grasp how this investment was engineered in conjunction with location production let's turn from the events and images that ring the film to move into the film itself.

A City Torn Apart I

Although ad copy varied for *Detroit 9000*, the most recurring tagline was: "A City Torn Apart." The statement cannily traded on Detroit's recent turmoil, promising its cinematic equivalent. It is clear that the bold solicitations made in exploitation publicity are often more exciting in what they promise than it what they deliver.[4] As mentioned above, *Detroit 9000* established itself as both a Blaxploitation film and a cop thriller, subtly winnowing its appeal according to the markets it was directing its publicity. What is notable, though, especially for a mode of filmmaking where narrative sophistication is unexpected, is that *Detroit 9000* in fact sustains a balance between these generic modes on the level of narrative as well, building an appeal to black inner-city audiences and white audiences into the very construction of its plot.

The film opens on the night of "The Hail Our Heroes Ball," a gathering of the city's black elites to celebrate servicemen that Senator Clayton co-opts to announce his candidacy and drum up support. Masked thieves, however, have infiltrated the hotel, and shortly surround the banquet demanding—via a pre-recorded message transmitted over the PA system—that attendees hand over their valuables. At a press conference the next day, a reporter's question subtly establishes both the investigative object and narrative drive of the film: was this, he asks, a crime of "blacks on blacks, or a honky caper to keep black power from taking over state government?" Discovering the racial identity of the criminals, in other words, will also establish their sociopolitical motive. In addition to its narrative function, the question functions extra-diegetically to subtly provoke the viewer to a question about what type of film they're watching: a Blaxploitation film that promotes a black power-style critique of white supremacy or a cop thriller in which white officers deal with the endemic chaos of the "urban jungle." Will this film resolve to satisfy black audiences who see inner-city problems perpetuated by white fiat, or white audiences who pathologize the inner city? Marks's comments to the actual Detroit press, as well as the film's advertising had already set up the possibility of both readings. The question then, could only be answered by following the (textual) investigation of the detectives, who, by discovering the race of the thieves, will also ultimately reveal the type of film the audience had just watched!

Unfortunately, the viewer who attentively tracks this thread will be disappointed as the narrative subtly tacks away from its initial premise. After a series of twists and blind-turns, the thieves are revealed to be a multiracial gang whose motives were far from political, the heist being "just another rip-off" rather than a political statement. As more than a few critics mentioned, the plotting of *Detroit 9000* is frequently obscure. The investigation into the heist that opens the film is compounded by the arrival of the floating body of an "Indian" with connections to the crime. Senator Clayton's political opportunism at the "Hail Our Heroes" ball initially suggests deeper forms of corruption, but as the story unfolds he is revealed merely as morally insipid, not a criminal. Sgt. Williams and Lt. Basset's pursuit of these leads serves to produce a networked image of the city: the detectives travel from the corridors of police headquarters to Indian Joe's hideout on Belle Isle Park, a brothel where visiting convention-goers frolic with prostitutes (and where, it is revealed, Basset is a regular), and, subsequently, to the office of a doctor who treats these prostitutes.

Though the sensational thesis of the reporter dissipates, racial politics are reintegrated on a personal-professional narrative through the developing relationship between the white and black lead detectives. Bassett initially chafes at his partnership with Williams, the order of a superior officer with whom he also has differences. Likewise, as the two work the case—the story dividing itself in focalization between them—Williams begins to wonder about the motivations of his white partner. Bassett is first introduced at a hospital where a doctor informs him that a good cure for his perpetual sinusitis would be to be "to get the hell out of this city." "The trouble with you," the doctor frankly informs him, "is you're allergic to Motown." Fleeing the city, however, isn't an option Bassett can afford. It is shortly revealed that he has been supporting the hospitalization of his wife at a local sanitarium. Her condition is never named, but it appears she suffers from a kind of racial hysteria—she complains of the black hospital workers touching her. Unlike so many other white Detroiters, therefore, Bassett's flight to the suburbs is circumscribed. Williams's girlfriend Helen (Ella Raino, née Edwards), speculates that Bassett's issue may be that, in Detroit, "He's a one to nine minority . . . It's a whole new turnaround situation for the honkies" This line was adapted into an advertising tagline that caused some objection from Mayor Gribbs: "It's Motortown . . . Where the Honky is the Minority!" Williams counters Helen's viewpoint though, suggesting that Bassett is a professional—an alignment with which Bassett, a well-educated, athletic, and community-minded officer, is also identified. He raises the possibility that Bassett may be a crooked cop looking to score the heist treasure himself, thus producing Bassett himself as an object of investigative scrutiny.

Inasmuch as this line of inquiry aligns us with Williams's point-of-view as he attempts to figure out the motivation of a white character, so too does this aspect of the narrative line up with the tendencies of a black-oriented film. In the film's penultimate scene, Bassett's undercover attempt to broker the stolen jewelry to an underworld contact are foiled when the contact pulls a gun and tells him that his only knowledge of his seller was that he would be black—Bassett's whiteness, therefore, blows his cover. Williams arrives at the exchange as Bassett is crumpling from a gunshot, wheezing "If only I was black. . . ." Moments later in an ambulance a dying Bassett bemoans losing out on the million-dollar bust—not because he intended to keep the money, but because it would have made his career (it is established earlier that Bassett has been repeatedly passed over for promotions). Williams, by his side, remains doubtful and presses his partner for the truth: was he really trying to bust the criminal ring or was he out to score himself? Unfortunately, Bassett's last words are to ask for his sinus sniffer. The film concludes with a press conference that lauds Williams's efforts and heralds Bassett as a fallen hero. Outside, Williams embraces Helen and, in a line that cues the closing credits, confesses that he'll always wonder if Bassett "was the worst cop I ever knew . . . or the best."

For its entire narrative course *Detroit 9000* locks itself to an ambiguity that is simultaneously structural and generic. The open-endedness of Bassett's motivation, that is, sustains its "wide-appeal" right until the end. By making a black lead the subject and a white lead the object of investigative scrutiny, the film aligns itself with Blaxploitation's centralization, and psychologization, of strong black characters. But the uncertainty surrounding Bassett's professional commitment to policing makes him a character with links to figures from the early 1970s super-cop cycle—like *The French Connection*'s Popeye Doyle or Frank Serpico in *Serpico*. Though the storyline is mostly confusing and somewhat haphazard, the structural complexity of *Detroit 9000* and its commitment to retaining this generic ambiguity is surprising for an exploitation film. On a certain level, its narrative twists and turns tie it to more critically lauded examples of the frustrated detective cycle like Robert Altman's *The Long Goodbye* (1973), and Roman Polanski's *Chinatown* (1974).

If all an exploitation film was ever expected to deliver was, as Marks himself admitted, sex and violence, why go to the trouble of building a film that clearly aspires to such narrative sophistication? Auguring this construction is an amplified sense of sociospatial discord within the film's urban setting. Bassett, now a minority, is "allergic" to the city, a fact we are reminded of whenever he pulls out his inhaler (which is almost every scene). This and other aspects of the film lean heavily on the collective memory of Detroit's 1967 riots, which, by the early 1970s, were increasingly being identified as symptomatic of life in the ghetto, rather than, say, symptomatic of a larger social system disinvesting from the inner city. *Detroit 9000* avoids the former by pointing to the broader demographic forces driving urban transformation, both in Detroit and in other cities. The "turnaround situation" that Helen mentions would have just as readily been found in Cleveland, Buffalo, and Chicago as in Detroit. The film also hints at positive developments within this change through its depiction of an ascendant black professional class; including Williams (who devotes time to coaching boys' basketball), Helen, a professor at Wayne State, Senator Aubrey Clayton, and Clayton's disenfranchised but aspirational aide (played by Detroit-area actor Council Cargle). Indeed, shortly after the film's premiere, the city would elect its first black mayor, Coleman Young, who would initiate a socially progressive, but business-minded vision for downtown. Yet, the film also exhibits a class-consciousness that tempers the affirmative cohesiveness of this emergent group from the very beginning. During the opening credit sequence, two black men warm themselves over barrels burning copies of *The Detroit News*. Observing the well-to-do black socialites arriving in expensive cars for the "Hail Our Heroes Ball" one says to the other: "Wanna know how all those rich motherfuckers got it together? By shafting the hell out of poor sons of bitches like us! Shaft on, brothers!"

In its publicity and in the outset of its narrative *Detroit 9000* positioned itself as taking on the one of the most complex and contentious social issues of its moment. In doing so, it sustained a tradition within American genre cinema; one of confronting and working through issues with currency for the movie-going public. Because urban discord was such a prevalent and on-going discussion, *Detroit 9000* did not even need to directly represent images of turmoil in the streets. The Detroit public is consistently evoked by police, reporters, and politicians in the film, but never are we shown crowds or street views that would establish a city "torn apart," fresh memory of the montage of images circulated in 1967 is sufficient. As with other popular confrontations of social reality, however, *Detroit 9000* stops short of identifying the systematic issues that shaped the urban crisis. These issues, are instead displaced onto the travails of the individual, namely William's puzzlement over what kind of person Bassett is. In the 1930s, this pivot away from social contradiction to individual conflict was so identifiable it was nicknamed "Burbanking" by *Variety*, after the studios at Warner Brothers where *I Am a Fugitive from a Chain Gang* and *Black Fury* (1935) were made.

Forms of narrative displacement, in fact, have longer roots within genres of melodramatic action, where the focus might also shift from the social to the environmental. For example, the conclusion to D. W. Griffith's *Way Down East* (1920) in which a spectacular chase through a snowstorm and onto an ice floe encourages the spectator to forget the unjust treatment of Anna (Lillian Gish) by the morally upstanding Squire Bartlett (Burr McIntosh) and instead focus on a suspenseful battle against natural elements. *Detroit 9000* likewise features an extensive chase sequence, one that helps the film dodge the question of the political motivations behind the heist raised earlier in the narrative. However, the film's turn toward physical action across the urban landscape was not necessarily a turn away from urban crisis itself. Instead, the chase offered the opportunity to explore and display a concatenation of urban forms related to de-industrialization and blight, and to nurture black crime cinema's continuing readjustment of the visuality of urban crisis.

The City Torn Apart II

The motivation behind Marks's decision to locate the story in Detroit were material and narrative, but it is clear that they also had to do with the physicality of the city itself, a factor which comes into focus through the film's mise-en-scène. *Detroit 9000*'s late-winter climate, brownish-green pallet, and attendance to decrepit settings aesthetically align it with other popular crime films of the period. This physicality, however, is more than just generic iconography, it also fulfills a key plot function. The location named in Hampton's original screenplay, "The Holly Hill Caper," appears in the film as the name of an abandoned parochial school. The school is visited by Williams and his partner following a clue whispered by Robey (Vonetta McGee) before she dies at the hands of the gang behind the heist. Williams and Robey had been childhood friends and lovers, and Robey's words "After Holly Hill . . . so sweet . . . so nice," are initially taken by him as a dying memory of their teenage romance. On a hunch, Williams visits Holly Hill Tabernacle, now abandoned and in a state of ruin. Pondering Robey's final words, Williams wanders through the demolished site after pausing briefly to regard the surrounding neighborhood, which is similarly run-down. Taking in the environs, Williams comes to understand that Robey's memory was in fact also a clue to the criminal gang's whereabouts. "After Holly Hill," he and Robey had gone to train station nearby. This moment is both sentimental and complex: as Williams wanders through the shattered remains of the church, the soundtrack replays Robey's dying words accompanied by the dulcet gospel sung by Laura Lee earlier.

The film remarkably conveys the fact that, for Williams, Holly Hill is a *place*—a site named and delimited, with particular meaning and association. And yet, of course, Holly Hill is very fictional location, *emplaced* by a series of fictional supports: a sign reading Holly Hill is placed outside a ruined church, a layered sound mix cues us to Williams's mood, a series of reverse shots creates a sense of his view of the now shambolic neighborhood. As he is transported into memory, so too is a shared urban geography perceived by the spectator, linking Williams and Robey's past to a train station where they once had a romantic interlude. Like Holly Hill and its surrounding neighborhood, the train station too is abandoned and, it is shortly revealed that Robey has used this memory to convey that it is this train station that is the location of the thieves' hideout. Williams's recollection spurs the construction of a small geography, through a shot/reverse-shot relay, that will play out in the action of the following scenes. From where he stands, he spies the station (shot at the Union Depot) and the Elmwood Cemetery. No matter that these sites—as metro Detroit spectators would surely notice—are actually miles apart, in the sequence that follows, they will be integrated through the action of chase, with police chasing the band of criminals from their hideout in all directions. Yet just prior to the moment that the film pivots its narrative toward kinetic, physical action, we are given, through Williams's ruminating detection, a moment in which spatial fiction opens toward familiar feeling—a feeling that anyone returning to a neighborhood undergoing change or demolition was likely to be familiar with.

Yet, this is an action film, and such moments are ephemeral interruptions to the business of sensation. In appearing to resolve itself on a centerpiece chase action sequence, *Detroit 9000* bears striking similarities with an earlier script by Orville Hampton entitled *The Big Chase* (1954), a "B" police procedural that delivers on its sensational title only in the final 15 minutes of its 60-minute running time. Like *The Big Chase*, *Detroit 9000* promoted "out of sight chase scenes" on its posters and publicity featured images from the film of Hari Rhodes dashing down open railway track. *Detroit 9000* was more liberal in is offerings, however, and features two other chases. One is a short foot chase through Belle Isle Park that evolves into a motorboat pursuit along the Detroit River. The other, a foot chase through a dilapidated residential area, was actually shot near downtown Los Angeles—another example of the generic nature of the urban space the film constructs. The climactic chase sequence of the film, however, was shot in Detroit and, taking up approximately eleven minutes of screen time, is both spatially and temporally extensive.

Chase sequences, of course, enjoy a long history in American cinema, especially in the crime film, and so *Detroit 9000* was in a certain sense performing a generic duty. At the same time, the specific features of its chase sequence corresponded with more contemporaneous crime genre trends, both in Blaxploitation and police thrillers. Films such as *Sweet Sweetback's Baadasssss Song*, *Shaft's Big Score*, *Across 110th Street*, *Black Caesar*, *The French Connection*, and *The Seven-Ups*, all employed the trope of a chase sequence traversing zones of urban blight and decay, their heroes negotiating hollowed out warehouses, fields of rusting machinery, junk-strewn lots, and the marginal spaces that accumulate beside, beneath, and around transport infrastructure. The obligatory nature of this climactic pursuit was hardly lost on the press: it was mentioned by almost every review of the film, and the *Chicago Tribune*, in its caption to a publicity still of Hari Rhodes in action, blithely noted the film's "inevitable chase scene" ("At the Movies" [16 September 1973] F16).

Although it may have appeared as tediously routine to critics (and perhaps even to contemporary viewers), the final chase sequence for *Detroit 9000* was incredibly complex. In order to differentiate the film from its competitors, Marks resolved to construct a four-pronged pursuit that would split the action in four directions. Though subsequently it is often difficult to follow, there is a geographic logic to this decision. Moving from the disused train station, across decaying platforms, and out along rail beds, the fleeing paths taken by the criminals are initially defined by the vestiges of railway infrastructure. The Fort Street Union Depot, situated close to downtown, would have been immediately recognizable to Detroiters. Built in 1891, the red sandstone, neo-Romanesque building was closed in 1971 and demolished just a year after *Detroit 9000* was filmed on its premises. For spectators unfamiliar with the actual building, the station's clock face and main tower, arches, and conical spires serve as a point of departure and an iconic reference point for the multiple vectors of action that spike out from it. Following the four individual men on their separate getaway routes, the sequence begins with a series of fairly consistent geographic reversals: shots of the fleeing criminals face west along the track beds, a view of the Ambassador Bridge frequently visible on the horizon. A number of aerial views are also inserted here, perhaps taken using the police helicopter which also makes several appearances. The police forces that converge on the criminals are most often shown using an eastward facing camera, reinforcing the station as the site of egress and catching fragmented views of downtown skyscrapers. The general movement of the pursuit therefore, as regards the geography of Detroit, is from the city's verticalized central business district, toward low-lying warehouses, broken-down residential zones and empty lots, disused industrial areas along the river, and, tellingly, a cemetery.

As much as certain sites within the film were offered up to Detroiters, so too is the urban mise-en-scène of the film, and particularly it chase sequences, meant to convey the general states of decay pervading American cities. As each leg of pursuit moves further from the station it becomes increasingly, so to speak, derailed. Not only do the criminals find themselves trapped, surrounded by police, and violently shot down in hails of gunfire, but the locales they escape through become marked by degradation and indecipherability (figure 3.2). Hopping into a car, one gang member careens down a corridor of loading docks, swerving to avoid squad cars and a transport truck, before slamming into a cluster of rusting, abandoned cars. Moving toward the cemetery another criminal must first negotiate a lot strewn with the wreckage of a demolished house before hopping a fence. Each of the criminals' forking paths brings into view the dense strata of railway infrastructure: wooden frames, iron girders, and embankments that support the rails; fences, and walls that border the track; overpasses that allow the rails to be transected by highway. For Detroiters, a key flash of site recognition occurs as one criminal runs past large green highway signs denoting the junction of the Lodge Expressway to the 75/Fisher Freeway. Yet though moments like this might signal where in the city a particular shot was taken, and even a sense that however much the city was desolate and confusing it retained a coordinated system of traffic management, in the frenzy of an eleven-minute sequence of pursuit these sites merely add to the mixed bag of urban forms on display. Over the course of this time, with locales distended and added on, we begin to experience a dizzying explosion of site and spaces. Going further from, under, and around the skeletal features of the railway, these infrastructural forms become a brown-green-gray kaleidoscopic jumble. Thus, as the final gang member, pursued closely and fired on by Williams, scrambles up from the tracks along a craggy embankment dotted by withering shrubs and broken concrete block (figure 3.3), it seems as if not only could this landscape go on forever, but so too would it continue to offer endless variations of structural decay. It becomes possible to see here how Cleveland or Buffalo, other rust-belt cities experiencing the effects of de-industrialization and racial conflict, might have slipped in as equivalents.

Running Men

There is no doubt that *Detroit 9000*'s expansive chase sequences were practical for narrative, generic, and promotional purposes. However, they also intersected, perhaps unconsciously, with a current of cultural meanings relating to the place and mobility of inner-city men. Edward Dimendberg claims that the itinerant images of film noir are ways of getting at the nostalgia and fragmentation endemic to the subjective experience of metropolitan modernity. As a whole, the original noir cycle coincides with the beginning of the collapse of urban modernism and a

Figure 3.2. A criminal negotiates urban blight in *Detroit 9000*'s final chase sequence.

Figure 3.3. More detritus in *Detroit 9000*'s final chase.

spatial disintegration that will continue into the 1970s. Such disintegration is evinced within noir both through wandering passages through the central city, and the emergent experiences of centrifugal space that begins to pull urban life through highway systems, networks of instantaneous communication, and the suburban periphery. By the early 1970s this collapse was ongoing and familiar, but mutated. Following urban renewal, white suburbanization, a decline in domestic manufacturing, and the emergence of a racial underclass, abandoned buildings and streets begin to signify a different type of terrain. In the rhetoric of journalism and the popular press, images of blight unquestionably connoted racial conflict. Yet for the people of color who lived in these spaces, these same images would come to take on different cultural meanings, meanings related to survival and cunning.

Peter Stanfield argues that street walking is a cardinal trope in the Blaxploitation cycle—boldly exemplified in the opening sequence of *Shaft*—because "gaining dominion over the urban space of the street holds out the promise of escape from the confinement of ghetto life"; life that is circumscribed by the boundaries of the ghetto and, in the allegorical narratives of Blaxploitation, the control of white crime syndicates (284). Although Blaxploitation film is filled with images of the nightclubs, street-corners, and other commercial spaces that form the pulsating cultural topoi of inner-city life, its action scenes typically play out through the liminal spaces formed by abandonment and demolition.

In these scenes, running, not walking, is the prinicipal mode of transit and suspense, not contemplation, is the affective register.

Whereas walking connotes existential quest, running indicates a different mode of cognition. Running, jumping, tumbling, ducking, hiding—maneuvers common to the chase sequence—were forms of physical action correspondent with a post-riot, crime addled inner city. In "A Journey Into the Mind of Watts," the novelist Thomas Pynchon surveyed the state of the post-riot Los Angeles neighborhood:

> Watts is tough; has been able to resist the unreal. If there is any drift away from reality, it is by way of mythmaking. As this summer warms up, last August's riot is being remembered less as chaos and more as art. Some talk now of a balletic quality to it, a coordinated drawing of cops away from the center of the action, a scattering of The Man's power, either with real incidents or false alarms . . . Others remember it in terms of music. . . . (*New York Times* [12 June 1966] 84)

The "unreal" here refers to Pynchon's characterization of the mass mediated spectacle of the "L.A. scene." In contrast to other environs around Los Angeles, the only unreal aspects afforded by Watts are the mythical memory of the riot, discussed in the expressive terms of art, ballet, music. In many ways the Blaxploitation cycle met the desire for a popular black imaginary that emerged through the confluence of civil rights, urban revolt, and black power. The type of figuration Pynchon describes immediately recalls the types of movement on display in Blaxploitation; including the sophisticated promenades of black heroes, but also more heart-pumping flights.

Running and escape are forms of movement with significant roots in the African-American folk tradition. In his book on "The Mecklenburg Six,"—inmates who escaped a prison in Virginia touted as escape-proof—Daryl Cumber Dance points out that "in the Black folk lexicon, noted for its flexibility, its originality, and its vivid metaphors, there is no idea that has so many different words to express it as the idea of leaving, fleeing, running,"—these include "backtrack, beat it, blow, breeze, brush of . . . dodge, drift, duck out . . . slip, skivver, slide . . . trilly walk, tort, truck, truck it . . ." and so on (3, 169n3). Other expressions of bodily movement include the many songs and stories that describe fleeing from the bondage of slavery. Many interpolate the phrase "run, nigger, run" and impart not just the necessity of literal escape, but also extraordinary running skill:

Take dis old hammer an' carry it
to the cap'n
And tell him I'm gone.
IF he ask you was I runnin', tell him
no, I was might' near flyin'.
(*American Negro Folklore*, qtd in Cumber Dance 3)

The Great Migration that brought millions of African Americans to northern cities from the South was also, fittingly, accompanied by lyrics of flight from the oppression of the South (4). When different forms of racism and struggle also emerged in northern cities, so too were themes of flight sustained, even as horizons of movement became more limited.

The key cinematic mediation of the inner-city's myths of movement is *Sweet Sweetback's Baadasssss Song*, frequently credited as inaugurating the Blaxploitation cycle. Set in Watts and other areas around Los Angeles and wholly built around the flight of one man (Sweetback, played by the director Melvin Van Peebles) from white authorities, *Sweet Sweetback* is expressively staged through montage that multiplies views of its hero traversing the endless forms of Los Angeles' built environment: underpasses, overpasses, muddy lots, crumbling residential areas, viaducts. The kinetics of this movement are amplified through Van Peeble's jazz-funk score and the recurring visual motif of a silhouette of Sweetback's running legs, superimposed on the mise-en-scène (figure 3.4). Like the myths of riot-

Figure 3.4. Sweetback's running silhouette superimposed on a Los Angeles streetscape in *Sweet Sweetback's Baadasssss Song*.

ers balletic diversion of police, Sweetback evades his pursuers through an unrelenting motion.

Images of pursuit through spaces of urban blight and de-industrialization are a recurring trope in both Blaxploitation and police thrillers of the 1970s. The motif of Los Angeles blight as playground is taken up again at the end of the Blaxploitation era in Charles Burnett's neo-realist independent film, *The Killer of Sheep* (1976) as well as the teen melodrama *Youngblood* (1978). In *Killer of Sheep*, the melancholy of the working poor is punctuated by scenes of inner-city boys and girls playing in open dirt lots, on train tracks, alleys, and around amongst partially demolished buildings. In one scene, a group of children clamber on the roofs of a housing complex, a low angle camera capturing them as they leap between buildings. The physical exuberance of the children is tinged with both playfulness and energetic possibility—particularly when one considers the ways that rap and riot will continue to shape, and be shaped by this environment.

From *Sweetback* to *The French Connection* through *Black Caesar*, *Shaft's Big Score*, *Across 110th Street*, *Killer of Sheep*, and *Youngblood*, images of black bodies dashing through inhospitable urban environments, often chased by police, becomes a recurring trope in popular film. *Detroit 9000* too deploys this trope, and in stretching it to the limit reveals more space and more motion—exploitation cinema's logic of more acting to put more of Detroit on screen. These images, again, were designed to have general appeal, but they would also have particular resonance with inner-city Detroiters, not just because they might recognize the sites depicted, but because, like urban blacks across the country, they were struggling with an increasingly oppressive and violent police force. But, just as the revolt in Watts would produce myth and folk heroes, so too would Black Detroiters' ongoing conflicts with the city's savage police force produce its own set of heroes. Although these heroes would not be directly represented in *Detroit 9000*, the film would place itself at the very center of the conflict between Black Detroiters and the city's police force.

The Detroit Police Department was not just exemplary of general trends in inner-city law enforcement, it was also at the avant garde of national trends that would define inner-city policing in the succeeding decades. As Fine notes, like many other police departments in major cities, the Detroit Police Department largely regarded the riots of 1967 not as symptomatic of inner-city living conditions, but as the illegitimate action of discrete groups. This perspective led them to request budget increases from the city that would allow the purchase of an array of firepower, including sniper rifles, tactical equipment for crowd control, and a helicopter. Much like William Parker's LAPD in the 1950s and

1960s, the DPD adopted a militaristic outlook toward inner-city conflict (an approach that has persisted within American policing). Though the DPD's requests for supplementary tactical equipment were initially denied by the city, they eventually found ways to get at least some of what they asked for, as some of these items are on full display in *Detroit 9000.*

Prior to and during the production of *Detroit 9000*, the Detroit Police Department was facing increasing public, and national, scrutiny over increasingly violent incidents and reports surrounding the STRESS (Stop the Robberies Enjoy Safe Streets) unit. In an exposé for *Ramparts*, Howard Kohn wrote that STRESS had been responsible for over 20 civilian deaths and over 500 unwarranted raids between 1971 and 1973. Not unlike NYPD's undercover Street Crime Unit (discussed in chapter 2), STRESS was nominally a sting team operating in downtown Detroit whose stated strategy involved offering up vulnerable-appearing victims (actually police agents) as bait to muggers who would be, in turn, apprehended. As Kohn reported, however "In actuality, the decoy setup was only part of an overall clandestine operation that included extra-legal searches and surveillance on a wide range of "criminal suspects—among them militant Vietnam veterans and radical auto workers" (39).

In fact, the routine activities of the poorly trained unit involved the violent harassment of inner-city residents, activities that all too often led to deadly confrontations. These included the widely reported "Rochester Massacre" of March 1972, in which a STRESS raid on a late night card game turned into a shootout. The card players, it turned out, were Wayne County Sheriff's deputies, one of whom died in the conflagration. Eight days later, STRESS officers shot and killed a 15-year-old boy suspected of a mugging.

The inefficacy and brutality of STRESS inspired strident opposition, and not just amongst political activists. Edward Bell, the circuit court judge who had invested in *Detroit 9000*, accused the unit of "creating a state of terror in the city," and a group of black police officers known as the Michigan Guardians, as well as area NAACP leaders called for the unit to be investigated or dissolved (Kohn 39; "Gribbs Orders Changes for STRESS" *Detroit News* [17 March 1972] A3). An anti-STRESS rally was attended by 2,000 people, fomenting opposition to both the DPD and its ongoing support of STRESS. In 1973, Coleman Young ran on a platform that promised the immediate dissolution of STRESS. His opponents included Bell (who would later drop out) and John Nichols, the cop very much responsible for the state of the DPD and STRESS.

When Young became mayor in November of 1973, *Detroit 9000* was still in theaters. It is tempting but difficult to ascribe historical agency to the film in relation to these local matters, or even to definitively suggest that the film is either pro-police or pro-black. As discussed above, the film deviously evades a strict reading in order to widen its appeal. Certainly, the film was made with the support of the DPD and the film as a whole could be construed as an endorsement. An audience member polled by the *Detroit Free Press* after the premiere understood the movie to endorse the Detroit cops, saying "any film honoring the Detroit police is an insult to my intelligence." But other viewers seemed to be able to overlook these faults, one saying that he could "relate to that scene" (Gary Blontson "Bloody 'Detroit 9000' Bows and the Profit Dash is On [13 August 1973] A3). Around the time of the film's release Gottlieb and Marks indicated that a sequel to *Detroit 9000* was in the production budget for the following year that would center on the STRESS unit (*Daily Variety* [10 September 1973]: 1). The film, however, was never made.

Detroit 9000's overt support for the police was nominal at best. A few lines about professionalization amongst the rank-and-file here, John Nichols appearing conciliatory on "Buzz the Fuzz" there; and then, bombastic displays of police force—displays that to inner-city residents harangued by violent and overbearing law enforcement could be a visceral experience. Hari Rhodes's portrayal of Jesse Williams as a handsome, athletic, and individualistic black cop could potentially split audiences torn between aspiration and indignation. To account for the appeals the film could hold for inner-city audiences worn down by this police apparatus, it is necessary to look, however, with a more diffuse lens, at the images of physical motion the film provided and the ways these linked to the contemporary myths of escape and flight.

However fantastical the games of cops and robbers were on film, foot chases through Detroit streets were a fairly regular occurrence and thus not far from anyone's mind, on screen or off. The bizarre episode that cemented the demise of STRESS, and likely helped to carry Coleman Young into office, was a city-wide manhunt that occurred just months before *Detroit 9000* was filmed and almost seems lifted directly from an action film of the period. The drama began with a shootout between STRESS officers and a small group of ex-military vigilantes, some with training from the Black Panthers, who had elected to take on drug dealers in their neighborhood (a plot, such as it is, almost identical to Ossie Davis's *Gordon's War*). Led by a man named Hayward Brown, the group was sneaking up on a local heroin dealer when they were spotted by a STRESS unit. As Brown and his men gave chase to the dealer in their car, the police gave chase to the vigilantes. The police unit pinned the vigilante's vehicle, but was then surprised when the men went on counterattack, wounding the four officers and then escaping unscathed. The group would subsequently evade the police in two additional confrontations on city streets.

Appearing on WQLB's "Buzz the Fuzz," in the midst of the search for the men, John Nichols angrily snarled: "We're doing everything we can to get those mad-dog killers." Nichols' epithet would be repeated again and again as the story of the manhunt was picked up in the national press. The aggression of the police during the weeks-long, city-wide pursuit that followed only served to swell opposition to the Detroit Police. Brown was finally captured in early January, but his two remaining partners managed to slip through the police dragnet disguised as a priest and a nun. They died weeks later in a police shootout in the South, en route to Atlanta. The radical, charismatic, and increasingly popular Detroit lawyer Kenneth Cockerel, an important grassroots political figure in the anti-STRESS opposition, defended Brown in court. He pleaded self-defense, claiming that he was shot at by STRESS officers in one confrontation, and, in another, he was worried he'd be executed by police after arrest if he gave himself up. Cockerel cleared him of charges in three separate trials. Not only were juries sympathetic to his story of battling STRESS officers, he shortly became a folk hero for the embattled Detroit public (Kohn 38–41).

Given the patterns of police injustice in Detroit and across America, it is not difficult to see how the rioters of Watts, Hayward Brown, and even Van Peebles' Sweetback could gain mythical traction amongst urban populations in the early 1970s. Images of running are the converse element of the confident swagger of Richard Roundtree's John Shaft or Ron O'Neal's Priest (*Super Fly*), indexing a culture abundantly aware of the continuing imperative to bolt. Advertising for *Detroit 9000* implicitly referenced the recent travails of the Detroit police, proclaiming "a sock-o-action story of the black heist of the decade, and Detroit's own cops in the manhunt of the century." *Detroit 9000* drew on the mythic energy of black men in motion, but shuffled and mixed its signifiers in order to sustain multiple appeals. In the film it is the police—infamous locally and nationally for their endemic racism—who are led by a black hero (Rhodes), giving chase to a racially mixed gang across the city. Less an allegory of contemporary racism, *Detroit 9000* could be read as an endorsement of police power.

With a meandering storyline, the apparent endorsement of the DPD, and, in turn, a swiftly evaporating critique of white power in its narrative, *Detroit 9000* hardly sustains the political force of its predecessors in 1970s black-themed cinema, nor of many of the other entries into the Blaxploitation cycle. It does however, employ similar means to access and unfurl the urban environment that the cycle was founded on, exposing an incipient poetics of urban representation that was making its way into many forms of American popular culture. Its final chase sequence literalizes the film's promise to show a city "torn apart" by describing a passage from an identifiable, though abandoned, architectural form, a train station, out into spaces that are less and less identifiable but whose endless piles of rust, waste, and concrete seem to resemble a city in the process of pushing up spaces of production and utility. At the same time, police and thieves swarm over this space, running, shooting, riding horses, flying a helicopter, jumping into and crashing cars, leaping fences, spilling down hills. The sheer proliferation of police across this terrain, in fact, reflects a total police mobilization that inner-city Detroiters had grown accustomed to in the years following the riot. These familiar scenarios, this familiar de-industrialized space, were overlaid by the mythical figure of the black man on the run.

As both a narrative that binds images of the blighted city and a publicity phenomenon exploiting the same, *Detroit 9000* was shot through by the contradictions of popular urban representation during its era. Although the film's attempt to integrate its appeals was confusing and haphazard, in its blatant attempt to please the widest possible demographic, it unfastened the rhetoric surrounding the image of the city—as fallen, as abandoned—allowing viewers to see, to borrow a cinematically inflected phrase from decades earlier, the naked city. *Detroit 9000* presents, in its action sequences, a terrain composed of transport infrastructure, sites of productivity fallen into disuse, residential areas in the process of demolition, and an array of undifferentiated pockets where waste gathers—in essence, spaces that seem to lack the vibrant culture of the street that had been identified with the vitality of the city.

In fact, the depopulated zones that *Detroit 9000* enlists for its chase sequences were shortly becoming a significant spatial figure in landscape photography of the time. Robert Smithson's "A Tour of the Monuments of Passaic, New Jersey," published in *Artforum* in 1967 chronicled the artist's expedition through a depopulated built environment composed of rusting bridges and pipes, a "zero panorama," an "anti-romantic mise-en-scène" that seemed to contain "ruins in reverse" (Smithson 54–56). A similar type of anti-scenic aesthetic was developed within the photographic works associated with the New Topographics movement, which depicted "man-altered landscapes" nonetheless devoid of human bodies: corners of industrial buildings and suburbs, parking lots, and agricultural structures.

The architect and theorist Ignasi de Solà-Morales Rubió has defined the types of spaces depicted in this work, to which popular film should undoubtedly be added, as "*terrain vague*," writing:

> In these apparently forgotten spaces, the memory of the past seems to predominate over the present. Here only a few

> residual values survive, despite the total disaffection from the activity of the city. These strange places exist outside the city's effective circuits and productive structures. From the economic point of view, industrial areas, railway stations, ports, unsafe residential neighborhoods, and contaminated places are where the city is no longer. (120)

In accounting for the fascination elicited by these spaces for urban photographers, Morales suggests that they confront us with the strangeness endemic to late-capitalism:

> Strangers in our own land, strangers in our city, we inhabitants of the metropolis feel the spaces not dominated by architecture as reflections of our own insecurity, of our vague wanderings through limitless spaces that, in our position external to the urban system, to power, to activity, constitute both a physical expression of the other, the alternative, the utopian, the future. (121)

The image of the *terrain vague* then, is not simply an expression of disorder and negativity, but a space of strangeness that offers the possibility of something else.

For Detroit, possibility and its foreclosure would come in short order. As part of a vision for a revitalized downtown, Henry Ford II assembled a conglomerate of private investors to fund the building of the Renaissance Center on the banks of the Detroit River. The megastructure was designed by developer-architect John Portman (whom Ford hired) and featured a 73-story cylindrical glass tower surrounded by four 39-story office towers. Paired with plans for the Detroit People Mover, an elevated light-rail train that encircled the city center, it was hoped that the Renaissance Center and developments like it would spur the growth of a "new Detroit" that would attract business and the middle classes back downtown. Through the 1980s, however, Detroit's fortunes would continue to dwindle as its metro population receded apace and unemployment and crime rose proportionately.

In recent years the image of Detroit's ruin and abandonment has become so acute as to become a well-known cliché: ruin porn (see Leary). Photographers, both amateur and professional, have converged on the city to explore and take pictures of the formerly majestic train stations, skyscrapers, and factories that once made Detroit the lodestar of modernity. However, in the coffee-table photo books and even the many Detroit-focused documentaries, there is a stillness to these scenes and a noticeable lack of human bodies within them. The motion of running individuals no longer traverses the wide-angle views of these landscapes. So too then does a new myth of landscape come into visibility: the idea that Detroit, like other rust-belt cities, has been fully surrendered to nature.

A predisposition toward large-scale urban tragedy so beloved by urban photographers, however, obscures an unrelenting pulse. Even as Detroit became visually emblematic of urban decay, it was electronically recalibrating the soul music it had helped innovate into synthesized funk. In the globally influential music of Detroit Techno, the ballet of foot pursuit through urban blight is converted into looping rhythms that reassemble the noise-pieces of industry and the beat of the freeway into a forward-looking, unrelenting motion. For a moment in the 1970s, this same motion was captured on film and broadcast to the nation in the coded images of *Detroit 9000*; the first Hollywood Midwestern made in Detroit.

4

Bystander Effects

Death Wish and *The Taking of Pelham One Two Three*

Bystander Apathy as Sociological Vignette

THE 1967 FILM *THE INCIDENT* portrays late night passengers on a New York subway car terrorized by a pair of carousing punks. Out for violent kicks, Joe and Artie (Martin Sheen and Tony Musante), anarchically spin around and prowl the car, finding ways to humiliate each rider in turn. A young gay man (Robert Fields) is harassed and led around the train by his tie; another young man on a date (Victor Arnold) is pointedly asked about the sexual experience of his girlfriend (Donna Mills). When a young African American (Brock Peters) expresses his approval of the men's torture of the white riders, Joe and Artie turn to bait him: they call him "nigger" and threaten to break his sister's (Ruby Dee) arm. Imprisoned on the train by the sadistic pair, these passengers have no means of escape, but more importantly for the force of the message of this film, they cannot find a way, either individually or collectively, to stop the baiters' obnoxious insults and increasingly violent harassment. Eventually, Felix (Beau Bridges), a soldier with a broken arm who is visiting New York for the first time, can bear it no longer. When Joe turns his attention to a young child slumbering in her father's arms, attempting sadistically to wake her up, Felix bellows and rises to confront him. Sustaining a knife wound, Felix beats Joe senseless—using his plaster cast as a weapon—then delivers a similar beating to Artie before collapsing on the floor. The car finally stops and the police are called. One-by-one, the passengers disembark in silence.

An adaptation of the teleplay "Ride With Terror" (1963) written by Nicholas Baehr, *The Incident* is intended as a parable dramatizing what social psychology of the period identified as "the bystander effect." The bystander effect (or bystander apathy) described a phenomenon endemic to modern urban societies, that in situations of danger or emergency occurring within public places strangers were unlikely to come to each other's aid. The seeming detachment of urban culture of course has long been a theme within sociological thought. Georg Simmel identified similar tendencies within metropolitan life around the turn of the century and the theme of urban alienation was taken up in studies of crowd behavior and conformity by thinkers such as Gustave Le Bon, Elias Canneti, David Riesman, Theodor Adorno, and Max Horkheimer, C. Wright Mills, and others. Such currents animated sociological inquiry in the postwar era particularly in the context of America's economic expansion, suburban development, and paranoid cold-war culture.

However, the idea that urban America had become isolated, atomized, numb, indifferent, and apathetic gained special popular attention and intensified appeal in the sensational aftermath of the murder of Kitty Genovese in March of 1964. Genovese, a bar manager, was killed by a stranger while walking home at night in the Kew Gardens area of Queens, a white, middle-class neighborhood crowded with high-rises. The crime was initially alleged to have been witnessed by thirty-eight different residents of an apartment building facing the street (this number becomes reduced in later accounts). Despite Genovese's cries for help and the extended period of time over which the attack took place (35 minutes, according to reports), not one of these residents came to her aid, nor did any telephone the police. When the story broke, intense scrutiny and interpretation was focused on the seeming indifference of the witnesses, as well as the spatial conditions, if any, that had prevented them from assisting Genovese or relaying her calls for help. A pull-quote from one of the witnesses became a by-word for bystander apathy: "I don't want to get involved." Coverage of the event and its mute witnesses flashed internationally. In 1965, Martin Gansberg, the *New York Times* reporter who had spearheaded the story, wrote: "In Istanbul and Moscow, in San Francisco and Miami, in Berlin and elsewhere people read about the 38" (12 March 1965, 35).

The perils of involvement that the Genovese murder revealed spurred the creation of a sociological vignette that would, with minor variations, be replayed by journalists, researchers, and on film again and again: anonymous strangers in a public setting presented with an unfolding incidence of malice or violence, the strangers' response to this Genovese-like scenario, or lack thereof, occasioning a diagnosis on the state of American civic life. The short television film *The Detached Americans* (1964) used the case to delve into a broad critique of social atomization, suburbanization, alienated labor, commodification, and the rote nature of the educational system. The Genovese scenario was fictionalized for the very popular "Perry Mason" in 1965 ("The Case of the Silent 6") and later in the 1975 TV movie *Death Scream*. That same year, when the Federal Government refused a bankrupt New York City financial aid and the *New York Post* printed its famous headline "Ford to City: Drop Dead," the *Los Angeles Times* printed an editorial cartoon that depicted a slumped woman's body, labeled as "Kitty Genovese," at the door to the Oval office, a sign hanging on the door reading: "We don't want to get involved"—a poignant, if rare, moment in bi-coastal, inter-city solidarity.

The Genovese trope was so popular it migrated into social science. Noting the growing number of Americans "concerned about their lack of concern" Bibb Latané and John M. Darley conducted a series of experiments throughout the 1960s investigating the phenomenon of bystander apathy (63). Eschewing commonsense explications related to anomie, the dehumanizing effects of modern life, indifference, or authoritarianism, Latané and Darley pointed instead to the fact that bystander intervention in emergency situations was less and less likely the more bystanders were present. Thus, they argued, the belief of "safety in numbers" was entirely misleading. "Modern city dwellers," they wrote of city-dwellers' misapprehensions, "shun deserted streets, empty subway cars, and lonely walks in dark parks, preferring instead to go where others are or to stay at home" (88). However, as in the Genovese case, a crowd does not necessarily increase the likelihood of help in an emergency: "In fact, the opposite seems to be true. A victim may be more likely to get help, or an emergency be reported, the fewer people who are available to take action" (89). Although they were alone in their apartments, the residents of Kew Gardens, Bibb and Latané held, assumed that someone other than themselves would come to Genovese's aid.

Of course, it is difficult to ignore the fact that Americans' emergent attunement to indifference was occurring against the historical backdrop of new configurations of the urban crowd: on-the-streets civil rights marches, antiwar protests, and a burgeoning left-wing/countercultural youth culture on college campuses. In a certain sense, the bystander effect refracted the anxieties of a middle-class that was "standing by," keeping safe, as tectonic shifts seemed to be occurring all around them in American culture. The dissolution of the liberal consensus in the face of this fracturing left them on uncertain ground. Carrie Renstchler, a scholar of media coverage of the Genovese case, suggests that the murder and the speculation it generated provided a foundation for the insurgent law and order, crime-in-the-streets rhetoric adopted by Republican presidential candidate Barry Goldwater in the 1960s, eventuating ultimately in the "fearing subjects" that would shiveringly make up Richard M Nixon's base (312–13). As Rentschler points out, the Kitty Genovese reportage focused on the psychological interiority of the witnesses and on the streets and buildings around which the crime took place, rather than taking a more conventional approach focusing on victim and perpetrator. She notes that the photographs accompanying the Genovese story obsessively reconstructed the perspective of the witness-residents toward the street-level crime, again and again working through the enabling of indifference by examining the precise conditions of the physical arrangement of the space: the street, its alleys, the nearby parking lot for the Long Island Railroad depot. The search here was for an explication that could somehow mitigate the implications of the resident's failure to act. Notably, the Genovese story is also a significant thread in the visual imagery used in *LIFE*'s "The Cities Lock Up," which features the silhouetted image of a female figure glaringly backlit by inhospitable urban terrain visible through her barred window—the perfect image of a detached witness who will choose not to get involved.

The role of optics and visuality in the Genovese incident assumed a curious importance, one that would be carried over into the reconstructions of bystander apathy scenarios by social psychologists. As Rentschler demonstrates, in the explosion of media coverage following the murder of Kitty Genovese, the most circulated images were a photograph of Genovese and views of the street in Kew Gardens where the crime took place. In these latter images intense descriptive and diagrammatic attention was paid to the position and scale of buildings and alleys, and the types of sightlines offered to the thirty-eight residents that were said to have witnessed the crime. As a mostly white neighborhood that stood on the midway point of the Long Island Railway connecting the suburbs to the city, Kew Gardens was both urban and suburban, a geographic identity that enabled the coverage to connote a "signal crime" (a crime with an outsized impact on social fears) with wide-ranging implications for both urban and suburban white middle classes (Rentschler 321). The photographs of Austin Street and its environs were presented as documentary evidence of a highly visible stage for crime. Taken during the day, on empty streets, these images "depict a depopulated crime scene from the perspective from which witnesses ideally could have seen it," showing "witnessing the crime after the fact as an act of seeing exteriorized" (317). In the coverage of the Genovese murder and in the massive body of social psychology that builds on it, a process of abstraction likewise works to remove the contingencies and uncertainties of perception that trouble the act of witnessing and the interpretation of events in order to make moral claims about the mental life of cities. As Renstschler points out, the bystander effect as theorized by Latané, Darleyn is primarily operative in anonymous cities, rather than in putatively safer suburban-like settings where only one or two bystanders are present (322). Of course, the anti-urban/pro-suburban thesis of bystander apathy falls apart if one understands the suburbs not as new type of small-town community, but rather a cellular extension of anonymous urban life, replete—much like Kew Gardens—with its own situational forms of alienation and anomie.

By probing and commenting on the material conditions of individual detachment the Genovese reportage and the studies of the bystander effect that followed it put pressure on the ability of urban citizens to fully withdraw from the outside urban environment. When sightlines from apartment windows were put into play, the limits of this withdrawal were objectified and defined. Latané and Darley's conceptualization of the bystander effect was based on data from experiments in which unwitting subjects witnessed a variety of staged scenarios of danger, personal injury, or theft. For example, two subjects were placed in an exam room with an air vent that slowly emitted smoke; or in a room adjoining an office where an "injured" woman called out for help. Another experimental scenario involved directing subjects to a store where actors "stole" beer while the clerk was away from the counter. The researchers sought to repudiate "such vague cultural . . . concepts as 'alienation due to urbanization,'" and replace them with "situational factors . . . involving the immediate social environment." Thus,

> [o]ur results may explain why the failure to intervene seems to be more characteristic of large cities than rural areas. Bystanders to urban emergencies are more likely to be, or at least think they are, in the presence of other bystanders than witnesses of non-urban emergencies. Bystanders to urban emergencies are less likely to know each other or to know the victim than are witnesses of non-urban emergencies. When an emergency occurs in a large city, a crowd is likely to gather; the crowd members are likely to be strangers; and it is likely that no one will be acquainted with the victim. These are exactly the conditions that made the helping response least likely in our experiments. (89–90)

As much as it differed with established sociological notions of alienation and anomie, Latané and Darley's studies promulgated a familiar anti-urban thesis about the urban crowd: in the big city, don't count on anybody to help you out.

Although they presented their work as bringing rigorous scientific clarity and empirical data into to the bystander apathy discourse, in dramatization and representation Latané and Darley's experiments in fact shared much with the cultural productions, from "Perry Mason" to *The Incident*, that were also working through the bystander effect. First, there was a curious elision: in an age of white flight and mass suburbanization, their allusion to *Gemeinschaft/Gesellshaft* oppositions between "modern city dwellers" and rural areas rings antiquated, if not wholly false. The poverty of this opposition is further shown by the experimental scenarios conducted in offices and waiting rooms—generic sites just as likely to be found in suburban areas as in large cities. In fact, these experiments are hardly about modern cities at all, but rather the more extensive urban/suburban *topoi* of everyday life in the 1960s. Most of the sites chosen for the Latané/Darley experiments were semi-public, allowing the researchers to neatly bracket out the sensory conditions typifying the experience of big cities. Sensorial ambiguity could be removed from situations of emergency in order to more clearly pose the moment of inaction and non-engagement. In order to achieve the clarity necessary to reproduce and observe the bystander effect, the experiments needed their scripts to unfold apart from the crowded and messy flux of the public realm.

This displacement of ambiguous factors continued in a 1970 article for *Science* by the renowned social psychologist Stanley Milgram which referenced Latané and Bibb's research, that of others who had sought to empirically define aspects of urban behavior, and introduced new findings based on experiments much like Bibb and Latané's.[1] Milgram also assumed a fundamental structural opposition between the big city and the small town or rural area, again bracketing suburban or metropolitan categories. So too did he agree with Latané and Darley that personality was not the factor in characteristic urban unhelpfulness; instead "contrasts between city and rural behavior probably reflect the responses of similar people to very different situations, rather than intrinsic differences in the personalities of rural and city dwellers" (1465). And Milgram also sought to dramatize this state of affairs in the form of vignettes. The educational film *The City and the Self* (1972), written by Milgram and directed by Harry From, mixes documentary footage and dramatization to more fully integrate the conclusions of bystander-effect studies with the realities of an urban fabric. An extended opening sequence depicts a morning commute by subway, often from a first-person perspective, before recounting the Kitty Genovese case and moving through dramatizations of some of Latané and Darley's experiments. Here documentary footage of the urban sites mixes with dramatization and other expressive modes of display in a visual rhetoric meant to enmesh the bystander effect within a contemporary urban scene.

Couched in empiricism, the social psychological studies of urban bystander effect are linked with cultural production stirred by the Genovese murder, which works through, replays, and examines the conditions under which such an incident could have happened. Illustrated here are the outlines of an emergent mode of urban visualization filling journalistic discourse, scientific research, and cultural mythology and expression at once, a mode that seems to increasingly preoccupy middle-class Americans at the time: a desire not only to look, read, and comprehend urban spaces and "situational conditions" but also to impose clarifying, normative, and also perhaps self-interested, frameworks of understanding. *The Incident*, Latané and Darley's experiments, and Milgram's study, in fact, echo research carried out in the 1940s by the American Jewish Committee's Studies in Prejudice projects. As Johannes Von Moltke recounts, in addition to a number of books, most famously *The Authoritarian Personality*, the AJC's Department of Scientific Research also planned to make a test film taking place on a subway car, concocting a scenario that bears unmistakable outlines to *The Incident*. The film was conceived by a group of researchers, including Paul Lazarsfeld, Margaret Mead, Robert K. Merton, and (at some distance), Siegfried Kracauer. The unproduced film, Von Moltke writes,

> was to have staged a dramatic scene in a crowded subway, which would have culminated in a woman getting pushed out of a the moving car. Several characters would have been introduced in the run-up to this incident as possible perpetrators—a "tough guy," a club-footed man, and a character who in different versions of the film would be cast alternately as a Jew, an African American, a German, or an Englishman. During a blackout, passengers would have sought to assign blame for the incident in ways reminiscent of the political discussion at the end of Brecht's *Kuhle Wampe* (1931); then the lights were to have come back on—first in the film, where the woman turned out to be unharmed, and then in the theater, where audience members would have been asked to respond to a questionnaire. "You too, have been eye-witnesses of the accident," the final title was to proclaim. "What is your opinion?" (120)

Whether Baehr was familiar with this unmade test film or not, *The Incident* bears unmistakable traces of its impulse toward social-psychological analysis via a filmic imaginary, even as it sharpens the melodramatic aspects and deepens characterization.

The Incident's pre-credit sequence establishes the social deviance of Artie and Joe as they wild their way through a pool hall, then accost late night pedestrians, mugging one of them in an alley. Before the victimization on the train begins the film sketches the background of each passenger. Flipping between glimpses of their itineraries prior to boarding, the film defines these characters primarily through personal or interpersonal conflicts: Bill and Helen Wilks (Ed McMahon and Helen van der Vlis) arguing over family finances; Douglas (Gary Merrill) struggling with alcoholic temptation whilst in the same bar Kenneth faces up to his sexual urges. After leaving a cocktail party Muriel Purvis (Jan Sterling) needles her husband's (Mike Kellin) lack of ambition. The elderly Beckermans (Jack Gilford and Thelma Ritter) quarrel over their son's ingratitude. By the time Artie and Joe board, we have been given a synoptic overview of the diverse personalities that make up this train's ridership as well as the private conflicts that individualize them sociologically.

This arbitrary gathering of the dramatis personae seemed far too obvious to the film's reviewers. A number of critics commented negatively on the construction of types and on the film's pretenses toward rendering a social microcosm, one calling it a "carload of clichés" (Terry). Charles Champlin admired the film but noted, however, that the story device was as "old as the hills": "Throw a wildly diversified group of people together in a tight space and expose them to a crisis that reveals the weaknesses (or the strengths) beneath the facades" (1967). In fact, *The Incident* anticipated the formula that would be repeated again and again in the disaster cycle of the early 1970s: an assembly of people putatively from different "walks of life" bound together by transit or infrastructure (see *Airport* [1970], *The Poseidon Adventure* [1972], *The Towering Inferno* [1974], *The Cassandra Crossing* [1976], *Rollercoaster* [1977]) and forced to deal with an emergency together. In essence, a dramatic test of democracy. As a dramatic speculation on the bystander effect, the neatness of this construction within *The Incident* makes sense. The film is trying to illustrate and work through the conditions that enable non-engagement—it is, in a sense, an abstraction of urban life, rather than a naturalistic slice of it. As in to the Genovese reporting, and the later *LIFE* cover, the riders are portrayed as locked into private antagonisms that prevent connection or collectivity, each rider a variation on the "detached American" conceptualization.

The selection of the subway as the film's setting, and of Artie and Joe's unqualifiedly vicious characterization makes more sense in the context of the aesthetic dimension of the bystander-effect studies. Especially after Artie sticks his shoe in the door to prevent riders from disembarking, the subway car provides an enclosed theater ensuring that everyone inside endures and witnesses a complete situation clearly, rather than taking the kind of partial or distanced view that marred the generalizability of the Genovese murder. Not one of them arrives late on the scene, nor is a single potential witness allowed to leave before the violence is done. The film's extended prologue, one of the features that differentiated it from the earlier teleplay, may be seen as a way of compensating for the potentially stagy (that is, problematic for cinematic construction) single setting of the story's main action. Whereas the subway-car section was shot on a set in New York's Biograph Studios, other scenes were shot nearby on nighttime Bronx streets, producing a sense of locational authenticity. Although several Bronx stations are visible (Mosholu Parkway, for example), precise narrative locations are not explicitly named. We are also given interiors of a pool hall, the late-night bar haunted by Kenneth, Doug, and a smattering of other nighthawks (a haven where alcoholic and homosexual angsts burn and aggravate together), and a high-rise cocktail party in a toney apartment, all of which settings suggest the socially variegated urban night world from which the characters converge. Once everyone has arrived the subway-car set allows for the action that unfolds to be seen and experienced unambiguously by the characters, similarly to what happens in Latané and Darley's experimental scenarios. Though its interior lights authentically flicker when the train is in motion, the car is generally brightly lit, providing clear views. Sitting in seats facing the inside of the car, the passengers provide a perfectly placed audience for Artie and Joe's performative antics as they roam the car, twirl athletically around its poles, and yelp wildly, offering anarchic contrast to the sociological straightness the other characters.

Critics—especially those that found the rest of the ensemble rather staid—in fact admired the commanding malevolence of Musante and Sheen. In his review for the *Chicago Tribune*, Terry Clifford wrote that Artie and Joe represented a new film type: "the professional punk; and that Musante and Sheen's characterization of this type was the most refined aspect of the film." As Terry surmised, the punk-types on display in *The Incident* updated the amateurism of the 1950s juvenile-delinquent films and presaged the more career-focused urban thugs of *Dirty Harry* and *Death Wish*. The "creatively evil" Sheen and his partner were a welcome antidote to the balance of the cast. "[Director Larry] Peerce's puppets blurt out their individual hang-ups in a kind of psychological Show and Tell," but this changes when the "cardboard cast" is joined by "the troublemaking tandem, supercharged with booze and brass, teasing and tormenting, breaking up over their self-styled cleverness" (8 January 1968, B5). The preternatural ability of the punks to identify, expose, and exploit the passengers' private fears and anxieties makes them projective fantasies rather than psychologically "authentic" (or in the case of this apparent critical failure, cardboard) characters.

Thus, a formal tension emerges between the film's intended social realism and the almost supernatural expressionism represented by Artie and Joe, who are nightmares in a very literal sense. Aside from establishing Artie and Joe's propensity for violence, then, the function of the pre-credit sequence may be to re-balance the shocked impression of their fantastical qualities by emplacing them within an urban context, making the two into realistic urban types. Yet here, too, they come to embody the deepest bourgeois fears of the city street: that they are populated by amoral lower-class cretins who thrive on "kicks," a new, less romantic mutation of the youths depicted in *West Side Story* (1961).

As much as *The Incident* aligns with the anti-urban theses of bystander-effect criticism, it is also a film that in the location photography of its opening strives to render a naturalistic picture of the texture of the modern urban environment. It works, using naturalistic detail and description, to subsume the obviousness of the subway car as a narrative device and its normative sociological abstraction (that the riders are a representative, middle-class group of social types). For Champlin, *The Incident* represented an emergent style he called the "New York" film, a film defined by "considerable use of locations" and "a toughness, rather than slickness of surface" (1967). Indeed, director Larry Peerce emphasized early on the importance of the film's location production, stating that it "will be shot mostly on location in the Bronx and, if we get the OK from the Mayor's office, on actual subways and in stations, as well as at the old Biograph studios in the Bronx" (*Globe and Mail* 22 May 1967, 20). In Peerce's framing, ironically, the historically significant studio of D. W. Griffith's first films offers a site of authenticity homologous to the streets of the Bronx, rather than a site prefiguring the Hollywood slickness to which Champlin claims *The Incident* is a reaction.

In dramatically (and cinematographically) working through the bystander-effect phenomenon catalyzed by the Kitty Genovese case, *The Incident* reveals the paradoxical nature of anti-urbanism as a cultural structure of feeling: paradoxical because paradigms for understanding the dysfunction of urban society are also methods for looking at, studying, and even finding visual pleasure in urban spaces. This paradox takes objective form in the succession of New York films that followed in the wake of John V. Lindsay's establishment of the Mayor's Office of Film, Theatre, and Broadcasting in 1968, still only a nascent operation when

The Incident was filmed. From *Midnight Cowboy* and *Panic in Needle Park* to *The Out-of-Towners*, *Little Murders*, and *Law and Disorder*, New York was pictured as crowded, messy, and chaotic, conforming to anti-urban sentiment even as its location photography invited audiences to look with curiosity at the city's various spaces of degradation; from the streetscape of "the Deuce" around 42nd Street and tenement shooting galleries, to the isolation of modernist apartment towers. In effect, throughout the 1960s bystanders and film spectators come to be conjoined. As such, social-scientific frameworks and location photography mixed in with popular discourse on urban life to form a heady, often contradictory, stew of urban cinematic representation.

Hollywood's Sensational Urban Sociology

The dialectic of documentary, sociological interest, and sensation that characterized urban-based New Hollywood cinema in many ways resembles the rich media environment that accompanied the mass migration to urban centers in the nineteenth and early twentieth centuries. As Ben Singer has shown, the shocks of urban life during this time—the crowds, the traffic, the multiple forms of visual and bodily stimulation—were reproduced in a variety of popular entertainments (59–99). Illustrated newspapers of the period depicted, often in grotesque detail, an overwhelming world of visual sensation and the variety of gruesome accidents that could befall the human body subject to traffic accidents or other random occurrences.

In a certain sense, the concerns animating portions of urban sociological thought in the 1960s and 1970s are not substantially dissimilar from underlying currents of thought and feeling at the turn of the century. The abstract figure envisaged in the bystander effect recalls Simmel's conception of the blasé individual, protected from the shocks of urban life by shielding out stimulus through indifference. Sociological interest in the modern urban condition was sustained by writers like William Whyte, Jane Jacobs, Lewis Mumford, and Jonathan Raban, as well as by Richard Sennett (who built upon the Chicago School of Urban Sociology) and the ethnographically focused sociology of the journal *Urban Life and Culture*. The cover and frontispiece of *Urbanman: The Psychology of Urban Survival* (1973), an anthology of social science research that includes entries from Latané and Darley, Stanley Milgram, and others, offers an updated illustration of the blasé individual who exteriorizes these shielding mechanisms: a cartoonish illustration image depicting a man wearing a gas mask, helmet, spiked kneepads, roller skates, and a variety of quasi-militaristic accoutrements mixed in with white-collar elements (brief case, tennis racket). The levity of the *Urbanman* cover in some ways cuts against the apparent sobriety of the book's content, even as it references the social upheavals characterizing urban life as inconveniences within the life world of the white-collar worker. The word "Urbanman" suggests a superhero, and the plastic effect that is reinforced by block lettering surrounded by yellow dots suggests a movie marquee. As much as the subject matter it contains, the book itself in essence indicates a white, middle-class culture of lively engagement with urban social issues, one that emplaced contemporary social psychology within the neighborhood of *New York* magazine covers and think-pieces on mugging, Jules Feiffer's darkly satirical 1967 play *Little Murders* (remade as a film that *Newsweek* called "Funny in a new and frightening way!"), big-city cop shows, and, of course, crime movies.

Whether they lived in the cities or not, Americans were reading about urban crisis and crime in newspapers and magazines. The differences between the sensational culture of urban modernity that Singer delineates and 1970s urban culture relate to emergent configurations of living brought on by suburbanization. Middle-class Americans would often learn about urban crime in contexts at a geographical remove from the sites being described. An evening's television could begin with a news broadcast bringing updates from Vietnam as well as reports on urban decline, followed by city-based programming like "Adam-12," showing LAPD officers cruising sun-drenched streets; (NBC, 1968–1975), "The Odd Couple," with Tony Randall and Jack Klugman bickering in a New York apartment (ABC, 1970–1975), then "The Rookies" (ABC, 1972–1976), "The Streets of San Francisco" (ABC, 1972–1977), "Kojak" (CBS 1973–1978), or even "Shaft" (CBS, 1973–1975) with Richard Roundtree reprising his film role as a black detective circulating within the matrix of urban ghetto life. Despite ongoing suburbanization, then, images and dramas of urban culture were still central to the American visual media landscape. Like the charged media environment Singer describes, the visual culture of 1970s urbanity was resolutely contemporaneous and sensational—stocked with a richly divergent cast of police, black revolutionaries, hippies, and LSD gurus. Hollywood could play a distinctive part in this culture. Televisual representations were still mostly tied to studio sets, so, excepting outliers like the heavily location-based "Streets of San Francisco," their mise-en-scène typically consisted of a dynamic opening montage of actual urban spaces followed by a drama unfolding mostly on a series of soundstage interiors rather than crowded streets. The key role that Hollywood could play in popular urban culture then, was tied to a capital investment in production value. What is often reductively called "spectacle" amounts in this case to (at the very least): distinctive locations, recognizable stars, and a compelling screen story that meshed with sensational urban visual culture.

Two films released in 1974 partake of this sensational culture, and the currents of the bystander-effect discourse interweave them in ways that are alternately thrilling and frightening. These films ultimately gained traction not just within a society focused on what was happening in American cities but also within the more specific context of a vivid and contemporaneous urban sociological imagination. In *Death Wish*, an everyman is provoked by home invasion and mugging to become an urban vigilante, one who somewhat indiscriminately guns down thieves on New York streets and subways thence inconceivably becoming a city-wide—then national—folk hero and even an international celebrity. *The Taking of Pelham One Two Three*, like *The Incident*, also played on fears of insecurity on the subway but pushed them further, portraying the highly organized hi-jacking of a carful of passengers and the subsequent response by the various agencies responsible for subway operations (The New York Transit Authority and its police force, the NYPD, the Mayor's Office). Both films thematize the bystander effect, but in different ways, each partaking of a contemporary culture of urban sensation and endowing previously more abstract sociological notions with cinematic energy and effect.

Death Wish and the Age of the Mugger

Fearing that a film with "death" in the title would be a box office disaster, producer Dino De Laurentiis initially titled his film—based on the novel *Death Wish* by Brian Garfield—*Sidewalk Vigilante* (Winner 201–02). In fact De Laurentiis need not have worried. The film's opening weekend was wildly successful, and it became one of the top-grossing films of the year. The narrative of urban vigilantism rode the violent currents of Sam Peckinpah's *Straw Dogs* (1971) and Stanley Kubrick's *A Clockwork Orange* (1971) as well as those of *The French Connection* and *Dirty Harry*. It also aligned with a burgeoning vogue for revenge films, a cycle that heretofore included *Point Blank* (1967), *Billy Jack* (1971), *Jeremiah Johnson* (1972), *Coffy* (1973), *Walking Tall* (1973), and *White Lightning* (1973), not to mention other films also starring Bronson like *Cold Sweat* (1970) and *Mr. Majestyk* (1974). Merging with the revenge trend, *Death Wish* also carried—particularly through the brutality of its violence—the movement of filmmaking styles previously associated with exploitation into the mainstream of genre entertainment (Cook 259).

The plot of *Death Wish* turns on the reaction of a mild-mannered architect, Paul Kersey (Bronson), to a savage home invasion in which his wife (Hope Lange) is beaten and his daughter raped. The gang perpetrating these crimes is led by wiry and skittish Jeff Goldblum, sustaining the "cute"/sadistic punk typage of Artie and Joe from *The Incident*. When his wife later dies from her trauma, Kersey self-transforms into a vigilante, seeking out and shooting muggers on the street. Kersey's exploits gain the attention of the police, the city authorities, the mayor, and the news media. Fearing a public outcry if he arrests Kersey, and following orders from higher up, the investigating police detective (Vincent Gardenia) convinces our protagonist to quietly leave New York. The end of the film shows Kersey arriving at Union Station in Chicago, instantly spotting a new set of thugs in need of violent dispatch.

As a result of its topicality, its simplicity, or both, *Death Wish* became a hit with audiences, and this success became in turn a widely discussed phenomenon in its own right. Cited in editorials and think-pieces, the film came to be used as a sociological prop, one that provided critics and commentators across the political spectrum a readymade speculative framework for discussing the dire consequences of increasing urban crime. Advertisements for the film became dense with critical text written by reviewers who stressed the film's timeliness, or trumpeted it as a bellwether of a significant societal shift. Its topical condensation of urban fear was one reason for the film's immediate popularity, but equally fascinating for the press was its enthusiastic reception by audiences. Even though critics were on the whole ambivalent about the quality of the film, they were forced to acknowledge that audiences felt differently, crowds reportedly filling theaters with loud cheering at sight of Bronson's armed assault on street crime. Under the headline "What Do They See in 'Death Wish'?" (1 September 1974, Section 2: 1, 9) *New York Times* reporter Judy Klemesrud polled audiences at two of the downtown Manhattan Loews theaters where the film was playing, finding that "it was hard to find anyone critical of the film." *Death Wish*, like the vigilante it created, was a phenomenon unto itself.

Some of the controversy—which was indeed to a certain extent media-generated—centered on the film's sadism and the dangerous imitation it was sure to inspire outside theaters. "Tho I hesitate to become hysterical about this movie," wrote Clarence Petersen in the *Chicago Tribune*, "it worries me enough that I am rethinking an adult lifetime of opposition to censorship of any kind." Vincent Canby was likewise vociferous in his denunciation, in both his initial review and a subsequent article entitled "Death Wish Exploits Fear Irresponsibly" (4 August 1974, 85). From Klemesrud's report, it seemed the film was "equal-opportunity" in its appeal: the reporter found that "women applaud the actions more than men," and that spectators of various ethnicities and races were likewise exhilarated.

Death Wish is a film riddled with oddity—most abundantly, in a series of visual non sequiturs designed to heighten a sense of the surrealism of urban life—but one of the more striking elements is its treatment of race: although some of the muggers accosting Kersey are people of color, many are not. For all the vengeful brutality toward black street criminals the film displayed, many reporters—even Canby—maintained that the film was not racist. It was noted that Kersey is accosted by mixed groups of thieves, black, Latino, and white, a particularly curious point to make for reviewers who so astutely laid out the film's representational inaccuracies (that the muggers Kersey attacks never seem to carry firearms themselves). The film's casting of mixed-race gangs of criminals was clearly a ploy to excuse it from accusations of racism and incitement to race-based violence. Greg Mims, the reviewer for the black-oriented *New Pittsburgh Courier*, was sharply attuned to the bizarrely mixed-race street gangs, noting ironically that "fully integrated Equal Opportunity teams of muggers roam the streets" (21 September 1974, 17). Mims also pointed out that *Death Wish* was simply a "whitesploitation" film, mimicking as it did similar scenarios in Pam Grier and Jim Brown films of the same period (such as *Coffy* and *Slaughter's Big Rip-Off* [1973]). Black and brown audiences would not only have been familiar with the revenge-narrative framework from Blaxploitation films of the era, they were also part of urban populations as much—if not more—afflicted by street crime than white populations. The key difference was that white victimization tended to be treated as newsworthy where black and Latino victimization did not. Further, in the discourses of the news media, street crime was frequently coded in terms that alluded to entrenched racial geographies. Crime, it was said, was "encroaching"—moving from areas where it is natural and expected (racial ghettos like Harlem and the Bronx) to areas where it was intruding, a matter for concern.

The skewed casting of the criminal element in *Death Wish* directly echoed the rhetoric of law and order conservatives. As noted in chapter 2, the rhetoric of "crime in the streets" promulgated by conservatives strategically condensed a concatenation of social types understood "always already" as deviant, subversive, or non-normative: white hippies, drug addicts, homosexuals, and insurrectionary blacks. Although critics often failed to make the connection between the grab-bag quality of the *Death Wish*'s criminals and the right-wing urban imagination, the film's general law and order ideology was duly noted. Maureen Orth wrote in *Newsweek*: "Every law-and-order type—including many who may not have considered themselves as such—is bound to be captivated by the story of a 'bleeding heart liberal turned vigilante killer'" (26 August 1974, 82). As Orth's review indicates, the topicality of the film inhered not simply in its depiction of the problem of urban crime but in its vivid and, as we shall see, augmented animation of conservative images and narratives. The idea of the "streets" was pivotal in this discourse and the event of mugging became a key scenario for a shift of political consciousness.

Philadelphia Mayor Frank Rizzo, a former police commissioner known for espousing extreme law and order views, often quipped that "a conservative is a liberal who was mugged the night before." The statement is a reconfiguration of one of Barry Goldwater's famous campaign slogans—"Goldwater: In Your Heart You Know He's Right"—in its opposition of liberal surface to conservative essence. This strategy of playing on liberal doubts precisely defines the characterizations in, and narrative structure of, *Death Wish*, in which Kersey, a self-proclaimed "bleeding heart liberal," who abhors guns and preaches the values of tolerance to his co-workers, is converted into a crusading killer. For critics like Canby and Petersen who fretted over the film's deleterious effects, the danger of *Death Wish* was that it was a mechanism for producing approval of, and incitement to, vigilantism. Rex Reed's review for *The New York Daily News* breathlessly embodied these critic's fears, re-duplicating the film's elaboration of Rizzo's maxim. "Rarely have I found myself so caught like a horse in midstream, between my own gut reactions and intellectual reservations," Reed wrote. Though he admitted that the film's message was "so far right-wing it lands somewhere to the right of Attila the Hun," it was also so effectively designed that "[e]ven the most militant liberals are applauding like kids at Saturday afternoon Punch and Judy show" (26 July 1974, 62). For others, the film was as much a tool of conservative propaganda as an innocuous form of catharsis. A forty-seven-year-old poet interviewed by Klemesrud admitted that he had now seen *Death Wish* twice. "It's very entertaining and very lively, and tremendously well done. I don't necessarily agree with the vigilante philosophy, but the movie is so entertaining that I don't bother with the morality." Like Reed, reviewers balked at the film's politics and obscenity while acknowledging its pleasures. The larger question that could be posed here was whether the passivity of the viewing experience would lull audiences to entertain baser impulses, thus opening them to the ideologies of mythic violence on which law-and-order conservatism thrived.

Even prior to the release of *Death Wish*, there was within cities a pervasive concern that spiking levels of street crime could have drastic sociopolitical implications, a situation allegorized in the violent conclusion of the *The Incident* when Felix's beating of Artie and Joe both solves an immediate problem and indicates a pervading undercurrent of barbarism lurking below putatively civil society. In *Incident*, however, Felix's final act was ambiguous—a point of departure and discussion, rather than a conclusion. In a 1972 opinion piece for the *Village Voice*, Columbia University sociologist Amitai Etzioni noticed an apparent change in mugging and New Yorkers' attitudes toward it, after he returned from being away from the city for only four months (12 October 1972, 13). Thieves, he noted, had changed their m.o., graduating from straightforward street stick-ups to home invasions. Many accounts of mugging detail attacks that took place in the corridors, elevators, vestibules, and stairwells of apartment buildings, enclosures previously thought to be safe from predation. Reflected in *Death Wish*—which opens with Kersey and his wife returning to wintry New York from a sun-dappled tropical vacation—was a vision of Etzioni's own time away. What could happen, he mused, if the street crime situation continued without resolution:

> People discussing crime used to be concerned, worried, angry. They used to talk about types of locks, alarms, and dogs. Now the tone is bitter and desperate. The police, people seem to have concluded from stories circulating in the past few months, are corrupt and ineffectual [he's referring here to the Knapp Commission hearings] . . . people are undergoing what, to my sociological eyes, is an unmistakable transformation. The impact of the experience of having so many of those one knows come to harm is difficult to overestimate. In comparison, all other experiences pale. The war in Vietnam reaches us mainly via the press, radio, and television. I, for example, know no one personally who has been killed in Vietnam or who has kin who have been. But I know quite well at least 20 people who have been killed, knifed, bashed, threatened, assaulted, or merely burglarized. . . . What the hell do the city's, the nations, the state's, and the nation's leaders expect will happen when the citizens conclude there is no way one can safely drink a cup of coffee in one's own kitchen, not to mention sleep in one's bedroom? . . . People may abandon the streets and turn their homes into fortresses, but if each time the door is opened to a spouse, he or she might be accompanied by a mugger—who may or may not hurt one's child—who will stand for that? And thus, in my judgment, this city is a festering sore, which, if not rapidly drained through *effective* means of curbing crime, will explode in an ugly wave of fenced-in neighborhoods, private police forces, vigilantes, and blind support for whoever waves a fist aimed at the real or alleged sources of crime. Mile-long phalanxes of citizens ready to support practically anybody who promises measures to return safety to their homes are

> about to form. If no rational help comes soon, can irrational demagogic leadership be far behind? (13)

In this piece Etzioni offers a more nuanced take on the issue of law and order in the streets, giving equal weight to perceptions of crime on one hand and their possible political effects on the other. Some of those effects would indeed come to pass.

A critic for the *Wall Street Journal* adopted a line of thought similar to Etzioni's in her joint review of *Death Wish* and *The Education of Sonny Carson* (1974), a black-oriented film with revenge themes released at the same time:

> [T]hese films not only describe [a] retreat from civilized behavior, but in fact support it. More importantly their audiences support it too. For the kinds of remedies our society is offering for the social problems they face—better lighting on city streets; improved education and employment opportunities for blacks—are partial and long-term. And neither the trembling white middle class nor the angry blacks seem willing to accept such half-way, though civilized measures, what each group wants instead is an immediate and total solution. (Boyum 9)

In this instance, the right-wing disposition of *Death Wish* and its seeming endorsement of a "total" solution to crime in the streets were antithetical to band-aid liberal solutions like improved street lighting, and education—lighting being, as we shall see, one of *Death Wish*'s most significant motifs and aesthetic undercurrents.

The canniness of *Death Wish* was its very precise exploitation of extant urban fears, the way that it churned the ambivalence of urban audiences. Further, the film manufactures its own sociocultural significance by diegetically thematizing its protagonist's growing media celebrity. When Kersey's anonymous vigilantism gains the attention of the press, he becomes a media phenomenon as prolific as the Kitty Genovese incident to which the film ostensibly responds. Stories about his exploits are published in newspapers and magazines, advertising for which repeatedly appears on billboards and on the side of city buses within the film's mise-en-scène. The stack of magazines in Kersey's home indicates that he reads about himself, just as he watches television news stories about the reverberating effects of his actions. A televised news broadcast within the film reports that enlivened citizens have begun to strike back against their attackers but then, illogically, cuts to "footage" showing muggings in progress foiled by pedestrians and construction workers. No effort is made to explain how these scenes might have happened to be caught in the moment by television cameras. It is truly one of the film's odder moments, but it also reinforces the oneiric qualities of the whole, and reinforces the idea that this is a film that subordinates urban reality to urban fantasy. Kersey's celebrity even extends across the sea, with German news outlets arriving to report on how city hall and the New York police are dealing with his well-regarded initiative. As far-fetched as is this scenario, the media storm within the film punctures the diegesis, creating a porous intertextual space that allows the film to permeate into the discourse and imagery of crime already coursing through the real-life media environment.

As much as it was taken up within conservative quarters, the right wing could not claim a monopoly on the discourse and culture that emerged around urban crime. Called the "The Age of the Mugger" in a *New York Times* piece revisiting the era (24 October 2004, CY1), mugging accounts and strategies for avoiding being mugged proliferated within popular media of the period. *LIFE* published a feature on mugging that included a one-page "survival" guide with tips on how to deal with mugging. Articles like "Mugging as a Way of Life" (Freeman 1970) in *New York* and "A Dollar for the Mugger" (Mooney 1970) and "Portrait of a Mugger" (Willwerth 1974) in *Harper's* sought to give insight into anti-mugging tactics and the mugger's psyche. "Portrait of a Mugger" was shortly followed by James Willwerth's book of the same name, detailing time he spent talking and following a dyed-in-the-wool mugger through the streets of New York. For a more academic sociological account, one could turn to the recently launched journal *Urban Life and Culture* to read Robert Lejeune and Nicholas Alex's "On Being Mugged: The Event and Its Aftermath" (1973). *New York* magazine became central to this discussion, even publishing a cover story by George Alexander on "The Mugging Hour" (1971): the time of day that New Yorkers were most likely to get mugged (figure 4.1 on page 168). In this context the image of the armored businessman used on the cover of the *Urbanman* anthology begins to make sense.

Perhaps the strangest piece of urban survival ephemera was the "Welcome to Fear City" pamphlet published by the New York Police and Fire Departments. To oppose layoffs proposed by Mayor Abraham Beame, the police and fire unions formed the "Committee of Public Safety," which put the pamphlet together to be handed out at airports and tourist areas. Emblazoned with a death's head shroud (figure 4.2 on page 169), the text described the adverse effects of budget cuts to the police and fire departments and warned of their dire consequences for civic life. Designed as an ersatz "survival guide," the pamphlet listed an alarming series of tips for visitors to the "dangerous" city that included suggestions like, "Do not walk," and "Avoid public transportation." The pamphlet was designed to be hyperbolic not informational, a tactic to

Figure 4.1. *New York* cover illustration for "Mugging Hour" feature.

Figure 4.2. Welcome to Fear City pamphlet released by New York police and fire departments.

scare the Beame administration by way of threatening much relied-upon tourist dollars. Yet, like *Death Wish* this publicity material was also rooted in very real and growing fears of city street experience. Like the film, it added itself to a burgeoning culture of urban sensation.

As much as *Death Wish* partook of fear culture, so too did it transform it. In particular, *Death Wish* distinguished itself within the crowded field of mugging discourse by expanding on a latent image of "striking back" against attackers, in this way expanding on and filling out the fantasy scenario that was only guardedly presented by Felix at the end of *The Incident*. As many critics noted, the casting of a performer like Bronson as a man putatively struggling with pacifist commitments already cued viewers in this direction. Hardly ever seen in films or publicity of the era *without* a gun, there was never a doubt that Bronson would take up arms against criminal antagonists.

In addition to Bronson's presence, however, was an imaginative restaging of conventional mugging imagery. In mugging discourse one of the key sources of trauma was the suddenness and violent intimacy of robbery, in particular when this involved a man assaulting a woman. Popular depictions of mugging frequently framed a conventional picture: a shadowy figure assaulting someone from behind, rather than head on. *New York*'s cover illustration for its "Mugging Hour" piece exemplifies the dynamics of intimacy and invisibility characterizing a mugging (with S&M overtones no less): a close-up view of a gloved hand (with a wristwatch to convey that the attacker operates by the clock) covering a woman's mouth, her eyes straining but unable to see the figure behind her. The difficulty of seeing, or remembering seeing, one's attackers is a recurring trope in mugging accounts, in which the aggressor seems to appear out of nowhere in the most unexpected locations, or is embodied by only a voice, a sharp jab, or a flash of steel. Whether because of the trauma of the act or the ingenuity of the robbers, a mugging becomes defined by partial objects. In *Harper's* Ruth Mooney writes: "My pocketbook strap suddenly left my hand; I turned, and saw the man's back just before he vanished behind a six-foot-high ramp of excavated dirt across the street" (26). Similarly fragmentary portrayals can be found on the covers of trade paperbacks like Morton Hunt's *The Mugging* (1972) or the 1975 Ballantine reprint of Ed McBain's *The Mugger*. The cover of *The Mugging* features a disembodied hand holding a knife, seemingly blurred by motion, and a blurb from the *New York Daily News*: "The Anatomy of a Mugging—The sudden savage assault by a stranger who leaps from the shadows touches a raw nerve."

The poster publicity for *Death Wish* both references and reverses the typical modes of representing mugging. In the most oft-used design (figure 4.3), Bronson is shown on the concrete steps of a public park. Although his feet are planted forward his torso has turned, and his gun is raised to take aim at whomever may be approaching from behind him, out of frame. Most significant perhaps is the scale of the image. Rather than a fragmentary close-up, we are given a clearly rendered full-body

Figure 4.3. *Death Wish* Poster.

view. The image not only succinctly and physiologically communicates the reversal of feeling that Bronson's character experiences in the film narrative, it also iconically represents the stance of a citizen able in a public setting to anticipate a mugger's attack. Under the tagline, "Vigilante—city-style. Judge, jury, and executioner," Bronson's twisting frame forcefully renders an urban dweller who catches a full view of a mugger presumably advancing just out of view. *Death Wish* in effect responded to an undercurrent of desire for intelligibility and involvement that coursed through the imagery and narratives surrounding the Genovese murder, the discourse on the bystander effect, and films like *The Incident*. We know what muggers are; we see them coming; we know how to handle them.

To understand how this desire for knowledge and capacity for involvement was met by the film requires attending to Bronson's interaction with a subtle, but recurring element: the street light.

Designs for Night

The poster for *Death Wish* prominently displays a practical feature of mise-en-scène that joins Kersey on almost all of his violent nocturnal sojourns: the burning globe of a street lamp. In a certain sense the street lamp simply fills out the urban setting, playing the part of a motivated lighting source. But in an almost unconscious way, its presence in the poster alludes to the patterns of street lighting that play a consistent accomplice to Kersey's vigilantism, both within the seen space of the drama and as the ostensible diegetic lighting just outside the frame. These night lights, as it were, at once serve the film's aesthetic of legibility—no matter how dark it is when people get mugged, in movies we have to be able to see in order to have visual pleasure—and allude to the role of the material urban infrastructures that were thrust into the foreground with surging urban crime rates.

The first street mugging sequence in the film occurs after Kersey has decided to arm himself with a sock full of quarters and is returning home from work in the evening. Exiting a subway along a well-lit main thoroughfare, he is greeted by the newsstand operator in a neighborly way (an exchange that suggests this is Kersey's street) before he continues down a side street. Passing a small alley there, Kersey is startled to hear the sound of a match being struck and turns to see a figure leaning against a wall. The loiterer turns out to be non-threatening, but we have been signaled to be aware of the immediate surroundings and the denizens lurking there. A Herbie Hancock musical cue helps to raise the tension for a moment, then drops down, sustaining the mood at a lower octave. As Kersey continues to move down the street we are given a handheld point-of-view shot showing hesitant forward motion along the sidewalk. This side street is noticeably darker than the thoroughfare at the beginning of the sequence and becomes darker still as Kersey progresses, much of the frame filled with inky patches and the opposite side of the street, initially well lit, dropping into darkness. As the street gradually grows dimmer, so too does its topography become more ominous, shifting from a zone of amiable neighborliness to one of uncertainty and illegibility. Suddenly, a man jumps out from behind a low wall and, sticking a knife into Kersey's back says, "Turn around, you son-of-a-bitch!" Kersey turns, swinging his sock of quarters at the attacker's face, and both men race away in opposite directions. In this first mugging scene, then, we are provided the outlines of the typical mugging scenario, albeit one which has been unduly thwarted by a man who has, it seems, nothing to lose.

Like *The French Connection*, *Death Wish* emphasizes the anxious semiotics of the street, the necessity of reading a scene and the people in it to distinguish between threat and non-threat. Director Michael Winner tweaks this game, however, loading the film's mise-en-scène with characters that seem to signify or carry meaning but whose only function is to suggest a bizarre and unreadable—thus in many ways unbearable—city. These types include, for example, a man in a purple jacket and brown floppy hat listening to a radio in a police precinct, seen only from the back, who calls out to an officer, "Why haven't you found my dog? He's vital to my income, he paints such marvelous pictures with his paws!" Two scenes open with groups of nuns passing in the foreground, another with a group of nighttime revelers dressed up as characters from *The Wizard of Oz*. All of these pointedly invite decoding or decipherment but hardly fit into any overarching system of signification. The urban world, it seems, is incomprehensible. As Kersey's persona transforms, however, so too do certain aspects of the city's inscrutability. More specifically, the light design molds the city to conform to Kersey's vigilante perception.

When Kersey emerges as a full-fledged vigilante, the lighting pattern of the mugging sequence evolves. Instead of being cloaked in darkness Kersey's attackers become strongly lit. Walking toward the river on a path dotted with lamps in Riverside Park, Kersey observes a man in a brown jacket, yards away atop an embankment, walking parallel to him and returning his gaze. In the deep space of these tracking shots, the embankment between the men is covered with dark brush, but the man in Kersey's sights, who is seeing him, is fully illuminated by white overhead light. Kersey's aggressor here is never covered by darkness. Nor could we say that, as in the technique of day-for-night shooting, the scene is *generally* luminous. It is not. Large swaths of darkness take up significant portions of the screen, particularly along the scrubby embankment. What is shown most clearly in these shots is Kersey and the man who seems to be following him with malignant purpose. Unlike the staging of Kersey's first mugging, not to mention the popular image of mugging, the thief's presence is constantly held in view by movement and bright white light, and hence the man's interest in Kersey is unambiguous, as "plain as day."

This lighting design continues, and is even diegetically acknowledged, in a third sequence where Kersey interrupts the beating of a man in an alley. Again, though shadows stretch around the central action, the action itself is lit with a hard, white overhead light (figure 4.4). To set this up, Kersey first passes the alley along the street, with a reverse-angle supplying his point-of-view on the skirmish. Centered in the frame, and illuminated as if by a spotlight from above, the attack is presented as a highly visible event. Kersey need only turn his head to see precisely what is happening. Once again, of course, he violently dispenses of the criminals. Later, when the police arrive and the elderly victim refuses to give them the name of his vigilante protector, a detective presses him by protesting: "C'mon, they were under 'dat street light!" In the world of *Death Wish*, illumination and knowledge are the same. Here in such brilliance ignorance is impossible, so the clouding memory that often accompanies a mugging—is converted by the rescued victim as a way of protecting Kersey—completely visible within the mise-en-scène—from police identification.

In the mugging sequences of *Death Wish* lighting serves to illuminate the figures in the environment, rather than the environment itself.

Figure 4.4. *Death Wish*. A mugging in progress shown from Kersey's point-of-view.

While a number of reviewers at the time of the film's release ridiculed the ease with which Kersey happened upon would-be criminals, few picked up on the way Winner supported this rhetoric of visibility. The film delineates an urban nightworld in which Kersey is offered unobstructed sight of his targets, eliminating for the audience any sense that the vigilante could misconstrue or miscomprehend his nocturnal predators—that is, catch innocent civilians by mistake. To be labelled by Kersey is to be labelled correctly, since Kersey's point-of-view is always furnished by superabundant street lighting. More, lighting is clearly subordinated to action rather than put in the service of completing the portraiture of a credible nighttime world. For, if this world was too naturalistic, the ambiguity produced could potentially compromise perceptual certitude, detracting from the fantasy of striking back with perfectly unerring skill. Thus, Winner develops and augments a contradictory impulse that first emerges in the aftermath of the Genovese murder, a tendency—seen in both bystander-effect studies and *The Incident*—to clear away or bracket the ambiguity and over-stimulation that in many ways constitute the urban public realm in order to be able to show it more clearly.

In subtly redesigning Kersey's nighttime environs, however, *Death Wish* was also inserting itself into another much broader ongoing conversation regarding the safety of city streets, one that, while not as prominent as the media surrounding mugging or law and order conservatives, had ramifications for navigating and experiencing the urban night. I refer to here to electric street lighting, particularly the roles it was understood to play in urban nightlife. Within this lighting discourse, as in the Genovese murder, the precise relationship between individual indifference and the material obscurity of the urban realm comes under clearer examination.

Electric Streets

Wolfgang Schivelbusch and David Nye—both cultural historians of electricity and light—have shown that the history of nighttime urban illumination has been divided into two primary projects: that of amusement, entertainment, and spectacle, and that of surveillance, control, and public security. Schivelbusch demonstrates in *Disenchanted Night* that the lighting of city streets, particularly in its electric forms, has always been conjoined to discourses of policing and improvements to safety (79–114 and *passim*). With the advent of electric arc lighting, cities such as Flint, Detroit, and San José built towers to considerable heights, showering whole segments of the city in light (124–27) before moving to the more conventional street-by-street lighting patterns used today. As Nye points out in *Electrifying America*, public lighting was seen as a symbol of civic progress and cities and towns across America competed with each other by emulating the lights of Broadway with "Great White Ways" of their own that were installed by General Electric and Westinghouse (54–57). Lighting was seen as a tool to both increase consumer traffic on commercial thoroughfares and deter crime, and between 1900 and 1920 almost every city made improvements to its street lighting on this basis. Every few years, GE introduced new models of public lighting, marketing them as improvements on older systems.

Through the 1950s and 1960s, electrical companies promoted crime-deterrent lighting improvements with a powerful ally, J. Edgar Hoover. Writing guest editorials for a *General Federation Clubwoman* (1963) and *Street and Highway Lighting* (1970), Hoover praised the crime-fighting abilities of street lighting in no uncertain terms:

> While moonlit nights and twinkling stars may be the joy of poets and lovers, those with crime on their minds much prefer dark, moonless nights for their activities. Darkness, naturally, is an ally to crime, since most criminals prefer to creep stealthily through gloomy, moonless, and unlighted streets and byways, to enter homes, offices, schools, business establishments and even churches, and make off with anything of value on which they can lay their greedy hands. . . . A prudent person must conclude, then that while darkness invites crime, light deters it. (Hoover 5)

Citing FBI statistics, Hoover also made the point that lighting not only provides a shelter from crime-generating darkness, it also equips citizens with visibility. He specifically singles out the apathy understood to surround the Genovese case: "Crime flourishes not only in the darkness created by unlighted streets and buildings, but in what might be called the mental darkness of indifferent citizens." The solution: "The Nation needs an aroused citizenry, whose eyes will serve as floodlights to pierce the darkest reaches of the underground" (5). Crime is endowed not just by the obscurity of unlighted spaces but by dim citizens whose perception has eroded.

An article in *Coronet* magazine entitled "How Bright Lights Reduce Crime" was more direct in its formulation, unequivocally touting the power of illumination-based crime fighting and thoroughly aligning crime with darkness and infrastructures of light with the elimination of threat. "Today, with modern lights, our streets can be made bright, shadowless—and *safe*," the article states, extending Schivelbusch's report into the mid-twentieth-century. For good measure the article provided a "before and after" picture of a street scene, its caption reading "Dimly lit streets in McPherson[,] Kansas hid crime;" below a picture of a typical night-time street scene. Then, above a significantly brighter version of the same scene: "new lights illumined burglaries out of existence." Commentaries by town officials and sheriffs bolster the argument, but the concluding commentary by a GE engineer hints at the particular economic interests underlying the promotion of infrastructural change.

By the early 1970s, New York City was once again seeking to change its public lighting systems, announcing the gradual replacement of mercury vapor lights with the newer technology of sodium lighting in an effort to increase security. The new sodium lighting technology was said to double the brightness of the older street lights. As main arteries were slowly upgraded, block associations also raised their own funds to install better lights on their streets. In the summer of 1972, the *New York Times* reported that the residents of 84th Street between West End Ave. and Riverside Dr. (roughly the neighborhood where *Death Wish* is narratively set), who had once "locked themselves behind their doors for fear of crime in the streets and theft in their homes," installed seven high sodium lights on their street, converting it to "an after dark playground." The *Times* interviewed residents, including the artist Peter Max and the actor Jerry Stiller on the changes to their street. Max was appreciative of the aesthetic effects of the new temperature: "The streets have taken on a nice yellow-green aura, and the whole street has a golden glow that gives people a nice secure feeling." Stiller added: "Through that phosphorescent glow, my children think I'm immortal."

Reports and discussions such as this about street lighting illustrate the ways that urban infrastructure, so often invisible and mundane, moves into the foreground in times of crisis. In the 1977 blackout, of course, crisis erupted around a breakdown of the electrical infrastructure itself. The vandalism and arson that ensued were a reminder for many of the civilizing bulwark of street lighting systems, even as citizens in Midtown spontaneously began to direct traffic in the absence of streetlights.[2] In the mounting crisis surrounding street crime, attention was paid both to the individual perpetrators and to the material environments that endowed the act itself. Much of the media surrounding mugging discusses the act as an environmental phenomenon, rather than a strictly sociocriminological one. *New York*'s piece on the "Mugging Hour" updates the reader on when muggings have recently been tending to occur (between 6:00 and 7:00 p.m.) and where (in elevators and vestibules), in a manner not unlike a traffic or weather report. In many cases, the phenomenon of mugging thrust the material life of urbanity into focus; and it is here perhaps that some fine distinctions can be made in the rhetorical figuration of "crime in the streets." For those who lived within the everyday reality of mugging as opposed to only reading about it, or who briefly visited it (as comically depicted in, for example, *The Out-of-Towners*) crime in the streets meant attunement to the street as a material field of threat and opportunity, and awareness of the structured dimension of urban experience.

Like the geographic ambiguity of Kew Gardens, the cinematic topography of *Death Wish* embodies the broader processes of urbanization at play during this era. The suburbs and urban planning play a curious role in *Death Wish*. It is through Kersey's visit to a suburban developer in Arizona that he comes to be convinced to abandon his liberal pacificism. Yet, Kersey also refuses his son-in-law's pleas to leave the city for the suburbs. His profession as an architect and urban developer conflates with his vigilantism, the latter in many ways an extension of the totalizing vision of the master planner. Just as the profession of urban planning itself was shifting from the large-scale visions of Le Corbusier and Robert Moses to the street-level preoccupations of Jane Jacobs and Kevin Lynch, so too does Kersey recalibrate his own focus closer to the ground.

And although they were clearly filmed in the streets of New York (particularly its Upper West Side white enclaves), Kersey's nighttime journeys can appear as depopulated as sleepy suburban streets. His ability to place himself in an ideal position for witnessing—to become the hero that bystander rhetoric openly wished Kitty Genovese's watchers could have been—ensures that, however excessive, his gunplay is clearly justified. Like the experiments used to hypothesize the bystander effect, *Death Wish* suspends illegibility in favor of unambiguous scenarios that present clear pathways to intervention. Perhaps this is what makes the film both so effective and yet so strange and fascinating to a viewer otherwise opposed to its ideology. Both Roger Ebert and Vincent Canby, who objected to the film, also confessed that its visuality was intriguing. Ebert admitted an "eerie kind of fascination," and thought the film depicted a New York that "doesn't look like 1974, but more like one of those bloody future cities in science fiction novels about anarchy in the twenty-first century." Likewise Canby noted that the city looked "to be about three years from now"—a fascinating observation when one considers precisely how difficult it would be to intentionally portray such a small increment of futurity within a film's setting. In many ways, what these critics were noticing was the cinematic iteration of a practice that had been very common at the turn of the century. Nye comments that the electric illumination that created the Great White Ways around the nation "made possible a new kind of visual text, one that expressed an argument or view of the world without writing, solely through suppressing some features of a site and emphasizing others. This new rhetoric of night space edited the city down to a few idealized essentials" (60). In *Death Wish* this editing takes the form of night-spaces designed to elaborate the idealized view of law and order.

In *Death Wish* the structure and infrastructure of the urban environment—what urban dwellers move through, perceive, and think about everyday—is bent to the will of a single man. In this bending, a familiar physical landscape is made strange. And a strange new landscape of violence is made familiar. Perhaps too it was *because* this is a film made by tourists and outsiders (British Michael Winner, Italian Dino de Laurentiis, non-New Yorker Charles Bronson, who reportedly disliked the city) that it became so popular. It allowed spectators to repeatedly engage in a touristic fantasy of the streets on which they lived—the arousing fantasy of violent clarity.

The Taking of Pelham One Two Three: Subway Scene and System

Adjacent to and contiguous with city streets, subways were a significant site of urban crime in the postwar era. And, like the infrastructure of electric street light, the subway's physical plant offered innumerable "situational conditions" that contributed to danger. In 1974, the *New York Times* commented on the growth of "Subway Terror," citing escalating crime rates as well as films like *Death Wish*, *The Incident*, and the 1973 novel *The Taking of Pelham One Two Three* by John Godey (the film version was yet to be released) as indicators in a shift in sensibility toward the subway ("About New York: Subway Myths, Subway Terror," 2 August 1974, 15). The piece noted that fear of subway transit was a departure from depictions of it in musicals like *Subways are For Sleeping* (1961–62) or *On the Town* (produced for Broadway 1944, filmed 1949), which celebrated the vitality of underground transport. A more recent security measure announced by Mayor Beame, the article reported, would have the connecting doors between subway cars locked at night so that passengers would have to bunch together in the same car "like a wagon train on the Great Plains, the settlers looking for Sioux" (15). Negative thoughts about subway riding also dovetailed with the ongoing fiscal problems facing New York and the way this affected essential city services. If crime topped the list of the city's "worst ills" in 1974, worry about an increased subway fare came in fourth on the list, just below inflation and above education at 19 percent (David Burnham "Most Call Crime City's Worst Ill," 16 January 1974: 1). Although the Transit Authority reported that New York's subway was the safest in the world, a fire in August trapped hundreds of riders underground for two hours and prompted worry about the structural strength of the system and its procedures for dealing with accidents (Robert Lindsey "For Those with Inner Peace, Subways are Safe," 25 August 1974, 173). The Fear City pamphlet put the problem in no uncertain terms. Noting that cuts to the Transit Patrol could increase crime, it stated: "You should never ride the subway for any reason whatsoever."

It was thus apposite that filmmakers took advantage of New York's generous new location production policies to depict the dangers and surreal nature of the subway system. Paul Kersey, for example, dispatches muggers both on train platforms and on an empty late night car. In *Bananas* (1971), Woody Allen recreates an *Incident*-like situation for comedic effect, striking back against leather-jacketed punks (one played by Sylvester Stallone) and in turn being chased by them, all to a slapstick piano score. *Little Murders* shows Elliott Gould's character wandering catatonically onto a train in a blood-spattered white shirt to the indifference of the crowded carful of passengers. Again and again in these films, iterations of Artie and Joe from *The Incident* appear to harass subway citizens, motivated solely—like Alex and the Droogs from *A Clockwork Orange* (1971)—by an anarchic urge for violent kicks.

In a sense all of these films drew on and developed what would become a generic New York subway scene: a diverse group of riders enclosed within a clearly bounded space, confronted by criminality and a delirious collage of societal malfunctions. The austere anomie of urban life depicted in the George Tooker's painting "The Subway" (1950) and Walker Evans's surreptitious subway photography give way to kaleidoscopic portrayals along the lines of Paul Cadmus's hyperbolic "Subway Symphony" (1975–76) or Ralph Bakshi's *Heavy Traffic* (1973). In Cadmus's painting the subway platform becomes an overflowing conflagration of caricatured faces and bodies (many corpulent), an assortment of MTA detritus vying with Day-Glo countercultural flash. In the foreground a black man with an afro and dashiki embraces a blonde white woman, their racial polarity accentuated (he wears dark brown colors, she is skimpily attired in bright white halter top and shorts) and drawing the gaze of others in the scene. The only non-cartoonish figure in the scene, a beautiful blond Adonis in the right bottom corner, alludes to the painter's understanding of the subway platform as a site of gay visual pleasure. In the *New York Times* the critic Alfred Kazin offered a similar take on the subway scene in the form of an elegiac literary montage:

> I think at random of elderly crippled and blind saxophonists wheezing out "When Irish Eyes are Smiling." Fat ladies with 17 shopping bags who can find no resting place for the sharp

> steel point of their soggy umbrellas but in your *kishkes*. Eager-beaver students dropping their breakfast on your pants as they enjoy an informal repast while standing over you on a crowded express train. The lovely relaxing bass scream of a train siren the transit cops on the next platform know that there has been a little commotion on this train—like, for example, a stabbing. The young man wearing (so help me) nothing but a blanket as he sat with this head bent to the grimy floor all the way from West 79th Street to Park Place . . . The terror in the face of a woman at 8 in the evening as she walks toward the rear exit on the East 33d Street Station (Lexington Avenue IRT) only to discover that the exit no longer exits and that she has to walk back the whole length of the deserted platform to the front exit. . . . A Japanese visitor to our fair city trying in a crowded hurtling train to read the subway map half hidden by someone's hat, a subway map that would look like a diagram of a television's set's insides even if the glass over it weren't encrusted with spray paint informing you that Peco was here. . . ." (25 March 1973, 10: 1)

Kazin's piece is accompanied by sketches from Miriam Troop, who in an adjacent article describes riding the subway as being like "rummaging through an addled anthropologist's mind," the car becoming "a wide-screen smorgasbord of splintered citizenry . . . men in their bizarre reality" (25 March 1973, 10: 1).

In concert with other voices of the time, the emergent visuality of the subway scene was a topos that not only underlined but formally reproduced the obscurity and delightful disorder of the modern city. In a sense, this was a bystander's discourse, one that, like Winner's gaze in *Death Wish*, produced surreal and bizarre observations to underscore the illegibility and chaos of the post-1960s city. Yet, while it amply supplied an appropriate backdrop for such imagery, the subway could also be seen as a very specific chronotope—a time-space that determined narrative possibility. While other New York-set films of the 1970s tended to use the subway as an iconic marker of city life, only *The Taking of Pelham One Two Three* attempted to create an affectionate portrait of the New York subway scene while also integrating the infrastructural logic of urban transit into film narrative.

Pelham's depiction of the response of various city agencies to a subway hi-jacking ("Pelham" designates the origin of the hijacked Lexington Avenue IRT train at Pelham Bay station, "1-2-3" designates the time [1:23] the train left this station) offers the opportunity for a dispersed, rather than narrowed, narrative perspective, one that moves between the hi-jacked car, the agents and control rooms of the transit authority and transit police, the subway riders across the city affected by the delay, and Gracie mansion, where the mayor (Lee Wallace) consults his advisors on how to respond to the situation. Alternating between all of the sites and people affected by the hi-jacking, the film produces the outlines of an integral image capturing the complexity of the subway system, one which imbricates people and technology, politics and infrastructure. Proffered through this image is a new sense of what it means to be a by-stander or to get involved. The scale of the subway system, the hi-jacking delay, and the required response mean that the involvement or non-involvement of any one person is less important than the overall functioning of an elaborate sociotechnical mechanism. Where *Death Wish* intervenes in the discourse of bystander apathy by way of fantasy, *Pelham* puts into motion an epistemological narrative, one which demonstrates all of the ways that the people of New York were entangled within a mechanism greater than any one or two of them—a complex of city employees, departments, civil engineering, railway technology, and communication that individual perception could only ever partially take in.

Perhaps more so than other sites in big cities, urban transit constitutes a phenomenological experience divided between part and whole. Sitting on a bus, waiting on a platform, zooming through a tunnel, we may reflect on how our immediate life-world is connected to all other parts of the city, and that this connection is in turn dependent on mechanisms not immediate to us. For example, we experience arrivals and departures of busses and trains but never the entirety of the schedule itself. But how common are such unharried reflections on a habitual commute? We experience delays and curse a malfunctioning system, but rarely would we comment on a speedy journey or a smooth transfer between different lines. Again, infrastructure becomes most palpable in moments of breakdown, remaining relatively invisible when functioning well.

Pelham uses hi-jacking as a plot device to render transit infrastructure and operations visible. Hi-jackings were common in the 1970s, although airplanes were the preferred target, so this device was indeed timely. Within the film the hi-jacking is coded with the artifice of fiction rather than in a realist manner, the criminal team belonging to no political/national movement or terrorist organization but being simply a collection of crooks—not unlike those assembled in postwar heist films like *The Asphalt Jungle* (1950), *The Killing* (1956), or *Ocean's 11* (1960). These men have been brought together by "Mr. Blue," (Robert Shaw), a British soldier of fortune. The various disguises—wool coats, felt hats, fake glasses, and moustaches—are as cartoonish as their kindergarten code names: "Mr. Blue," "Mr. Green" (Martin Balsam), "Mr. Grey" (Hector Elizondo), and "Mr. Brown" (Earl Hindman). This somewhat theatrical affectation integrates with the overall tone of the film, which matched suspense with the breezy comedy of a caper, the caustic back-and-forth of city workers, and an amusing tapestry of genuine New York types. The hi-jackers are not unlike Artie and Joe in *The Incident*—as narrative functionaries, they stand out from a naturalistically depicted urban environment. But in *Pelham*, the function of criminality is not limited to the sphere of the subway car itself. While the train carries and drives the narrative, the hi-jacking is signaled as a pretext for animating the lines of communication between agents at various nodes in the system, and for developing various pockets (or windows) of characterization.

One such pocket depicts a young conductor-in-training (Jerry Holland), who at one point rhymes off door closing protocols and memorized facts to his supervisor (Walter Jones): "Wanna hear somethin'? Every car on the IRT is seventy-two feet long. Costs $150,000, weighs 75,000 pounds." Another shows the small team of comptrollers in the cramped Grand Central Tower. Led by Kas Dolowicz (Tom Pedi), who objects to a new policy allowing women in the workplace, the Grand Central Tower team are the ones who first notice that the Pelham 1-2-3 train is delayed, sending notice along to Lt. Garber (Walter Matthau) in the main Transit Authority control center. The MTA command center is its own self-contained pocket, and—via a tour given to the well-bespoke visiting directors of the Tokyo Metropolitan Subway system—Garber communicates still more facts about the MTA's operations. The hi-jacked train car is itself another pocket, one not unlike that of *The Incident*, in that it contains passengers from a spectrum of social groups. Another pocket: Gracie Mansion, where a flu-ridden mayor frets over the financial and political implications of caving into the hi-jackers' demands. As the hi-jacking unfolds, relations form between all of these pockets.

This networked narrative style is consonant with a generic cycle that *Pelham* straddled. For in addition to falling in with the cycle of location-based urban crime thrillers, *Pelham* was also a disaster movie. In the fall of 1974 one could see not only *Death Wish* and other revenge films in their local theaters but also possibly *Airport 1975* (1974) the second installment of a series of films based on Arthur Hailey's novels depicting large-scale airplane emergencies; as well as Richard Lester's *Juggernaut* (1974), about an ocean liner with on-board bombs that are set to go off unless a ransom is paid. Like those of *The Poseidon Adventure*, *The Towering Inferno*, *Earthquake* (1974), *Black Sunday* (1977), and others. *Pelham*'s narrative unfolded a threat to a large-scale structural complex, necessarily weaving between different sites and individuals. The subway system was thus an apposite choice, not only because subways were sites of insecurity or because economic crisis in New York loomed but because, like an ocean liner, a skyscraper, or a sports stadium the subway was a multi-sited structure where any kind of emergency could have strikingly distributed effects.

As Michael Brooks notes in his exploration of the literary and artistic history of New York's subway, threats to personal security on the city's trains began to emerge as a pervasive fear beginning in the 1950s (Brooks 190). These fears were heightened by the fact that neither the Transit Authority nor the NYPD had introduced adequate measures to address growing concerns about crime on both the subway platforms and the trains. After a stabbing incident in 1965, the Transit Authority, writes Brooks, "experimented with a pathetic system in which a toll-booth attendant, aware of a crime in progress, would press a pedal with his or her foot, thus setting an amber light blinking on the street level, which it was hoped, would be noticed by a passing pedestrian "who, it is expected, will then call the police" (194). Because during the 1965 stabbing this system was not yet in place, "the motorman of the train on which Mormile [the stabbing victim] lay dying had to blow loud whistle blasts at each station he passed in an effort to summon aid" (194). The inadequacy of this "Rube Goldberg device" as Brooks puts it, with its dependence on a flimsy chain of alarms to signal trouble on what is in fact a mobile crime scene, seems self-evident.

Yet the logic of the Rube Goldberg-style alarm system is analogous to the way the operations of the subway system rely on the functioning of chains of signifiers, from the navigation of complex maps by passengers—maps of the system, and maps of the network of platforms that make up key junctions—to the reading of track lights by motormen. In *Pelham*, the interruption of this system occasions an opportunity to visualize its complexity. The crime of hi-jacking—different from mugging in both scale and process—becomes a medium for exploring the relationship between the flow of trains and their systems of management. The hi-jackers manipulate the subway system according to a strict plan that takes into account every detail of a subway train's operations. Signaled by an alarm in a command center, the interruption of the schedule quickly becomes apparent, mobilizing a response that involves relays of communication between satellite sites and the coordination of movement around the train. None of the primary actors in the film have the synoptic view of the situation offered to the film viewer, neither the Transit Police chief Garber nor the hi-jacking leader "Mr, Blue" nor any of the passengers, transit employees, police, or city officials. In fact the suspense of film relies on the limited perspectives inherent to the primary sites between which the narrative alternates: the fluorescently lit subway control center, the dim stolen subway car, and the platforms, tunnels, and streets above.

It is worth giving attention to that viewer's panoptical view. In their online project *Paris: Invisible City* Bruno Latour and Emilie Hermant challenge the notion of the panopticon as the techno-architectural apparatus dominating modern urban life. They propose instead we think of Paris's systems of traffic and water as oligoptic (from the Greek "oligo," or little). The panopticon has traditionally been conceived as an all-powerful mechanism that sees everything, a conception that, according to Latour and Hermant, produces at opposite ends a megalomania of control and a paranoia of domination. Oligopticons are defined by a narrow view, a view which limits what can be seen in order to see one thing better:

> Water, electricity, telephony, traffic, meteorology, geography, town planning: all have their oligopticon, a huge control panel in a closed control room. From there very little can be seen at any one time, but everything appears with great precision owing to a dual network of signs, coming and going, rising and descending, watching over Parisian life night and day. (32)

The figure of the oligopticon has rich implications for studying the visual nature of urban systems, and Latour and Hermant use it to account for the administration of things like room scheduling at the École des Mines, the routing of water through Paris, and even elections. Whereas the panoptic confuses map and territory, encouraging both the megalomania of those who imagine that they "dominate the collection of traces" as well as "the paranoia of those who think they are dominated by them," the oligoptic retains the distinction between map and territory, acknowledging that the limited view the map supplies enables the management of the system in question (26). In this conceptualization, views of the city are always partial and so too is power.

Oligoptic visuality is useful for understanding the spatial relations and narrative suspense generated within *Pelham*. Closed control rooms filled with transit workers and obscure subway system maps are a signature and recurring feature of the film's mise-en-scène. The most prominent of these is the windowless Transit Authority command center with its scattering of trainmaster's desks, each with a microphone hanging from a small arm to enable communication with motormen and other control towers and all facing toward an elongated system map (figure 4.5). The set, built in Filmways Studios in New York, is introduced via the tour Garber provides to the emissaries from Tokyo. Dotted with horizontal lines representing various subway lines, the command center's map looks nothing like the public map passengers and tourists use to navigate the same system. A similar, though more conventional looking, light-board map is located in the Transit police headquarters, where it is used, Garber informs us, to locate patrolmen within the system. Yet another map, this one with strings of yellow and red LED lights, is shown in the cramped Grand Central Tower command center. Here, a smaller staff observes the flow of the particular subway trains that fall under its purview, their progressions between stations animated by lights that blink on and off. From this smaller satellite command center, the staff incredulously observes the Pelham 1-2-3 train stopped and then decoupled by the hi-jackers, indicated by a single LED that separates from its sequence.

As soon becomes clear, thanks to former motorman Mr. Green/ Harold Longman the hi-jackers have some understanding of the mechanics of the subway car and the system of signals and relays by which the MTA operates. After taking the car, they establish a line of communication with the Transit Authority command center, who, in turn, relays their demands to the adenoidal flu-ridden mayor. Once set in motion, the film bounces between settings: the hi-jacked car with Mr. Blue on the radio, the TA command center where Garber and Carrell manage the chaos; Transit Police HQ where Rico Patron (Jerry Stiller) monitors developments; the Grand Central Tower where movements of the Pelham 1-2-3

Figure 4.5. *Taking of Pelham One Two Three.* Transit Authority Central Command Center.

can be seen live on the model board; the dark tunnel where Patrolman James spies the subway car; the 28th Street subway platform where Chief Inspector Daniels (Julius Harris) waits with an NYPD Special Operations team; the street above where a borough commander (Kenneth McMillan) radios with the police commissioner (Rudy Bond), and Gracie Mansion, where the mayor, his top aide, Warren Lasalle (Tony Roberts), and wife (Doris Roberts) fret over what to do. Each set of characters becomes situationally bound to their setting, giving them a different and limited perspective on the hi-jacking The narrative itself, however, is mobile—it moves with the decisions, information, and action, tracing lines of spoken communication as they flow along wires and radio signals.

One example of location shifting, from late in the film, is the extensive relay sequence that conveys the implications of the city's decision to meet the hi-jackers' demands—conveys in the double sense of both moving diegetic information and moving viewers to different sites. The sick mayor and his aide summon the police commissioner, the Transit Authority chairman (Thomas Barbour), and the comptroller (Marvin Silbersher) to Gracie Mansion, and together with the Mayor's wife they decide, after briefly weighing the political pros and cons, to pay the one million dollars. Pithy pragmatism seals the deal: "Wise up, for Christ's sake. We're trying to run a city not a goddamn democracy!" On his return trip the chief of police calls Harry, the borough commander, who is supervising ground operations by police within and above the tunnel. Harry radios down to Inspector Daniels on the platform, and Daniels, switching from his police radio to a transmitter inside a waiting train, informs Garber at the TA command center. Garber then calls Mr. Blue and informs him of the agreement to pay. The action here, running in tension with the hi-jackers' clock, is driven by the necessary time it takes to communicate between various channels of city and subway administration. The communicative chain in this sequence is rendered more quickly than before, not only because what is going on is much clearer but also because the film has already taught us how to follow the thread of communication: we have learned to trace the networked connections and the pulses that fire between them.

The mode of perception initiated by *Pelham* sustains a pattern of parallel editing and alternation developed within the early years of narrative cinema, a logic described in detail in Raymond Bellour's analysis of D.W. Griffith's *The Lonedale Operator* (1911) (262–77). Like that film, the narrative system that *Pelham* develops relies on a familiarity with networks of transit and communication—in *The Lonedale Operator* these are the train and the telegraph, in *Pelham*, the subway and radio communication. In her study of the imbrication of the railroad and cinema,

Lynne Kirby notes a fundamental instability within both the mobility of rail transit and the moving image:

> The instability of the railroad lies . . . in the very experience of mobility, of a passenger's being once immobile and in rapid transit, lulled to sleep and yet capable of being shocked awake. It also lies in bringing together for a brief period individuals from all walks of life, while dynamizing and hence destabilizing relations among them . . . In cinema, instability is built into the basis of the filmgoing experience: the perceptual illusion of movement is tied to the physical immobility of the spectator and the sequential unfolding of a chain of still images that constitute the basis of every film. The degree to which that instability was either controlled or exploited is a central issue for both the railroad and the cinema during the silent film era. (3)

Kirby's ideas reference several familiar themes. As in earlier experiences of the railroad, the visual culture of the subway in the 1960s and 1970s, whether in *The Incident* or Paul Cadmus's "Subway Symphony" painting, assembles individuals from all walks of life. This is likewise true of the passengers who become hostages in *Pelham*, a gathering that includes an elderly Jewish gentleman, a mother and her two children, a hip young pimp, an Hispanic woman who speaks no English, a young political activist who translates for her, a hippie (who turns out to be a cop), a chic young black woman, and others. All of these characters are identified in a designated section of the credits "The Hostages": The Maid, The Mother, The Homosexual, The Delivery Boy, The Salesman, The Hooker, and so on. Oddly, the credits give the characters confusing designations: no character is definitively coded as gay man, and the "maid" seems merely to be an Hispanic woman. "The Alcoholic" (Louise Larabee) is in fact identical to the Gary Merrill character in *The Incident:* she sleeps through the entire ordeal. As in Kirby's conception, this social gathering is dynamized and de-stabilized by the hi-jacking.

All the passengers are of course bystanders: they variously react to, but are powerless to stop, the men who take them hostage. At the beginning of the film, the hi-jacking is well under way, car decoupled from train, before all (but the dozing alcoholic) have taken notice—each passenger habitually lulled into screening out whatever bizarre goings-on surround his or her regular commute. Wisely, none of the passengers rise against or strike back against the armed men. Yet, they are neither passive nor silent. They worry, they communicate with one another, they ask questions of the hi-jackers, and they talk back—these bystanders, as much as they are able, are *involved*. This relatively small bundle of social relationships constitutes only a fractional part of a greater whole, however. What these passengers cannot see is what only we can: that the action of many city agencies has been set into motion around them—this small car has suddenly become an Archimedean lever that moves an entire city. Here again, a dream common to the railway and the cinema appears: we are connected to everything.

Here, perhaps, is where the narratives of *Death Wish* and *Pelham* are most comparable, if divergent. In *Death Wish*, Kersey's vigilantism is designed to be both a diegetic and extra-diegetic media phenomenon, it galvanizes the populace within the film and extends off the screen, arousing a film audience made weary and dangerously suggestible by everyday street crime. *Pelham* is also designed for such an audience, but its narrative mode and its effects are much different. It pulls us back from the subway car and the platform scene, vivid as they are, to show us the system and shuttle us between the sites that make it work. If *Death Wish* offered a fantasy of mythic violence, *Pelham*—also violent in its own way—offered a more modest, epistemological, and sociological vision. Nora Sayre's *Times* review of *Pelham* approvingly cited it as a "fine piece of reporting," finding its primary fantasy to be "the implication that the city's departments could function so smoothly together" (3 October 1974, 50). Indeed, in *Pelham* the urban infrastructure that so many found to be flagging does—despite bumps and missteps along the way—basically work. The heroes of this film are the civil servants, chiefly Matthau's Garber—who labor in concert to ensure the safety of the passengers, and, in turn, produce the capture of the hi-jackers. The urban machine we see here is unlike the Moloch of Fritz Lang's *Metropolis* (1927) and Allen Ginsberg's "Howl," its maw is much more mundane. Operations supervisor Frank Correll, angry that the decision to pay the hi-jackers continues to disrupt the flow of trains, captures this banality when he complains: "What do they expect for their lousy thirty-five cents? To live forever?"

To further understand the implications of the differences between the films, we might turn again to the *Wall Street Journal*'s review of *Death Wish*, which suggested that, in 1974, the "partial and long-term solutions" on offer such as "better lighting on city streets and improved education and employment opportunities for blacks," were insufficient in the fearful context of urban insecurity, which demanded "immediate and total solutions." As I have argued above, however, this immediacy was purchased through a system of lighting engineering. *Death Wish* built its fantasy city on top of New York locations by overlaying an aesthetics of illumination that aligned with a perversion of the Enlightenment dream of light perfected sight—an identity of vision, certitude, mastery, and action. *Pelham* however, worked with a much different philosophy of light and mise-en-scène and it is instructive to more directly contrast their approaches in order to demonstrate these film's divergent understanding of urban bystanders.

Interviewed in *Millmeter* in 1975, Michael Winner claimed he had the ability to shoot more camera set-ups per day than any other director because he shot "exclusively on location." "Life is lived in real places," Winner declared, "and I shoot in real places" (Carcucci 18). Another key to efficiency, according to him, lay in his management of crews: "I will not permit the egomaniacs on some film crews, the lighting and sound men, to spend 2 hours lighting a shot that can be lit as well in 5 minutes." However, the idea that shooting on location could lend speed to a production was hardly one of consensus. Interviewed for the same issue of *Millimeter* was Owen Roizman, the cinematographer for *Pelham*. Ironically, Roizman offers precisely the opposite view (indicating that he is possibly among one of the very egomaniacs Winner is referring to). After describing the time he usually gets before a film's production to go over the technical ramifications of the chosen locations (2 to 3 weeks), Roizman states, "Most people today think you can save a lot of time and money shooting on actual locations . . . it's become vogue to get that 'real look,' but there are times when a studio-built set can save you. You can work faster and cover many more set-ups per day" (Benderoth 11). The starkly oppositional approaches sketched here are clearly evidenced in both films. The street scenes in *Death Wish* are shot in a high-key style that relies heavily on high-powered arc lighting positioned just outside the frame. Given the imposition of a tight time frame, this would likely have been the best strategy for cinematographer Arthur J. Ornitz.[3] Additionally, Ornitz could have replaced bulbs in the street lamps inside the frame with lights of a different candle power (brighter or dimmer) or swathed these lights to direct their glare and diminish the possibility they would burn out the film image. In the Riverside Park sequences, the inconsistency of the park lights—some burn out the image, others are very dim—seem to indicate hasty set-ups.

My intent here is not to presume the craftmanship of Roizman against a ham-fisted approach taken for *Death Wish*. It is unquestionable that Ornitz possessed considerable photographic expertise. In addition to the uncannily wide-angle interiors, Ornitz's New York scenography is often striking. The credit sequence that follows the Kerseys' return cab ride through New York traffic at dusk, for example, shows the city skyline seemingly rising from a branchy tree line, a synedochal image of the clash between nature and civilization in this modern urban "jungle" that the narrative will soon develop. Highly composed shots like this stand out, however, against the workmanlike lighting set-ups of Kersey's outdoor killing, which mostly follow a simple textbook approach to locational night lighting: lighting of the foreground while using available light in the background (see, for example, Malkiewicz 159). In *Millimeter*, Winner's comments suggest that his approach to the night scenes was blandly improvisational: "I instructed Arthur Ornitz in the effect I wished to achieve. The city helped, it's very visual. . . . We tried to show the work-a-day New York. I often said to Arthur, 'Give me a bit more light on that building down there,' or 'Silhouette it here'" (23).

Roizman's images for *Pelham* are much more consistent, the result of the cinematographer's deliberate and well-planned approach to the subway set (a downtown Brooklyn station that had closed in 1946). This involved supplementing fluorescent lights alongside the subway car's built-in lighting fixtures as well as adding florescent lights to the existing incandescent lighting on the subway platform. Further, because a significant part of the film was set in a subway car without power in a dark underground tunnel, Roizman would frequently be shooting in very low light levels. He arranged for Movielab to "flash" the film stock—partially expose it to light—before shooting, a technique that Roizman boasted had never before been done for an entire film (qtd in McNally 28). This process partially desaturated the color but allowed him to achieve considerable detail in dark images:

> My concept in all the tunnel shots was to keep it so dark that you couldn't see anything—but you could see everything. In other words, you could pick out objects and people in the shadowed areas but it still *felt* very, very dark. Most of that was done with flashing. If I hadn't flashed the film, the blacks would have stayed black. But this way there was transparency in the shadows. (McNally 28)

The desaturation also helped Roizman get "the natural look and kind of funky atmosphere" he was going for, "not exactly documentary, but still dismal and dingy, just as it would be down in the subways" (McNally 27, 28). The ultra-dark tunnel scenes stand out all the more when they are alternated with the hard and even fluorescent lighting of the Transit Authority Command Center. In several scenes when Garber converses with Mr. Blue on the radio, the scene cuts between the well-lit (yet still very drab and dingy) Command Center and a long-shot of Blue in the motorman's cab under low, honey-yellow light.

Like Gordon Willis's approach with *Klute*, Roizman explores the seemingly contradictory possibility of making darkness visible and shadows transparent. In so doing, he troubles a visual aesthetic predicated on the strict separation of light and dark, the former tied to clarity and certainty, the later to unknowability. In *Pelham*, we not only see behind the scenes into a windowless command-center world, decorated by light-boards, that controls the subway system but into dark spaces, either the dim luminescence of a train car with its power shut off or an obscure subway tunnel where, if we strain our eyes, we might see bodies shifting around in the darkness. In both well-lit and darkened spaces, yet always with only part of the picture, human agents struggle to understand what is going on.

Conclusion: Seeing in the Dark, Living in the Dark

Today *Death Wish* is regarded as kitsch. Eight years after its original release, Winner and Bronson were enlisted by schlock-producers Menahem Golan and Yoram Globus of Cannon Films to make *Death Wish II* (1982), which reproduced and even further amplified the plot of the original film, and saw Paul Kersey once again drawn to city streets, this time in the city that defined the 1980s: Los Angeles. Indeed, the original film spawned a cycle of urban revenge narratives including *The Exterminator* (1980), *Ms .45* (1981), *Striking Back* (1982), *Vigilante* (1983), *The Exterminator 2* (1984), and *Savage Streets* (1984). The 1980s brought more *Death Wish* sequels (1985, 1987, 1994) as well as the copycat television series "The Equalizer" (1985–89), Marvel's "The Punisher" comic series (1987–95) and films (1989, 2004) and, more recently, films like *Death Sentence* (2007), Neil Jordan's *The Brave One* (2007), and a movie remake of *The Equalizer* (2014) starring Denzel Washington. 2018 sees the release of a remake of the original *Death Wish* by horror auteur Eli Roth, with Bruce Willis playing Paul Kersey; a reflection perhaps of the renewed conservative energy of the present. All of these iterations follow the same familiar pattern: a meek person subjected to savage violence and trauma on city streets finds it in him- or herself to violently strike back in the name of justice.

The networked, procedural pattern of *Pelham* on the other hand, continued to be used for disaster and thriller films and, it could be argued, was even transformed in "The Wire" (2002–08), the Baltimore-based crime show that shuttled between a multitude of characters and institutional sites (drug dealers, police, the docks, the mayor's office, city schools). As with *Pelham*, the effect of "The Wire" was to elaborate the complexity and entanglement of urban systems, lifting us out of our immediacies to get a better—that is, fuller, less obstructed, less pointedly placed—view.

It would be difficult to trace the myriad ways that a "concern about the lack of concern" has evolved and transformed with the extension of

American urbanization and as geography and technologies of media put us into new relations with the nation and the world. Suffice it to say that the bystander effect is surely a distant relative of the discourse of empathy that preoccupies popular social thinking today. Perhaps though, it is worthwhile to remember how the social psychologists of the 1960s and 1970s, as much as they fed into a pervasive anti-urban bias, also encouraged us to look at the material, situational factors surrounding the individual, forces that defined (by sketching the limits of) how urban life could be lived. Perception and circulation, interrelated and intertwined in modern life, are indeed material factors in many ways external to isolated individual experience.

The idea that safety and street lighting are tightly correlated remains a commonsense idea today. But a report published by the Department of Justice in 1979 already revealed the ways that manufacturing and utility companies had conjured publicity campaigns to trumpet the crime-fighting capacities of improved street lighting technology, and published promotional brochures that made strained connections between reduced crime statistics and better lighting systems (Tien et al. 27). In their own evaluation of street-lighting projects, the DOJ was unable to match the correlations made by previous studies. Not only was there a lack of reliable data on whether street-lighting projects reduced or deterred criminal activity, there were also other factors clouding the issue, including the inconsistency in the design of street lighting projects, and a reliance on expert opinion rather than emergent scientific research (25–26). Yet the study did hold that lighting could help to alleviate fear of crime:

> Although it does not seem to impact the level of crime and may in fact displace crime, street lighting can be assumed to affect the fear of crime. Despite the fact that this assumption is based on very limited statistical evidence, one's intuitive sense that street lighting makes an environment less alien provides an overwhelming argument in support of the assumption. Certainly, in this day and age, a completely darkened street would make one quite fearful and concerned. On the other hand, raising the illumination level to say, daylight levels would not eliminate one's fear of being victimized, since crimes do occur during the day. Actually fear is probably not a linear function of light (i.e., whatever measure or combination of measures characterize light), but is a step-wise function of light; that is, the level of fear remains relatively constant between certain ranges of light and changes significantly at other ranges. (93–94)

In making the point that fear is not a "linear function of light" the DOJ's lighting projects study mitigated the crime-fighting properties of light that underlay the logic of *Death Wish*.

Through the various urban renewals and renaissances of the late 1970s and 1980s, there emerged a more dualistic city than ever before. As Mike Davis's critiques of the urbanism of Los Angeles have shown, fear was concretized by the architectural and infrastructural transformation of the city, which produced increased socio-spatial segregation, borders patrolled by private police, the "defensible space" of gated communities, and the increased policing and ghettoization of the poor and the homeless. These changes happened in the background of spectacular renovations to the city core such as the development of new hubs of global business and the construction of large-scale entertainment and shopping districts (Chelsea Pier in New York, Navy Pier in Chicago, Faneuil Hall in Boston to name a few). The dialectic of surveillance and spectacle that underpinned urban development was already abundantly evident in the visuality of *Death Wish*.

But urban decline also facilitated subcultures, forged in darkness, that would be propelled into the mainstream and transform American—and global—culture. The downtown art scene, the gay liberation movement, hip-hop, punk, and disco, and a new generation of underground film culture were all in their own way born in the shadows of the 1970s city. These subcultures were formed by participants who found possibility in the ambiguous spaces of the city, and whose social involvements were purposively illegible to a previous generation of bystanders.

Conclusion

The Lure of the City

This book expands on a series of snapshots drawn from a cluster of popular films: Bree alone in her apartment and wandering through a discotheque; Popeye Doyle catching the eye of his quarry through a glass window, Men scrambling across Detroit's disintegrating landscape, Paul Kersey with a gun under a street lamp, Lt. Garber of the Metro Transit Authority puzzling over flows of trains represented on a lightboard. Unfolded into their respective urban histories and contexts, it becomes possible to see a culture faced toward the city, encouraged to figure out what possibilities its surfaces held, and, in the process, being enticed into the city. How, though, did the city turn out? What, if anything did this cluster of films foretell?

As the 1970s continued into the 1980s, the American city did not recede from film screens, nor did the emergence of the blockbuster entirely eclipse the crime genre. Likewise, attitudes toward the city appeared to remain stable: a 1977 survey funded by Housing and Urban Development found, in the words of *AIA Journal*, that "the majority believes the nation would be worse off without cities, but does not want to live in them" ("How Americans See Cities" May 1978: 20).

Despite this seeming ambivalence, the 1970s does witness an important shift in urban consciousness. In the 1960s the questions posed by and to white Americans were about whether the city was suitable and sustainable for living in, and whether the central city as a form would survive at all. The answer to these questions was clearer toward the end of the 1970s. By the end of the decade, writes urban historian Jon C. Teaford, "journalists, planners, public officials, and scholars all seemed to believe that America's cities had turned the corner," the crisis, these boosters proclaimed, was over (116).

Yet a whole new series of questions emerged. The city was not the same and this was not an era that returned the city to the centralized formation of the past:

> The central city would not advance by asserting itself as the hub of all metropolitan life, the focus of all retailing, entertainment, business, and government. It would sell itself as offering an "urban" way of life different from the prevailing suburban norm, a lifestyle that would appeal to young, childless professionals, tourists, and convention goers. (Teaford 116)

At the same time, however, "urban" would also soon become a coded term for African-American and Latino/a communities; communities that in an increasingly formalized manner were being aggressively policed and separated from the rest of the city.

What has been widely called the "urban renaissance" of the 1980s and 1990s was in fact anchored by a series of cultural formations perhaps more internally divergent than Teaford describes. The 1970s and 1980s see the spontaneous growth of new forms of art and subculture within the interstitial space created by de-industrialization and de-population. At the same time, downtown areas were being renovated for the purposes of shopping, tourism, and business through large-scale real estate developments. Whereas the former largely rejected the values of the white suburbs in favor of the vitality of the urban realm, the latter would import and amplify suburban modes of consumerism and security to create new boundaries between social classes, and between inside and out. Where part of the new urban way of life was predicated on an openness to the possibilities that inhered within the socially and physically fragmented city—its open spaces and cultural blending—the other part would see the city as a tabula rasa for a new, largely white, consumer culture. The way of life that Teaford describes, in fact, pulled in the different directions evinced and explored by the urban crisis crime films: one direction outward-facing and generally open to possibility and exposure, the other inward-facing, fearful, and closed.

The reversal of white flight had already been forecast in 1951, when the 8th meeting of the Congres International d'Architecture Moderne (CIAM)—the body largely responsible, under the leadership of Le Corbusier, for espousing the modernist open space designs that had led to metropolitan sprawl—convened under the theme "The Heart of the City" to address the problem of downtown city centers. The architect credited with introducing the archetypal design of the indoor shopping mall, Victor Gruen, committed himself throughout the 1950s and 1960s to the uphill battle of creating pedestrian-centered shopping districts in the downtown cores of cities like Fort Worth, Kalamazoo, and Fresno (Wall, 2005, 126–77). In the mid-1970s, the developer and planner James Rouse, who had also previously designed suburban shopping plazas and residential areas, likewise shifted his gaze downtown to conceive "festival marketplaces" like Faneuil Hall in Boston and Harborplace in Baltimore. More successful than Gruen's designs, these developments repurposed disused sites of industry and architectural castoffs (Harborplace was built at a steamship terminal that had been dormant since 1950) for shopping arcades and entertainment.

On the cover of *Time* in 1981, Rouse was dubbed "the man who made cities fun again." Such boosterism was a strange echo of the ironic nickname given to New York City at the end of the 1960s: "Fun City." In the midst of the debilitating 1966 transit strike, Mayor John Lindsay had made the Pollyannaish remark "I still think it's a fun city," and the sobriquet stuck as a smirking reference to the various forms of the city's ruination. But by 1980, even as cities contended with increased crime, unemployment, and the nascent crack epidemic, a national magazine could now proclaim without irony that the cities were once again fun.

The fun cities of the 1980s however, were really just zones sealed off from larger downtown areas. The lustrous designs of architect-developer John Portman—Peachtree Center in Atlanta, The Bonaventure Hotel in downtown Los Angeles, and the unambiguously-named Renaissance Center in Detroit—were constructed as enclosed citadels, divided from the streets that surrounded them by earthen berms, obfuscated entrances, and skywalks that floated above streets and sidewalks. Such constructions, Mike Davis points out, are themselves reactions to swelling zones of an urban underclass:

> The wave of ghetto insurrections between 1964 and 1969 powerfully concentrated the attention of urban developers and corporate architects on the problem of cordoning off the downtown financial districts, and other zones of high property values, from inner-city residential neighborhoods. Genuine public spaces, whether as parks, streets, places of entertainment, or in urban transport, were devalued as amenities and redefined as planning problems to be eliminated or privatized. (Davis, 111)

Crossing the glossy thresholds of Portman's buildings, one enters a secure and air conditioned world of ersatz urbanism, dotted with tiered greenery, escalators, fountains, and shopping. Contrary to Frederic Jameson, Davis argues that Portman's postmodern aesthetic expresses not the cultural logic of a globally integrated capitalism, but a symptom of a global financial crisis with a proclivity for overbuilding (109), a "massified modernism" (113) and, more locally, an architecture of fear.

The fortification of urban architecture also extended into housing design, following the popularity of Oscar Newman's concept of "defensible space." After conducting studies on crime rates in apartment high-rises through the 1960s and 1970s, Newman proposed that insecurity could be mitigated through designs creating a perception of territory, a sense achieved through low-lying, inward facing complexes that afforded residents clear views of the surrounding streets and courtyards. Newman's ideas found context within the heightened concern over bystander apathy surrounding the murder of Kitty Genovese. His conjunction of design and surveillance also presage the development of gated communities, and the growing identification of the outside urban world with criminality.

James Q. Wilson and George L. Kelling's influential "Broken Windows Theory" of policing also extended this discourse, arguing that disorder in the material urban environment—such as broken windows in a building, or a vandalized and abandoned automobile—was homologous with the disorder caused by disruptive and disorderly individuals, from drug users to rowdy youths to muggers. Wilson and Kelling argued that if police could intervene at a relatively low level, they could substantially improve the safety of a community. These precepts were subsequently instilled within the aggressive policing practices of major cities, including New York's infamous "stop and frisk," and the "zero-tolerance" policies behind police violence against people of color across the country. These practices can in certain ways be traced back to the rhetorical fusion, within Wilson and Kelling's theory, of people with their physical surroundings. "The unchecked panhandler," they write, "is, in effect, the first broken window. Muggers and robbers, whether opportunistic or professional, believe they reduce their chances of being caught if they operate on streets where potential victims are already intimidated by prevailing conditions" (Web). Broken windows theory thus reproduces the haunting idea—developed and amplified through popular film—of crime as suffusing the urban environment, collapsing humans and the physical environment together to create an encompassing danger.

In areas adjacent to the downtown renaissance, vibrant forms of cultural production were taking shape and gaining notice within mass culture. Much of this production emanated from musically based subcultures like punk rock, disco, and hip-hop, but there was also significant activity from art practices, including experimental and independent filmmaking, dance, performance, new music, and various avant-garde combinations thereof. The incipient global pop cultural phenomenon that many of these practices would become in the 1980s and 1990s, not to mention the appropriation of their aesthetics by the culture industry, has blurred their common post-industrial urban context. In fact, all these practices were shaped within the physical spaces made newly available by white flight. Though Soho galleries, discos, and performance spaces would quickly become part of the white gentrification of downtown areas and absorbed within the commodification of urban lifestyles, for a short time they drew on the emancipatory ideas of the 1960s to create new kinds of collective experience.[1]

Likewise, but in different shapes, punk and hip-hop rooted themselves within the castoff spaces of the city. For punk, adopting an iconography of refuse and delinquency was largely conceptual, forming a subcultural language that identified with spaces of negation as a way of marking itself off from suburban culture. As the Los Angeles-based band FEAR would sing in "I Love Living in the City" (1978): "I spent my whole life in the city, where junk is king and the air smells shitty; People puking everywhere, Piles of blood, scabs, and hair; Bodies wasted in the streets, People dying on the streets; But the suburban scumbags they don't care; They just get fat and dye their hair."

In contrast to the largely white, occasionally decadent, phenomenon of downtown punk, hip-hop emerged from the Bronx, perhaps the area most physically devastated by urban renewal. Hip-hop's original pillars—turntablism, b-boying (breakdancing), rapping, and graffiti—encompass enterprising cultural practices that repurposed everyday materials into powerful expressive forms. For neighborhood block parties at which MC-ing over mixed and scratched records would take place, power for sound systems would be poached from lamp posts. Just as DJ-ing required only a handful of records, breakdancing required only a boom box and a cardboard pad; rapping only the skillful manipulation of one's voice; graffiti, a marker or aerosol paint easily purchased at a hardware store. Though widely stigmatized as a signifier of urban degeneration, many forms of graffiti added vibrant panels of color to the dull chromatics of decay. Applied to cross-town subway cars, this color could be set in motion, networking bold names throughout the city.

Though the boundaries between disco, punk, and hip-hop have often been reified in lay histories, in fact the mixed clientele, musical programming, and modes of performance at New York's 1980s nightclubs, including The Mudd Club, The Ritz, The Roxy, and Danceteria, afforded ample opportunity for cross-cultural dialogue and hybridity (see Lawrence 2016). Sociospatial differences were also provisionally overcome within the art world by groups of artists eager to depart from the formalism of the 1960s and 1970s. Much of the work of this crossing happened through activist-artist groups and galleries such as South Bronx-based Fashion Moda, and Collaborative Projects Inc. (Colab). Fashion Moda was established in 1978 by Stefan Eins as a way of bringing together

Bronx-based graffiti artists and breakdancers and artists from Lower Manhattan (Gumpert, 2006). The latter included Jon Fekner, who, like Keith Haring, Jean-Michel Basquiat, and Jenny Holzer, broke from the confines of traditional gallery space to use a range of city surfaces as a medium. In 1980, Fekner painted phrases like “Decay,” “Broken Promises/Falsas Promesas,” and “Save our School,” on decaying buildings on Charlotte Street in the Bronx, an area devastated by abandonment and ruin. Further south, the 1980 Times Square Show put together by Colab and Fashion Moda, took over an abandoned massage parlor, bringing together over a hundred artists including Kenny Scharf, Charles Ahearn, Holzer, Haring, and Basquiat and graffiti writers like Crash and Blaze to fill the space. The spirit of this time also finds expression in films like *Downtown 81* (1981), in which Basquiat plays a wandering protagonist, weaving through streets and nightclubs, playing his saxophone, painting on walls, as well in Ahearn’s Super-8mm proto no-wave production *Deadly Art of Survival* (1979), a DIY kung-fu story set in the Alfred E. Smith housing projects in the Bronx with an amateur cast of locals.

In music, art, and the variety of cultural practices associated with what was called the “downtown” scene in New York, a radical openness occurred, creating new forms of urbanism predicated on creatively remaking the city, overcoming divisions between inside and out, and generating points of contact between diverse socioeconomic groups. Such acts, in turn, could be iterated within the empty downtown area of any city. Though the examples above are New York-specific, regional downtown scenes and the construction of artists’ lofts took place in cities across the country (Jim Stratton’s how-to guide *Pioneering in the Urban Wilderness* [1977], for example, shared stories of loft construction in Chicago, Minneapolis, Denver, St. Louis, and a host of other cities).[2]

Between the downtown renaissance that physically resculpted downtowns while cleaving them from other parts of the city and the various urban subcultures that developed within and across de-industrialized spaces, it becomes possible to glimpse a larger cultural conflict between the external world of the city and the inward-facing mindset radiating from the suburbs. The recurring criticism of John Portman’s projects (and others like them) was that they “turn away” from their urban contexts. Such a gesture is repeated in fortress-like downtown structures that create vast blank walls facing the street and sidewalk, usually with little indication of what lies within. Skywalks and flyovers, in turn, create *Metropolis*-like effects that ensure that commuting white-collar workers and shoppers need rarely let their feet touch the street.

Yet while it is possible to distinguish a field of tension within urban culture on the ground, within the realm of popular and visual culture the role of the central city both its landscape and sociality, continued to be ambivalent, if also prized. In 1980, Ronald Reagan—the key progenitor of law and order conservatism—conducted a campaign dedicated to cultivating signifiers of (white) American tradition. Making a stop in the South Bronx, Reagan set up a press appearance in front of one of the gutted buildings onto which Jon Fekner had painted the word "Decay." Whereas Fekner's purpose was to inspire reflection on architectural desiccation, in Reagan's appropriation the message was simplified: cities = decay. No matter that Reagan was shouted down by local residents (whom he later vigorously argued with on camera), the opposition between the world Reagan was building and the urban way of life was made clear.

Within films, television, comic books, video games the "urban" became a site ready at hand to connote all the things the suburbs was not. Among other qualities, the urban assumed a textural quality introduced by 1970s crime films: grittiness. For his spoof of the "Daredevil" comic, "Grit!" Alan Moore writes an opening scene that charts the formal dimensions of the grit aesthetic (figure 5.1 on page 202). The parody involves hyperbolizing the apparent "grittiness" of the Daredevil series, especially its reliance on Hell's Kitchen as a setting. It begins by introducing "Dourdevil" in over-the-top New York vernacular:

> Noo Yawk is grim, and gritty, and realistic. There are big black buildings with little squares on [them], and water towers and manholes and lots of other gritty stuff . . . And giant black men. Hundreds of giant black men in vests and (sic) woollen hats carrying large radios. Gritty? Realistic? Buddy, you don't know the half of it. The city is a death trap, a suicide rap. Or is that New Jersey? I know its (sic) either one or the other. Which is the one with all the hookers and winos? Is that Noo Yawk? Wait a minute, am I thinking of Detroit? How gritty is Detroit?

Moore cannily identifies the formal elements that go into building the conventional gritty-city montage. In foregrounding declarations of its "realistic" nature and the compounding of "gritty" with "realistic" he satirizes the Daredevil series' (under the authorship of Frank Miller) hyperbolization of New York—the idea that if tall buildings with little white dots, water towers, black men, hookers, and winos are combined, a particularly gritty form of reality is created. In Moore's spoof, the blind superhero grossly misinterprets the urban scene he is emplaced in. Standing on the body of a dog on a seedy street corner covered in garbage and populated by hookers and a shirtless man with a boom box, Daredevil

Figure 5.1. Alan Moore and Mike Collins's *Daredevil* spoof "Grit!"

says to himself: "I smell expensive perfume . . . I'm standing on some sort of fur rug, there's music . . . I must be in the Playboy mansion!"

Whereas the contrasting ideas of urbanity and conventional forms for the city's representation have discernable outlines in the 1980s, scrolling backward through the previous decade tends to blur the boundaries. Surely, the crime films of the 1970s were fomented within a new stage in the longstanding tradition of anti-urbanism, but they also partook of the urban, both in their locations, and in their evocation of the lure of the city.

The snapshots this book assembles reveal a relationship between popular film and America's urban culture that has for too long been occluded by the unwieldy heading "neo-noir." Inasmuch as this designation outlines a highly referential or self-conscious filmmaking mode, rather than a mode that exploits the camera's predisposition toward physical reality to create worlds *within* everyday, contemporary life, it is a label that has failed to capture the unique relationship between crime film and urban life. The connection to the city generated by the crime films of the 1970s was not merely gained through their photographic documentation of urban locales, but rather the way these locales were enlisted into a formal armature of observation, encounter, and pursuit, a topicality of plot and theme, and translated through cinematographic technique and technology. As Moore's parody of the Daredevil comic reveals, the reality of urban representation was a recognizable aesthetic construction or effect. These films diverge from neo-noir in their expressed affinity for this particular effect, one dedicated to interpreting the world of now. Moreover, in contrast with films like *The Long Goodbye* and *Chinatown*, the urban-crisis crime films are pointedly anti-nostalgic. Instead of evoking a desire for a return to the past (a signature preoccupation of the Reagan era), these films root themselves within a strange present. Without valorizing the surfaces of the modern and new, these films portray life amongst ruins; both the physical ruins of decaying infrastructure and the ruins of a social landscape as relations of propinquity unravel.

Designed as thrillers, crime films are also marked by anticipation, forward movement, and inquisitive observation rather than a nostalgic thrum. Chase and pursuit align with an uncertainly advancing motility and mobile gaze. As much as detectives are hampered by a world that no longer offers unambiguous solutions, the motivation to move, spontaneously scramble, and actively explore is retained. Given this speculative orientation, it is no coincidence that the abandoned, decaying landscapes of the 1970s crime film would be subsequently taken up by science-fiction and fantasy films like *The Warriors* (1979), *Escape from New York* (1981), and *Blade Runner* (1982), that further expanded the urban imaginary.

In the Hollywood film of the Reagan era and beyond, the American city becomes a functional reserve of danger and sexual energy for suburbs. In *National Lampoon's Vacation* (1983), *Desperately Seeking Susan* (1985), *Ferris Bueller's Day Off* (1986), *Adventures in Babysitting* (1987), *Bonfire of the Vanities* (1990), *Grand Canyon* (1991), *Judgment Night* (1993), *Milk Money* (1994), and many others, the pleasures of the gritty city or the danger of an underworld milieu can be readily accessed from suburban enclaves via expressway and onramp. That is, within the geography of popular film, the "urban" that Teaford describes acts in concert with the suburbs, creating a Dionysian counterbalance always at hand, but occluding the sociopolitical conditions, and economic interdependence, that keep these spaces separate and materially unequal in actuality.

The approach taken in this book is to examine recurring tropes and situations, rather than narrative wholes because, I believe, for certain spectators (such as myself) it is possible to detach urban images from their narrative wholes, indulging in their sensation without necessarily internalizing their ideological implication. If I have suggested throughout that many of these films offer a sense of possibility it is never with the intent to claim they offer utopian visions of urban living, or that they can be redeemed to show a politically progressive blueprint for urban life. Rather, like the larger plots in which they appear, the topoi I examine skew to the edges of business as usual. Like the sociology of Erving Goffman, crime films frequently probe the heart-pounding border between subjective normality and the free-fall of alterity. Never mind that these film's resolutions might seem socially regressive, it is the tense sensation they offer that productively destabilizes. This is why, to make a naked value judgment, *The French Connection* is better than *Death Wish*. In the latter, our perception is relentlessly organized, directed toward one particular aim—the satisfyingly distanced ease of annihilation permitted by a weapon that always finds its target in unambiguous light. The strange energy at the core of *The French Connection* though is the ambiguity of appearance, the thrilling possibility of exposure, and of contact made across space. Where *Death Wish* violently installs social distances, *The French Connection* potentiates their shattering within the flux of urban streets.

For middle-class Americans, both those who live in the suburbs and those moving back to central cities, the word "crime" continues to summon a host of associations, settings, and scenarios drawn from cable news, videogames, television, comic books, and film. Given that the provenance of these associations rest as much within the realm of fiction and representation than firsthand experience, it is important to remember that within our culture, crime is a genre, an image, and a cliché.

Delving into this repository reveals how cinematic experience restlessly settles into the everyday. Crime in cinema and the discourse of crimes in society are ultimately very different, and yet both recombine within a spatial imaginary together to become, as Alexander Kluge put it, "the film in the spectator's head." (qtd in Hansen 2012, 249). Understanding crime as a medium that reveals aspects of the urban imagination rather than reflects urban actuality provides a way of thinking through the way that commercial film visually acts on and becomes part of our world. The persistence and modest popularity of the crime film, its flourishing in the early 1970s, and its continual fascination with the spaces of the city betrays a still unspoken bond between our mind and the urban form.

Notes

Introduction

1. New Hollywood's commitment to realism is argued by Robert Kaufman, "New Hollywood Sees Things as They Are," *Los Angeles Times*, December 14, 1969, R22. On the ways that various regions attempted to attract feature film production in the 1970s, see Phyllis Funke, "How You Gonna Keep 'em Down in Hollywood After They've Seen the Sticks: Filmmaking Far From Hollywood," *New York Times*, Sept. 22, 1974, 135.

2. On the history of this office, see James Sanders, Martin Scorsese, and Nora Ephron, *Scenes from the City: Filmmaking in New York, 1966–2006* (Rizzoli International Publications, 2006); and McLain Clutter, "Imaginary Apparatus: Film Production and Urban Planning in New York City, 1966–1975," *Grey Room* 35, Spring 2009, 58–89.

3. The 1938 manual includes the following provisions: "284 (3) Recommended restrictions include the following: . . . (g) Prohibition of the occupancy of properties except by the race for which they are intended"; and "289 (1) Adequacy of Civic, Social, and Commercial Centers . . . Schools should be appropriate to the needs of the new community, and they should not be attended in large numbers by inharmonious racial groups."

4. For a description of Willis's and Roizman's techniques, see interviews in *Masters of Light*, (Schaefer and Salvato, 1986).

5. Chicago is did not create a film commission and is rarely filmed in the 1970s for commercial features, reputedly because of Mayor Richard J. Daley's opposition to the possibility of a negative portrayal (Bernstein, *Hollywood on Lake Michigan: 100 Years of Chicago and the Movies*, 1998) and the city's historical association with criminality (Sobcynski, 2013, 28).

6. Christopher P. Wilson (2005) supplies a reading of Peter Maas's source novel and police politics of this era, connecting it to traditions of Progressivist police exposé such as Lincoln Steffens's *The Shame of the Cities* (1904).

7. On the relation between the literature of the flâneur/detective and urban spectatorship, see Dana Brand, *The Spectator and the City in 19th Century American Literature* (1991).

8. Flashback narration in noir is used less, in the manner of the whodunit, to logically explain a criminal act than by narrators explaining their deepening entanglement in criminal acts.

9. This tendency is corrected by James Naremore in *More than Night: Film Noir in its Contexts* (1998), as well as by Dimendberg.

10. Marc Vernet, for example, challenges the commonly accepted parameters of noir by pointing to the prevalent use of darkness in crime and mystery films of the 1930s ("Film noir on the Edge of Doom," in *Shades of Noir* [1993], 1–31).

11. Consider too that the term noir—first developed within French film criticism of the 1950s—was taken up by American critics in the late 1960s, but did not enter popular discourse for another decade, around the time that the early 1980s neo-noir films referred to by Silver and Ward and Jameson begin to appear. Between 1970 and 1976, *Variety* and the *New York Times* use the term noir only a handful of times (*Variety* uses it solely in reference to the noir program at the 1971 Los Angeles International Film Festival).

12. As Todorov points out, many of S. S. Van Dine's rules, which forbade love interests for the detective, the existence of secret societies, and long descriptive passages in favor of distilled exercises of deduction, would exclude the hardboiled thriller and most detective adventure forms.

13. The chase as a cinematic trope has been examined primarily within scholarship on early cinema. See, for example, Tom Gunning (1984), Richard Abel (1994) Nöel Burch (1990), Jonathan Auerbach (2007), André Gaudreault (2009).

14. See, for example, Rafter (2006).

15. As an example, consider this sweeping statement on 1970s police and detective films from Douglas Kellner and Michael Ryan's *Camera Politica* (1988): "As the decade progressed, the shortcomings of the liberal agenda became more emphatically marked, and the people eventually fled from an ineffectual Democrat to an affirmative Republican. Not surprisingly, perhaps, the detective genre swung back into line" (84).

16. Though broadly vilified in Robert Caro's extensive biography, *The Power Broker* (1974) and Berman's *All that Is Solid Melts into Air* (1988), recent appraisals of Moses' projects have been more nuanced. See the essays collected by Hillary Ballon and Kenneth T. Jackson in *Robert Moses and the Modern City: The Transformation of New York* (New York: W. W. Norton & Co., 2007), especially Robert Fishman's "Revolt of the Urbs: Robert Moses and His Critics" (122–129).

17. Most notably Erving Goffman, *The Presentation of Self in Everyday Life*, (Garden City, NY: Doubleday, 1959); *Behavior in Public Places: Notes on the Social Organization of Gatherings* (New York: Free Press of Glencoe, 1963); and *Relations in Public: Microstudies of the Public Order*, (New York: Harper & Row, 1972).

18. For fascinating documentation of the various artistic and photographic movements that inhabited major American cities between the 1960s and 1980s, see *The City Lost and Found: Capturing New York, Los Angeles and Chicago 1960–1980* (2014).

19. I follow the historical frame provided by Robert Beauregard in *Voices of Decline* (1993). Beauregard suggests that in the discourse on cities, the beginning

of the 1970s represents a transition from the period of urban decline to a period of urban crisis (1993, 130–33).

20. The literature debating the character, definition, and existence of postmodernism is vast, but it is worth pointing out that several key works were released within a roughly ten-year period between the 1970s and 1980s. Umberto Eco's *Il Costume Di Casa* was published in 1973 and translated into English in 1986 as *Faith in Fakes: Travels in Hyperreality*. In 1979 *The Postmodern Condition: A Report on Knowledge*, Jean François-Lyotard's report to the Conseil des universities du Quebec was published, which discerned an emergent "incredulity toward metanarratives." Jean Baudrillard publishes *Simulacra and Simulation* in 1981, and in 1984 *The New Left Review* publishes Jameson's essay "Postmodernism, or, the Cultural Logic of Late Capitalism."

21. In *The Cinema of Urban Crisis: Seventies Film and the Reinvention of the City* (2014), Webb traces a path similar to the one explored here, but expanding to take in the cinematic representations of a number of global cities and their relationship to historical developments of the 1970s.

Chapter 1

1. There is also a notable episode of "Seinfeld" (1989–1998) where the primary characters become lost in a parking garage, inducing existential angst.

2. The flame from the cigarette lighter in this scene is notably non-illuminating. It is a point of light that draws our attention and locates a figure in space, but does not serve to show the figure any more clearly.

3. Alan J. Pakula Papers, *All the President's Men* Production File, Folio 47, "Visual Research Materials." (Margaret Herrick Film Library, Los Angeles, CA).

4. Built in the 1960s, Century City sits, ironically on the former studio back lot of 20th Century Fox.

5. Gledhill's incisive critique reveals how despite depicting an ostensibly feminist lead, *Klute* reaffirms patriarchal ideology. Gledhill's structural analysis identifies the film's "picaresque" investigative movement, but suggests that its primary function is to realize the city along the lines of Bunyan's Vanity Fair, as a site of moral turpitude, rather than as a contingent historical space. Jameson writes of *Klute*, and Pakula's other conspiracy films, as exercises in "cognitive mapping," an allegorical form that models a way to grasp a contemporary geopolitical system of late capitalism whose vastness constantly eludes apprehension. For other analyses of *Klute* see Robin Wood, "Klute" (1972), Colin MacCabe "Realism: Notes on some Brechtian theses," (1974), and Diane Giddis "The Divided Woman: Bree Daniels in *Klute*" (1976).

6. Jenkins' designs for Bree's apartment are published in "Designed for Film: The Hollywood Art Director," *Film Comment*, 14 (3), May-June 1978, 53.

7. This deep dark aesthetic is often compromised by video and digital transfer. Even if one views *Klute* (or Willis's other work from this period) in a darkened room, the limited dynamic range of the digital transfers currently available do not capture the darkness that comes through the same images on celluloid.

8. Examples of psychedelic happenings abound within the various youth sub-genres of the 1960s and 1970s, especially those produced by Roger Corman at American International Pictures. (*Psych-Out* ([968], *Beyond the Valley of the Dolls* [1970]).

9. On Benjamin's conception of the prostitute, see also Susan Buck-Morss, *The Dialectics of Seeing* (Cambridge, MA, and London: MIT Press, 1991), 184–85.

10. Todd McCarthy argues that Willis's "obscurantist" tendencies actually irked the American cinematographic establishment, explaining why he was never nominated for an Academy Award in the 1970s, despite being widely appreciated by younger cinematographers (McCarthy, "Hollywood Style '84, *Film Comment*, 20 (2), March–April, 1984, 33).

11. Willis was arguably influenced by the style of Raoul Coutard, who filmed similar backlit images in his photography for Jean-Luc Godard.

12. The photo, for example, was used in the *Frontline* documentary *Watergate Plus 30* (Foster Wiley, 2003) as interviewees describe Nixon's resignation.

13. In "*Klute* Notes #11," Alan J. Pakula Papers, Margaret Herrick Film Library.

14. 140 Broadway was also significant, like the Seagram Building, for its incorporation of an open space plaza at its base. This plaza, not depicted in *Klute*, featured the dramatic sculpture, by Isamu Noguchi, of a large cube balanced on one of its corners.

15. For example, in the climax to the Atlanta-based cop film *Sharky's Machine* (1981), before the villain Billy Score (Henry Silva) crashes through an upper story window of John Portman's Peachtree Plaza building to his death, he is shot in silhouette against blinding outside sunlight, much in the manner of the examples I have been discussing.

Chapter 2

1. For a good history of the police procedural as a genre unto itself, see Haden Guest, *The Police Procedural Film: Law and Order in American Cinema 1930–1960* (PhD dissertation, University of California Los Angeles, 2005).

2. *Cops and Robbers* was directed by Aram Avakian, who also made the experimental countercultural film *End of the Road* in 1969.

3. Television at this time, however, was expanding the boundaries of acceptable content within a different set of economic and regulatory frameworks. See Elana Levine's book *Wallowing in Sex: The New Sexual Culture of 1970s American Television* (2007).

4. While they did attempt to follow in the footsteps of Eddie Egan, Hantz and Greenberg's super-cop celebrity would soon begin a slow fade. The 1973 Doubleday book by reporter Whittemore, fell in with a raft of other mass-market tomes capitalizing on true crime cops and the film received poor notices. The film release was accompanied by a one off comic for Red Circle (an imprint of Archie Comics) and, in 1975, a pilot for a TV series that was never picked up.

5. Robert M. Pavich, "That Little Old Lady May Be a Cop," *Detroit News*, January 31, 1971, 1A; Evan Maxwell, "Scenes from 'The Undercover Follies,' "

Boston Globe, April 21, 1974, 50. "Harriet Stix, 'Charlie's Ugly Angels' Fight Crime," *Los Angeles Times*, July 5, 1977, G1.

6. Ironically, this camera style would be taken up full-bore in the proto-reality procedural "COPS" (1989–present).

7. This letter is found in the William Friedkin papers held by the Margaret Herrick library, Los Angeles (folio #6 *French Connection* correspondence).

8. In this sense, the HBO series "The Wire" (2002–2008), which likewise maps the obscure global economic circuits that bring drugs into Baltimore, is an inheritor of *The French Connection*'s aesthetic.

9. See James J. Gibson and Anne D. Pick, "Perception of Another's Looking Behavior," (1963).

Chapter 3

1. On the changing racial geography of film exhibition during this time, see Gerald Butters *From Sweetback to Super Fly: Race and Film Audiences in Chicago's Loop* (2014).

2. There is also conflicting information on whether the soundtrack composed by Holland-Dozier-Holland exists. As late as August 2, 1973 (ten days before the premiere), *The L.A. Sentinel* reported that Motown was planning a promotional campaign for its release of the *Detroit 9000* soundtrack (and that this was a harbinger of a reunion between the record company and the writing team).

3. It has also been claimed the Daley's opposition to film production began after he saw the depiction of a Chicago police officer taking a bribe on the Chicago-based TV Show "M Squad" (1957–1960) (Sobczynski 28). A handful of films were shot in Chicago during this time, including *Medium Cool* (1968), *T.R Baskin* (1971), and even the Arthur Marks directed *Monkey Hu$tle* (1976). This policy begins to abate in the late 1970s and early 1980s, with the establishment of the Chicago Film Commission.

4. For another example of this practice see Peter Stanfield's discussion "Intent to Speed: Cyclical Production, Topicality, and the 1950s Hot Rod Movie," (2012), which discusses how the hot-rod cycle of the 1950s promised the vicarious thrill of street racing in bold promotional strategies only to offer banal montage on screen (9).

Chapter 4

1. Milgram, Darley, and Latané cite each other frequently in their respective research, indicating that they were at the very least professionally acquainted, if not close collaborators (as their congenial research constructs seem to suggest).

2. I witnessed a similar outcome during the Toronto blackout of 2003, when downtown intersections were directed by businessmen on one block, and a homeless person on the next.

3. There is, unfortunately, no account that I have found by Ornitz of his work on *Death Wish*.

Conclusion

1. Andy Warhol's Factory, of course, references the artist's avowed interest in mass production, but also the initial industrial character of the spaces the artist and his retinue occupied (the second space Warhol moved the factory to was formerly the building of a piano company). Aside from disco and various styles of art, lofts in New York City also fostered a burgeoning jazz scene that had been marginalized by the conservative booking practices at the city's more established venues (Gendron, 48).

2. See also Burrard et al. *The City Lost and Found.*

Bibliography

Abel, Richard. *The Ciné Goes to Town: French Cinema 1896–1914*. University of California Press, 1994.

Aletti, Vince. *The Disco Files 1973–78: New York's Underground, Week by Week*. DJhistory.com, 2009.

Altman, Rick. *Film/Genre*. BFI Publishing, 1999.

Andersen, Thom. "Red Hollywood," *Un-American Hollywood: Politics and Film in the Blacklist Era*, edited by Peter Stanfield, Frank Krutnik, Brian Neve, Steve Neale. Rutgers University Press, 2007, pp. 225–63.

Armstrong, Michael F. *They Wished They Were Honest the Knapp Commission and New York City Police Corruption*. Columbia University Press, 2012.

Auerbach, Jonathan. *Body Shots: Early Cinema's Incarnations*. University of California Press, 2007.

Avila, Eric. *Popular Culture in the Age of White Flight: Fear and Fantasy in Suburban Los Angeles*. University of California Press, 2004.

Bakhtin, M. M. *The Dialogic Imagination: Four Essays*, translated by Michael Holquist and Caryl Emerson. University of Texas Press, 1981.

Ballon, Hilary, and Kenneth T. Jackson. *Robert Moses and the Modern City: The Transformation of New York*. 1st ed. W. W. Norton & Co., 2007, 1972, pp. 30–36.

Baumgold, Julie. "Cop Couples: Till Death Do Us Part." *New York*, June 19, 1972, pp. 31–36.

Beauregard, Robert A. *Voices of Decline: The Post-War Fate of US Cities*. Blackwell, 1993.

Bellour, Raymond. *The Analysis of Film*, edited by Constance Penley. Indiana University Press, 2000.

Benderoth, Mick. "Cinematographer Rises to Challenge." *Millimeter* Feb. 1975, pp. 18–20.

Benjamin, Walter. *Selected Writings Vol. 4* (1938–1940), edited by Michael W. Jennings, Howard Eiland. Belknap Press, 1996.

Bernstein, Arnie. *Hollywood on Lake Michigan: 100 Years of Chicago and the Movies*. 1st ed. Lake Claremont Press, 1998.

Blake, Peter. *God's Own Junkyard; the Planned Deterioration of America's Landscape.* 1st ed.. Holt, Rinehart and Winston, 1964.
Blake, Richard Aloysius. *Street Smart: The New York of Lumet, Allen, Scorsese, and Lee.* University Press of Kentucky, 2005.
Blass, Thomas. *The Man Who Shocked the World: The Life and Legacy of Stanley Milgram.* 1st ed. Basic Books, 2004.
Brand, Dana. *The Spectator and the City in Nineteenth-Century American Literature.* Cambridge University Press, 1991.
Buck-Morss, Susan. *The Dialectics of Seeing: Walter Benjamin and the Arcades Project.* MIT Press, 1989.
Burch, Nöel. *Life to those Shadows*, translated and edited by Ben Brewster. University of California Press, 1990.
Bussard, Katherine A. et al. *The City Lost & Found: Capturing New York, Chicago, and Los Angeles, 1960–1980.* Princeton University Art Museum, 2014.
Butters, Gerald R. *From Sweetback to Super Fly: Race and Film Audiences in Chicago's Loop.* University of Missouri Press, 2014.
Carcucci, Mark. "Film Is Actually Painting with Money." *Millimeter* Feb. 1975, pp. 11–15.
Caro, Robert A. *The Power Broker: Robert Moses and the Fall of New York.* [1st ed.]. Knopf, 1974.
Castells, Manuel. "Wild City." *Kapitalistate*, 4–5, 1976, pp. 2–30.
Chauncey, George. *Gay New York: Gender, Urban Culture, and the Makings of the Gay Male World, 1890–1940.* Basic Books, 1994.
Chesterton, G. K. *The Defendant.* Dodd, Mead, 1902.
Ciment, Michel. "Entretien Avec Alan J. Pakula." *Positif*, 136, 1972, pp. 32–39.
Clutter, McLain. "Imaginary Apparatus: Film Production and Urban Planning in New York City 1966–1975." *Grey Room* 35, pp. 58–89.
Conn, Steven. *Americans against the City: Anti-Urbanism in the Twentieth Century.* Oxford University Press, 2014.
Cook, David A. *Lost Illusions: American Cinema in the Shadow of Watergate and Vietnam, 1970–1979.* Charles Scribner's Sons, 2000.
Copjec, Joan. *Shades of Noir: A Reader.* Verso, 1993.
Corkin, Stanley. *Starring New York: Filming the Grime and the Glamour of the Long 1970s.* Oxford University Press, 2011.
Cronon, William. *Nature's Metropolis: Chicago and the Great West.* W. W. Norton, 1991.
Cumber Dance, Daryl. *Long Gone: The Mecklenburg Six and the Theme of Escape in Black Folklore.* University of Tennessee Press, 1987.
Daley, Robert. *Prince of the City: The True Story of a Cop Who Knew Too Much.* Houghton Mifflin, 1978.
de Solà-Morales Rubió, Iganasi. "Terrain Vague." *Anyplace*, edited by Cynthia Davison. MIT Press, 1995.
Dimendberg, Edward. *Film Noir and the Spaces of Modernity.* Harvard University Press, 2004.

Dunstan, Roger. "Overview of New York City's Fiscal Crisis." CRB Note 3, 1, California State Library, March 1, 1995.

Etzioni, Amitai. "Mugging Now Number One Topic." *Village Voice*, Oct. 12, 1972, p. 13.

Federal Housing Administration, *Underwriting Manual*, 1936.

Fine, Sidney. *Violence in the Model City: The Cavanagh Administration, Race Relations, and the Detroit Riot of 1967*. University of Michigan Press, 1989.

Flamm, Michael W. *Law and Order: Street Crime, Civil Unrest, and the Crisis of Liberalism in the 1960s*. Columbia University Press, 2005.

Fogelson, Robert M. *Big-City Police*. Harvard University Press, 1977.

Gandal, Keith. *The Virtues of the Vicious: Jacob Riis, Stephen Crane, and the Spectacle of the Slum*. Oxford University Press, 1997.

Gaudreault, André. "1904–1905: Movies and Chasing the Missing Links." in *American Cinema 1890–1909: Themes and Variations*, edited by André Gaudreault. Rutgers University Press, 2009, pp. 133–57.

Gehl, Jan. *Life Between Buildings*, translated by Jo Koch. Van Nostrand Reinhold, 1987.

Gendron, Bernard. "The Downtown Music Scene," in *The Downtown Book: The New York Art Scene 1974–1984*, edited by Marvin J. Taylor. Princeton University Press, 2006.

Gibson, James J., and Anne D. Pick. "Perception of Another's Looking Behavior." *The American Journal of Psychology* 76, 3, 1963, pp. 386–94.

Giddens, Anthony. *The Consequences of Modernity*. Stanford University Press, 1990.

Giddis, Diane. "The Divided Woman: Bree Daniels in Klute." *Women in Film* 1, 3/4, 1973, pp. 57–61.

Giedion, S. *Space, Time and Architecture; the Growth of a New Tradition*. Harvard University Press, 1974.

Gledhill, Christine. "Klute 1: Contemporary Film Noir and Feminist Criticism." *Women in Film Noir*, edited by E. Ann Kaplan. 2nd ed. BFI Publishing, 2000a, pp. 20–34.

———. "Klute 2: Feminism and Klute." *Women in Film Noir*, edited by E. Ann Kaplan. BFI Publishing, 2000b, pp. 99–114.

Gleich, Joshua. "Hollywood Location Shooting in San Francisco and the Aesthetics of Urban Decline 1945–1975" (dissertation). University of Texas at Austin, 2014.

Glisserman, Marty. "Death Wish—Watch Out, Chicago." *Jump Cut*, 5, 1975, pp. 7–8.

Goffman, Erving. *The Presentation of Self in Everyday Life*. Doubleday Anchor, 1959.

———. *Relations in Public: Microstudies of the Public Order.* Basic Books, 1971.

Graeber, David. *The Utopia of Rules: On Technology, Stupidity, and the Secret Joys of Bureacracy*. Melville House, 2015.

Greenberg, Miriam. *Branding New York: How a City in Crisis Was Sold to the World.* Routledge, 2008.

Gregg, Steele. "On Location with 'The Godfather.'" *American Cinematographer*, June 1971, p. 568.

Grieveson, Lee, Esther Sonnet, and Peter Stanfield, eds. *Mob Culture: Hidden Histories of the American Gangster Film*. Rutgers University Press, 2005.

Guerrero, Ed. *Framing Blackness: The African American Image in Film*. Temple University Press, 1993.

Guest, Haden R. "The Police Procedural Film: Law and Order in the American Cinema, 1930–1960." PhD, University of California, Los Angeles, 2005.

Gumpert, Lynn. "Foreword," in *The Downtown Book: The New York Art Scene 1974–1984*, edited by Marvin J. Taylor. Princeton University Press, 2006.

Gunning, Tom. "Noncontinuity, Continuity, Discontinuity: A Theory of Genres in Early Film." *Iris* 2, 1, 1984, pp. 101–12.

———. "Tracing the Individual Body: Photography, Detectives, and Early Cinema," in *Cinema and the Invention of Modern Life*, edited by Leo Charney and Vanessa R. Schwartz. University of California Press, 1995. pp. 15–45.

———. "From the Kaleidoscope to the X-Ray: Urban Spectatorship, Poe, Benjamin, and Traffic in Souls (1913)." *Wide Angle* 19.4 (1997), pp. 25–57.

———. "Invisible Cities, Visible Cinema: Illuminating Shadows in Late Film Noir," *Comparative Critical Studies* 6.3, 2009. pp. 319–32.

Halper, Andrew, and Richard Ku. *New York City Police Street Crime Unit: An Exemplary Project*. National Institute of Law Enforcement and Criminal Justice, 1975.

Hansen, Miriam. *Cinema and Experience: Siegfried Kracauer, Walter Benjamin, and Theodor W. Adorno*. University of California Press, 2012.

Harris, Neil. *Humbug: The Art of P.T. Barnum*. University of Chicago Press, 1981.

Haskell, Molly. "Fastest Gun on the West Side." *Village Voice*, Aug. 1, 1974, p. 67.

Hebdige, Dick. *Subculture, the Meaning of Style*. Methuen, 1979.

Heller, Steven. "Julian Allen's Five Legacies." *Julian Allen: A Retrospective*. Museum of American Illustration at the Society of Illustrators, Maryland Institute College of Art, 2006.

———. *The Graphic Design Reader*. Allworth Press, 2002.

Helmer, John, and Neil A. Eddington, eds. *Urbanman: The Psychology of Urban Survival*. Free Press, 1973.

Hersey, John. *The Algiers Motel Incident*. Knopf, 1968.

Holleran, Andrew. *Dancer from the Dance: A Novel*. 1st ed. Morrow, 1978.

Horkheimer, Max, and Theodor Adorno. *The Dialectic of Enlightenment: Philosophical Fragments*, edited by Gunzelin Schmid Noerr, translated by Edmund Jephcott. Stanford University Press, 2002.

Hunt, Morton M. *The Mugging*. Atheneum, 1972.

Isenstadt, Sandy. "Four Views, Three of Them Through Glass." *Sites Unseen: Landscape & Vision*, edited by Dianne Suzette Harris, D. Fairchild Ruggles. University of Pittsburgh, 2007, pp. 213–40.

Jackson, Kenneth T. *Crabgrass Frontier: The Suburbanization of the United States*. Oxford University Press, 1985.

Jacobs, Steven. *The Wrong House: The Architecture of Alfred Hitchcock*. 010 Publishers, 2007.

Jameson, Fredric. *The Geopolitical Aesthetic: Cinema and Space in the World System*. Indiana University Press, 1992.

———. *The Cultural Turn: Selected Writings on the Postmodern 1983–1998*. Verso, 1998.

Jameson, Richard T. "The Pakula Parallax." *Film Comment* 12.5 (1976), pp. 8–12, 72.

Jansson, André, and Amanda Lagerkvist, eds. *Strange Spaces: Explorations into Mediated Obscurity*. Ashgate Pub., 2009.

Jencks, Charles. *The Language of Post-Modern Architecture*. 4th rev. enl. ed. Rizzoli, 1984.

Kael, Pauline. *Deeper into Movies*. 1st ed. Little, Brown, 1973.

———. "Urban Gothic." *New Yorker*, Oct. 30, 1971: p. 113.

Keating, Patrick. "Film Noir and the Culture of Electric Light," *Film History* 27, 1, 2015, pp. 58–84.

Kohn, Howard. "Detroit's Super Cops: Terror in the Streets." *Ramparts*, December 1973, pp. 38–41, 55.

Krutnik, Frank. *"Un-American" Hollywood Politics and Film in the Blacklist Era*. Rutgers University Press, 2007.

Kracauer, Siegfried. *From Caligari to Hitler: A Pyschological History of the German Film*. Princeton University Press, 1947, 1971.

———. *The Mass Ornament: Wiemar Essays*, translated and edited by Thomas Y. Levin. Harvard University Press, 1995.

———. *Theory of Film: The Redemption of Physical Reality*. Princeton University Press. 1960, 1997.

Lasch, Christopher. *The Culture of Narcissism: American Life in an Age of Diminishing Expectations*. 1st ed. Norton, 1978.

Latané, Bibb, and John M. Darley. "Bystander 'Apathy.' " *Urbanman: The Psychology of Urban Survival*. Eds. John Helmer, Neil A. Eddington. The Free Press, Macmillan Publishing, 1973, pp. 62–91.

Latour, Bruno. *Reassembling the Social: An Introduction to Actor-Network-Theory*. Oxford University Press, 2005.

Latour, Bruno, Emile Hermant, translated by Liz Carey-Libbrecht, and Valérie Pihet. *Paris: Invisible City*, http://www.bruno-latour.fr/virtual/EN/index.html.

Lawrence, Tim. "Beyond the Hustle: 1970s Social Dancing, Discotheque Culture, and the Emergence of the Contemporary Club Dancer." *Ballroom, Boogie, Shimmy Sham, Shake*, edited by Julie Manning. University of Illinois Press, 2009.

———. *Love Saves the Day: A History of American Dance Music Culture, 1970–1979*. Duke University Press, 2003.

———. *Life and Death on the New York Dance Floor 1980–1983*. Duke University Press, 2016.

Leary, John Patrick. "Detroitism: What does 'ruin porn' tell us about the motor city?," *Guernica*, January 15, 2011, https://www.guernicamag.com/leary_1_15_11/.

Lee, Murray. *Inventing Fear of Crime: Criminology and the Politics of Anxiety*. Willan Publishing, 2007.

Lefebvre, Henri. *The Production of Space*. Blackwell, 1991.

———. *The Urban Revolution*. University of Minnesota Press, 2003.
Leitch, Thomas M. *Crime Films*. Cambridge University Press, 2002.
Lejeune, Alex, and Nicholas Alex. "On Being Mugged: The Event and Its Aftermath." *Urban Life and Culture* 2, 3, pp. 259–287.
Levine, Elana. *Wallowing in Sex: The New Sexual Culture of 1970s American Television*. Duke University Press, 2007.
Lipset, Seymour Martin. "Why Cops Hate Liberals and Vice Versa." *The Atlantic*, March 1969, pp. 78-83.
Lynch, Kevin. *The Image of the City*. MIT Press, 1960.
Maas, Peter. *Serpico*. Viking Press, 1973.
MacCabe, Colin. "Realism and the Cinema: Notes on Some Brechtian Theses." *Screen*, 15, 2, 1974, pp. 7–37.
Macek, Steve. *Urban Nightmares: The Media, the Right, and the Moral Panic over the City*. University of Minnesota Press, 2006.
Malkiewicz, Kris. *Film Lighting: Talks with Hollywood's Cinematographers and Gaffers*. Prentice Hall, 1986.
Maltby, Richard. "As Close to Real Life as Hollywood Ever Gets: Headline Pictures, Topical Movies, Editorial Cinema, and Studio Realism in the 1930s." *The Wiley-Blackwell History of American Film Volume II 1929–1945*, edited by Cynthia Lucia, Roy Grundman, Art Simon. Wiley-Blackwell, 2012, pp. 76–111.
Manaugh, Geoff. *A Burglar's Guide to the City*. Farrar, Straus, Giroux, 2016.
Marx, Leo. "The Machine in the Garden; Technology and the Pastoral Ideal in America." Oxford University Press, 1964.
Massood, Paula J. *Black City Cinema: African American Urban Experiences in Film*. Temple University Press, 2003.
Matassa, Elizabeth Healy. "'From the Cracks in the Sidewalks of N.Y.C.': The Embodied Production of Urban Decline, Survival, and Renewal in New York's Fiscal-Crisis-Era Streets, 1977–1983," (dissertation). The George Washington University, 2014.
McArthur, Colin. *Underworld U.S.A.* Secker & Warburg, BFI, 1972. Cinema One.
McDonald, Shannon Sanders. *The Parking Garage: Design and Evolution of a Modern Urban Form*. Urban Land Institute, 2007.
McGarry, Eileen. "Dirty Harry." *Film Noir: An Encyclopedic Reference*, edited by Alain Silver and Elizaeth Ward. 3rd ed. Overlook Press, 1992.
Moore, Alan, and Mike Collins. "Grit!" *The Daredevils*. #8. Marvel Comics UK, 1983, pp. 14–17.
Moore, Robin. *The French Connection: The World's Most Crucial Narcotics Investigation*. [1st ed.]. Little, Brown and Company, 1969.
Moynihan, Daniel Patrick. *The Negro Family: A Case for National Action*. Office of Policy Planning and Research, United States Department of Labor, 1965.
Munby, Jonathan. *Public Enemies, Public Heroes Screening the Gangster from Little Caesar to Touch of Evil*. University of Chicago Press, 1999.
Murray, Don. "How Bright Lights Reduce Crime." *Coronet*, 47, 4, February 1960, pp. 29–33.
Naremore, James. *More Than Night: Film Noir in Its Contexts*. Updated and expanded ed. University of California Press, 2008.

Newman, Oscar. *Defensible Space: Crime Prevention through Urban Design*. Macmillan, 1972.

Nicolaides, Becky. "How Hell Moved from the City to the Suburbs: Urban Scholars and Changing Perceptions." *The New Suburban History*, edited by Thomas Sugrue. University of Chicago Press, pp. 80–98.

Nicolaides, Becky M., and Andrew Wiese, eds. *The Suburb Reader*. Routledge, 2006.

Nye, David E. *Electrifying America: Social Meanings of a New Technology, 1880–1940*. MIT Press, 1990.

Nystrom, Derek. *Hard Hats, Rednecks, and Macho Men: Class in 1970s American Cinema*. Oxford University Press, 2009.

Pike, David L. "Urban Nightmares and Future Visions: Life Beneath New York." *Wide Angle* 20, 4, 1998, pp. 9–50.

Pomerance, Murray. *City That Never Sleeps: New York and the Filmic Imagination*. Rutgers University Press, 2007.

———. "The Climb and the Chase: Film Noir and the Urban Scene—Representations of the City in Three Classic Noirs," in *A Companion to Film Noir*, edited by Andrew Spicer and Helen Hanson. Wiley Blackwell, 2013, pp. 405–19.

Procter, Mary, and William Matuszeski. *Gritty Cities*. Temple University Press. 1978.

Pynchon, Thomas. "A Journey Into The Mind of Watts." *New York Times*, June 12, 1966.

Raban, Jonathan. *Soft City*. Hamilton, 1974.

Rafter, Nicole. *Shots in the Mirror: Crime Films and Society*. Oxford University Press, 2006.

Rentschler, Carrie A. "An Urban Physiognomy of the 1964 Kitty Genovese Murder." *Space and Culture* 14, 3, 2011, pp. 310–29.

Rhodes, John David, and Elena Gorfinkel. *Taking Place: Location and the Moving Image*. University of Minnesota Press, 2011.

Rice, Charles. *Interior Urbanism: Architecture, John Portman and Downtown America*. Bloomsbury Academic, 2016.

Robbe-Grillet, Alain. *For a New Novel: Essays on Fiction*. Grove Press, 1966.

Rudofsky, Bernard. *Streets for People; a Primer for Americans*. [1st ed.]. Doubleday, 1969.

Ryan, Michael, and Douglas Kellner. *Camera Politica: The Politics and Ideology of Contemporary Hollywood Film*. Indiana University Press, 1988.

Sanders, James. *Celluloid Skyline: New York and the Movies*. New York: Alfred A. Knopf: Distributed by Random House, 2001.

Schaefer, Dennis, and Larry Salvato. *Masters of Light Conversations with Contemporary Cinematographers*. University of California Press, 1986.

Schivelbusch, Wolfgang. *Disenchanted Night: The Industrialization of Light in the Nineteenth Century*. University of California Press, 1988.

Schleier, Merrill. *Skyscraper Cinema: Architecture and Gender in American Film*. University of Minnesota Press, 2009.

Sennett, Richard. *The Uses of Disorder: Personal Identity & City Life*. [1st ed.]. Knopf, 1970.

———. "Plate Glass," *Raritan*, 1, 4, Spring, 1987, pp. 1-15.
———. *The Conscience of the Eye: The Design and Social Life of Cities*. 1st ed. Knopf, 1990.
Shapiro, Peter. *Turn the Beat Around: The Secret History of Disco*. 1st ed. Faber and Faber, 2005.
Silver, Alain, and Elizabeth Ward. *Film Noir: An Encyclopedic Reference to the American Style*. Overlook Press, 1992.
Simmel, Georg. "Two Essays: 'The Handle,' 'The Ruin,' *Hudson Review*, 11, 3, Autumn 1958, pp. 371–86.
Singer, Ben. *Melodrama and Modernity: Early Sensational Cinema and Its Contexts*. Columbia University Press, 2001.
Slotkin, Richard. *Regeneration through Violence: The Mythology of the American Frontier, 1600–1860*. HarperPerennial, 1996.
Smithson, Robert. "Tour of the Monuments of Passaic, New Jersey." *Artforum*, 6, 4, December 1967, pp. 52–57.
Sobcynski, Peter. "Mob City: A Brief Tour of Chicago as Seen in Its Gangster Films." *World Film Locations Chicago*. Intellect, 2013.
Sorrentino, Christopher. *Death Wish*. Soft Skull Press, 2010.
Stalter-Pace, Sunny. *Underground Movements: Modern Culture on the New York City Subway*. University of Massachusetts Press, 2013.
Stanfield, Peter. "Walking the Streets: Black Gangsters Ad the Abandoned City in the 1970s." *Mob Culture: The Hidden Histories of the American Gangster Film*, edited by Lee Grieveson, Esther Sonnett, Peter Stanfield. Rutgers University Press, pp. 281–300.
———. "Intent to Speed: Cyclical Production, Topicality, and the 1950s Hot Rod Movie." *New Review of Film and Television Studies* 11.1, 2012, pp. 34–55.
———. "Pix Biz Spurts with War Fever: Film and the Public Sphere—Cycles and Topicality," *Film History* 25.1–2, 2013, pp. 215–26.
Steffens, Lincoln. *The Shame of the Cities*. McClure, Phillips & Co., 1904.
Stern, Robert A. M., Thomas Mellins, and David Fishman. *New York 1960: Architecture and Urbanism between the Second World War and the Bicentennial*. Monacelli Press, 1995.
Straw, Will. "Urban Confidential: The Lurid City of the 1950s" in *The Cinematic City*, edited by David B. Clarke. Routledge, 2005, pp. 110–29.
Sugrue, Thomas J. *The Origins of the Urban Crisis: Race and Inequality in Postwar Detroit*. Princeton University Press, 2005.
Sverbeyeff, Elizabeth. "Six in the Arts and How They Live: Robert Indiana." *House Beautiful*, 112, 2, February 1970, pp. 52–55, 166.
Taylor, Marvin J. *The Downtown Book: The New York Art Scene, 1974–1984*. Princeton University Press, 2006.
Teaford, Jon C. *The Metropolitan Revolution the Rise of Post-Urban America*. Columbia University Press, 2006.
Thompson, Richard. "Mr. Pakula Goes to Washington." *Film Comment* 12, 5, 1976, pp. 12–19.
Tien, James et al. *Street Lighting Projects: Phase 1 Report*. National Institute of Law Enforcement and Criminal Justice, Law Enforcement Assistance Administration, U.S. Department of Justice, 1979.

Twilley, Nicola, and Krista Ninivaggi. "A Cocktail Party in the Street—An Interview with Alan Stillman." *New City Reader*. http://www.ediblegeography.com/a-cocktail-party-in-the-street-an-interview-with-alan-stillman/

United States. *Report of the National Advisory Commission on Civil Disorders*. Bantam Books, 1968.

U.S. Commission on Civil Rights. *Housing: 1961 Commission on Civil Rights Report*. Washington, DC, 1961.

Venturi, Robert. *Complexity and Contradiction in Architecture*. Vol. 1. Museum of Modern Art; distributed by Doubleday, Garden City, NY, 1966.

———, Denise Scott Brown, and Steven Izenvour. *Learning from Las Vegas*. MIT Press, 1972.

Von Moltke, Johannes. *The Curious Humanist: Siegfried Kracauer in America*. University of California Press, 2016.

Wall, Alex. *Victor Gruen: From Urban Shop to New City*. Actar, 2005.

Webb, Lawrence. *The Cinema of Urban Crisis: Seventies Film and the Reinvention of the City*. Amsterdam University Press, 2014.

Webber, Melvin M. *Explorations into Urban Structure*. University of Pennsylvania Press, 1964.

White, Hayden. "Historiography and Historiophoty." *American Historical Review* 93, 5, 1988, pp. 1193–1199.

White, Morton, and Lucia White. *The Intellectual Versus the City: From Thomas Jefferson to Frank Lloyd Wright*. Oxford University Press, 1977.

Whittemore, L. H. *The Super Cops: The True Story of the Cops Called Batman and Robin*. Stein and Day, 1973.

Whyte, William Hollingsworth. *The Organization Man*. Simon and Schuster, 1956.

——— (ed.). *The Exploding Metropolis*. [1st ed.]. Doubleday, 1958.

———. *The Social Life of Small Urban Spaces*. Conservation Foundation, 1980.

Williams, Linda. *On the Wire*. Duke University Press, 2014.

Willis, Gordon. "Photographing All the President's Men." *American Cinematographer*, May 1976, p. 551.

Wilson, Christopher P. "Undercover Police: White Ethnicity and Police Exposé in the 1970s." *American Literature* 77, 2, 2005, pp. 349–77.

Wilson, James Q., and George L. Kelling. "Broken Windows: Police and Neighborhood Safety." *The Atlantic*, 249, 3, March 1982, pp. 29–38.

Winner, Michael. *Winner Takes All: A Life of Sorts*. Anova Books, 2005.

Wojcik, Pamela Robertson. *The Apartment Plot: Urban Living in American Film and Popular Culture, 1945 to 1975*. Duke University Press, 2010.

Index

THE SUNY SERIES
HORIZONS OF CINEMA
MURRAY POMERANCE | EDITOR

Also in the series

William Rothman, editor, *Cavell on Film*
J. David Slocum, editor, *Rebel Without a Cause*
Joe McElhaney, *The Death of Classical Cinema*
Kirsten Moana Thompson, *Apocalyptic Dread*
Frances Gateward, editor, *Seoul Searching*
Michael Atkinson, editor, *Exile Cinema*
Paul S. Moore, *Now Playing*
Robin L. Murray and Joseph K. Heumann, *Ecology and Popular Film*
William Rothman, editor, *Three Documentary Filmmakers*
Sean Griffin, editor, *Hetero*
Jean-Michel Frodon, editor, *Cinema and the Shoah*
Carolyn Jess-Cooke and Constantine Verevis, editors, *Second Takes*
Matthew Solomon, editor, *Fantastic Voyages of the Cinematic Imagination*
R. Barton Palmer and David Boyd, editors, *Hitchcock at the Source*
William Rothman, *Hitchcock: The Murderous Gaze, Second Edition*
Joanna Hearne, *Native Recognition*
Marc Raymond, *Hollywood's New Yorker*
Steven Rybin and Will Scheibel, editors, *Lonely Places, Dangerous Ground*
Claire Perkins and Constantine Verevis, editors, *B Is for Bad Cinema*
Dominic Lennard, *Bad Seeds and Holy Terrors*
Rosie Thomas, *Bombay before Bollywood*
Scott M. MacDonald, *Binghamton Babylon*
Sudhir Mahadevan, *A Very Old Machine*
David Greven, *Ghost Faces*
James S. Williams, *Encounters with Godard*
William H. Epstein and R. Barton Palmer, editors, *Invented Lives, Imagined Communities*
Lee Carruthers, *Doing Time*
Rebecca Meyers, William Rothman, and Charles Warren, editors, *Looking with Robert Gardner*
Belinda Smaill, *Regarding Life*
Douglas McFarland and Wesley King, editors, *John Huston as Adaptor*

R. Barton Palmer, Homer B. Pettey, and Steven M. Sanders, editors, *Hitchcock's Moral Gaze*

Nenad Jovanovic, *Brechtian Cinemas*

Will Scheibel, *American Stranger*

Amy Rust, *Passionate Detachments*

Steven Rybin, *Gestures of Love*

Seth Friedman, *Are You Watching Closely?*

Roger Rawlings, *Ripping England!*

Michael DeAngelis, *Rx Hollywood*

Ricardo E. Zulueta, *Queer Art Camp Superstar*

John Caruana and Mark Cauchi, editors, *Immanent Frames*

Nathan Holmes, *Welcome to Fear City*